GANDHIAN THOUGHTS
VIEWS AND REVIEWS

GANDHIAN THOUGHTS
VIEWS AND REVIEWS

A.S. Pabla

CYBER TECH PUBLICATIONS
4264/3, Ansari Road, Daryaganj, New Delhi-110002 (India)
Ph.: 011-23244078. Fax: 011-23280028
E-Mail: cyberpublicationsdelhi@yahoo.com

Gandhian Thoughts: Views and Reviews

First Edition 2009

Reprint 2025

Published by G.S. Rawat
For Cyber Tech Publications
4264/3, Ansari Road, Daryaganj, New Delhi-110002
Ph.: 011-23244078. Fax: 011-23280028
E-Mail: cyberpublicationsdelhi@yahoo.com

Printed at
Amit Enterprises, Moujpur, Delhi, Ph. -9810878184

Preface

Mohandas Gandhi was born on October 2,1869, at Porbandar, on the western coast of India. His grandfather Uttamchand Gandhi and father Karamchand Gandhi occupied the high office of the diwan (Chief Minister) of Porbandar. To be Diwan of one of the princely states was on sinecure. Porbandar was one of some three hundred 'native' states in western India which were ruled by princes whom the accident of birth and the support of the British kept on the throne. To steer one's course safely between wayward Indian princes, the overbearing British 'Political Agent' of the suzerain power and the long-suffering subjects required a high degree of patience, diplomatic skill and commonsense. Both Uttamchand and Karamchand were good administrators. But they were also upright and honourable men. Loyal to their masters, they did not flinch from offering unpalatable advice. They paid the price for the courage of their convictions. Uttamchand Gandhi had his hose besieged and shelled by the ruler's troops and had to flee the State; his son Karamchand also preferred to leave Porbandar, rather than compromise with his principles.

Although the is no dearth of literature on the subject but this book has its own unique style and presentation and I hope that readers will find it interesting to read this book and will know more about Gandhi and his thoughts.

—Author

CONTENTS

1

INTRODUCTION

When Gandhi was born British rule had been established in India. The uprising of 1857, known as the Mutiny, had merely served to consolidate the British adventure into an empire. India had effectively passed under British tutelage, so effectively indeed, that instead of resenting alien rule the generation of educated Indians were eager to submit to the "Civilizing mission" of their foreign masters. Political subjection had been reinforced by intellectual and moral servility. It seemed that the British empire in India was safe for centuries.

When Gandhi died it was India, a free nation that mourned his loss. The disinherited had recovered their heritage and the "dumb millions" had found their voice. The disarmed had won a great battle and had in the process evolved a moral force such as to compel the attention, and to some degree, the admiration, of the world. The story of this miracle is also the story of Gandhi's life, for he, more than any other was the architect of this miracle. Ever since his grateful countrymen call him the Father of the Nation.

And yet it would be an exaggeration to say that Gandhi alone wrought this miracle. No single individual, however great and wonderful, can be the sole engineer of a historical process. A succession of remarkable predecessors and elder contemporaries had quarried and broken the stones which helped Gandhi to pave the way for India's independence. They had set in motion various trends in the intellectual, social and moral consciousness of the people which the genius Gandhi mobilized and directed in a grand march. Raja Rammohan Roy,

Ramkrishna Paramhamsa and his great disciple, Swami Vivekananda, Swami Dayananda Saraswati, Dadabhai Navroji, Badruddin Tyabji, Syed Ahmed Khan, Ranade, Gokhale, Tilak, Aurobindo Ghosh and Rabindranath Tagore, to name only a few. Each one of them, had in his own, field created a consciousness of India's destiny and helped to generate a spirit of sacrifice which, in Gandhi's hands, became the instruments of a vast political-cum-moral upheaval. Had Gandhi been born hundred years earlier he could hardly have achieved what he did. Nevertheless, it is true, that, but for Gandhi, India's political destiny would have been vastly different and her moral stature vastly inferior.

But though Gandhi lived, suffered and died in India for Indians, it is not in relation to India's destiny alone that his life has significance. Future generations will not only remember him as a patriot, politician and nation-builder but much more. He was essentially a moral force, whose appeal is to the conscience of man and therefore universal. He was the servant and friend of man as man and not as belonging to this or that nation, religion or race.

If he worked for Indians only, it was because he was born among them and because their humiliation and suffering supplied the necessary incentives to his moral sensibility. The lesson of his life therefore is for all to read. He founded no church and though he lived by faith he left behind no dogma for the faithful to quarrel over. He gave no attributes to God save Truth and prescribed no path for attaining it save honest and relentless search through means that injure no living thing. Who dare therefore claim Gandhi for his own except by claiming him for all?

Another lesson of his life which should be of universal interest is that he was not born a genius and did not exhibit in early life any extraordinary faculty that is not shared by the common run of men. He was no inspired bard like Rabindranath Tagore, he had no mystic visions like Ramakrishna Paramhamsa, he was no child prodigy like Shankara or Vivekananda. He was just an ordinary child like most of us. If there was anything extraordinary about him as a child, it was his shyness, a handicap from which he suffered for a long time. No doubt, something very extraordinary must have been latent in his spirit which later developed into an iron will and combined with a moral sensibility made him what he became, but there was little evidence of it in his childhood. We may therefore derive courage and inspiration from the knowledge that if he made himself what he was, there is no visible reason why we should not be able to do the same.

His genius, so to speak, was an infinite capacity for taking pains in fulfilment of a restless moral urge. His life was one continuous striving, an unremitting sadhana, a relentless search for truth, not abstract or metaphysical truth, but such truth as can be realized in human relations. He climbed step by step, each step no bigger than a man's, till when we saw him at the height he seemed more than a man. "Generations to come, it may be, will scarce believe", wrote Einstein, "that such a one as this, ever in flesh and blood walked upon this earth." If at the end he seemed like no other man, it is good to remember that when he began he was like any other man.

Such is the great lesson of his life. Fortunately, he has himself recorded for us the main incidents of his life till 1921 and described with scrupulous veracity the evolution of his moral and intellectual consciousness. Had he not done so, there would have been in India no dearth of devout chroniclers who would have invented divine portents at his birth and invested him with a halo from his childhood.

BIRTH AND UPBRINGING

Mohandas Karamchand Gandhi was born on October 2, 1869, at Porbandar, a small town on the western coast of India, which was then one of the many tiny states in Kathiawar. He was born in middle class family of Vaishya caste. His grandfather had risen to be the Dewan or Prime Minister of Porbandar and was succeeded by his son Karamchand who was the father of Mohandas. Putlibai, Mohandas's mother, was a saintly character, gentle and devout, and left a deep impress on her son's mind. Mohandas went to an elementary school in Porbandar, where he found it difficult to master the multiplication tables. "My intellect must have been sluggish and my memory raw", he recalled with candour many years later. He was seven when his family moved to Rajkot, another state in Kathiawar, where his father became Dewan. There he attended a primary school and later joined a high school. Though conscientious he was a "mediocre student" and was excessively shy and timid.

While his school record gave no indication of his future greatness, there was one incident which was significant. A British school inspector came to examine the boys and set a spelling test. Mohandas made a mistake which the class teacher noticed. The latter motioned to him to copy the correct spelling from his neighbour's slate. Mohandas refused to take the hint and was later chided for his "stupidity".

We can also discover in the little boy a hint of that passion for reforming others which later became so dominant a trait of the Mahatma, though in this case the zeal almost led him astray. Impelled by a desire to reform a friend of his elder brother's, one Sheikh Mehtab, he cultivated his company and imbibed habits which he had to regret later. This friend convinced him that the British could rule India because they lived on meat which gave them the necessary strength. So Mohandas who came on orthodox vegetarian family took to tasting meat clandestinely, for patriotic reasons. But apart from the inherited vegetarian sentiment which made him feel, after he had once swallowed a piece, as if "a live goat were bleating inside me", he had to wrestle with the knowledge that such clandestine repasts would have to be hidden from his parents which would entail falsehood on his part. This he was reluctant to do. And so after a few such experiments he gave up the idea, consoling himself with the reflection : "When they are no more and I have found my freedom, I will eat meat openly."

While he was still in high school, he was married, at the age of thirteen, to Kasturbai who was also of the same age. For a boy of that age marriage meant only a round of feasts, new clothes to wear and a strange and docile companion to play with. But he soon felt the impact of sex which he has described for us with admirable candour. The infinite tenderness and respect which were so marked a characteristic of his attitude in later life to Indian women may have owed something to his personal experience of "the cruel custom of child marriage", as he called it.

YOUTH AND STUDY IN ENGLAND

After Matriculating from the high school, Mohandas joined the Samaldas College in Bhavnagar, where he found the studies difficult and the atmosphere uncongenial, Meanwhile, his father had died in 1885. A friend of the family suggested that if the young Gandhi hoped to take his father's place in the state service he had better become a barrister which he could do in England in three years. Gandhi jumped at the idea. The mother's objection to his going abroad was overcome by the son's solemn vow not to touch wine, women and meat.

Gandhi went to Bombay to take the boat for England. In Bombay, his caste people, who looked upon crossing the ocean as contamination, threatened to excommunicate him if he persisted in going abroad. But Gandhi was adamant and was thus formally excommunicated by his caste. Undeterred, he sailed on September 4, 1888, for Southampton-aged eighteen. A few months earlier Kasturbai had borne him a son.

The first few days in London were miserable. "I would continually think of my home and country. . . Everything was strange-the people, their ways and even their dwellings. I was a complete novice in the matter of English etiquette, and continually had to be on my guard. There was the additional inconvenience of the vegetarian vow. Even the dishes that I could eat were tasteless and insipid."

The food difficulty was solved when one day he chanced upon a vegetarian restaurant in Farringdon Street where he also bought a copy of Salt's Plea for Vegetarianism and was greatly impressed by it. Hitherto he had been a vegetarian because of the vow he had taken. From now on he became a vegetarian by choice. He read many more books on vegetarianism and diet and was delighted to discover modern science confirm the practice of his forefathers. To spread vegetarianism became henceforward his mission, as he put it. During the early period of his stay in England Gandhi went through a phase which he has described as aping the English gentleman. He got new clothes made, purchased a silk hat costing nineteen shillings, "wasted ten pounds on an evening dress suit made in Bond Street" and flaunted a double watch-chain of gold. He took lessons in French and in elocution and spent three guineas to learn ball-room dancing. But he soon realized-and here is foreshadowed the real Gandhi-that if he could not become a gentleman by virtue of his character, the ambition was not worth cherishing.

Towards the end of his second year in London, he came across two theosophist brothers who introduced him to Sir Edwin Arnold's translation in English verse of the Gita-The Song Celestial priceless worth. He was deeply impressed. "The book struck me as one of priceless worth. This opinion of the Gita has ever since been growing on me, with the result that I regard it today as the supreme book for knowledge of Truth. It has afforded me invaluable help in my moments of gloom."

About the same time a Christian friend whom he had met in a vegetarian boarding house introduced him to the Bible. He found it difficult to wade through the Old Testament which put him to sleep, but he fell in love with the New Testament and specially with the Sermon on the Mount. He also read Sir Edwin Arnold's rendering of Buddha's life-The light of Asia-as well as the chapter on the Prophet of Islam in Carlyle's Heroes and Hero Worship. The attitude of respect for all religions and the desire to understand the best in each one of them were thus planted in his mind early in life.

Having passed his examinations Gandhi was called to the Bar on June 10, 1891, and sailed for India two days later.

ON THE THRESHOLD OF MANHOOD

When he reached Bombay he learnt to his profound sorrow that his mother had died. The news had been deliberately kept back from him to spare him the shock in a distant land.

After spending some time in Rajkot where with his usual earnestness he immediately took in hand the education of his little son and of his brother's children, he decided to set up in legal practice in Bombay. He stayed in Bombay for a few months but had only one small brief. When he rose to argue it in the court, his nerve failed him and he could not utter a word.

Having failed to establish himself in Bombay, Gandhi returned to Rajkot where he started again. But he did not make much headway and was unhappy and out of tune with the atmosphere of petty intrigue that was rampant in the small states of Kathiawar. In this predicament came an offer from Dada Abdulla & Co. to proceed to South Africa on their behalf to instruct their counsel in a lawsuit. It was a godsend. Gandhi jumped at it and sailed for South Africa in April 1893.

He little realized what he was letting himself in for and fondly imagined that he was escaping from an unpleasant situation in Rajkot and was going to make a little money after all. But fate had something different in store for him. It was in South Africa that this shy, timid youth of twenty-four, inexperienced, unaided, alone, came into clash with forces that obliged him to tap his hidden moral resources and turn misfortunes into creative spiritual experiences.

Dressed in a frock-coat and turban Gandhi landed in Durban where his client Abdulla Sheth received him. Almost the first thing he sensed on arrival was the oppressive atmosphere of racial snobbishness. Indians of whom large numbers were settled in South Africa, some as merchants, some in the professions, the large majority as indentured labourers or their descendants, were all looked down upon as pariahs by the white settlers and called coolies or samis. Thus a Hindu doctor was a coolie doctor and Gandhi himself a coolie barrister.

After about a week's stay in Durban Gandhi left for Pretoria, the capital of the Transvaal, where his presence was needed in connection with a lawsuit. A first class ticket was purchased for him by his client. When the train reached Maritzburg, the capital of Natal, at about 9 p.m. a white passenger who boarded the train objected to the presence of a "coloured" man in the compartment and Gandhi was ordered by a railway official to shift to a third class. When he refused to do so, a constable pushed him out and his luggage was taken away by the railway authorities. It was winter and bitterly cold. Gandhi sat and shivered the whole night in the waiting-room, thinking : 'Should I fight for my rights or go back to India?' He decided that it was cowardice to run away without fulfilling his obligations.

The next evening he continued the train journey-this time without a mishap. But a bigger mishap awaited him on the journey from Charlestown to Johannesburg which had to be covered by stagecoach. He was made to sit with the coachman on the box outside, while the white conductor sat inside with the white passengers.

Gandhi pocketed the insult for fear of missing the coach altogether. On the way the conductor who wanted a smoke spread a piece of dirty sackcloth on the footboard and ordered Gandhi to sit there so that the conductor could have Gandhi's seat and smoke. Gandhi refused. The conductor swore and rained blows on him, trying to throw him down. Gandhi clung to the brass rails of the coach box, refusing to yield and unwilling to retaliate. Some of the white passengers protested at this cowardly assault and the conductor was obliged to stop beating Gandhi who kept his seat.

Though his main concern in Pretoria was with the lawsuit, Gandhi's sense of social justice had been aroused by his personal experience of the indignities to which his countrymen were subject. He therefore lost no time, after making the necessary preliminary contacts, in calling a meeting of the Indian community in Pretoria which consisted largely of Muslim merchants. This was his first public speech successfully delivered. He exhorted his countrymen to observe truthfulness even in business and reminded them that their responsibility was all the greater since their country would be judged by their conduct in a foreign land. He asked them to forget all distinctions of religion and caste and to give up some of their insanitary habits. He suggested the formation of an association to look after the Indian settlers and offered his free time and services.

The position of Indians in the Transvaal was worse than in Natal. They were compelled to pay a poll tax of £3; they were not allowed to own land except in a specially allotted location, a kind of ghetto; they had no franchise, and were not allowed to walk on the pavement or move out of doors after 9 p.m. without special permit. One day Gandhi, who had received from the State Attorney a letter authorizing him to be out of doors all hours, was having his usual walk. As he passed near President Kruger's house, the policeman on duty, suddenly and without any warning , pushed him off the pavement and kicked him into the street. Mr. coates, an English Quaker who knew Gandhi, happened to pass by and saw the incident. He advised Gandhi to proceed against the man and offered himself as witness. But Gandhi declined the offer saying that he had made it a rule not to go to court in respect of a personal grievance.

In the meanwhile he had been working hard at the lawsuit and had gained a sound knowledge of legal practice. He made two discoveries: one was that facts are three fourth of the law; the other, that litigation was ruinous to both parties in a suit and therefore the duty of a lawyer was to bring them together in a settlement out of court. In this particular case he succeeded in persuading both Abdulla Sheth and the opposing party, Tyeb Sheth, to accept arbitration.

Having completed his work in Pretoria, Gandhi returned to Durban and prepared to sail home. But at a farewell dinner given in his honour some one showed him a news item in Natal Mercury that the Natal Government proposed to introduce a bill to disfranchise Indians. Gandhi immediately understood the ominous implications of this bill which, as he said, "is the first nail into our coffin" and advised his compatriots to resist it by concerned action. But they pleaded their helplessness without him and begged him to stay on for another month. He agreed, little realizing that this one month would grow into twenty years.

With his usual earnestness Gandhi then and there turned the farewell dinner into an action committee and drafted a petition to the Natal Legislative Assembly. Volunteers came forward to make copies of the petition and to collect signatures-all during the night. The petition received good publicity in the press the following morning. The bill was however passed.

Undeterred, Gandhi set to work on another petition to Lord Ripon, the Secretary of State for Colonies. Within a month the mammoth petition with ten thousand signatures was sent to Lord Ripon and a thousand copies printed for distribution. Even The Times admitted the justice of the Indian claim, and for the first time the people in India came to know of the hard lot of their compatriots in South Africa. Gandhi insisted that if he had to extend his stay in South Africa he would accept no remuneration for his public services and since he still thought it necessary to live as befitted a barrister he needed about £300 to meet his expenses. He therefore enrolled as an advocate of the Supreme Court of Natal.

Emergence of Mahatma

Three years' stay in South Africa persuaded Gandhi that he could not now desert a cause he had so warmly espoused. He therefore took six months' leave to visit India and bring his family back. But it was no holiday. He visited many cities in India and worked hard to interest the editors of papers and eminent public men in the unfortunate condition of Indians in South Africa. He published a small pamphlet on the subject. Though it was a very sober and restrained statement of the Indian case, a distorted summary cabled by Reuters created considerable misunderstanding in Natal which was to have unpleasant consequences later.

When plague broke out in Rajkot, Gandhi volunteered his services and visited every locality, including the quarters of the untouchables, to inspect the latrines and teach the residents better methods of sanitation.

During this visit, he made the acquaintance of veteran leaders like Badruddin Tyabji, Pherozeshah Mehta, Surendranath Banerjee and the great savant and patriot, Tilak. He met the wise and noble-hearted Gokhale and was greatly attracted to him. He addressed a large public meeting in Bombay. He was due to speak in Calcutta also, but before he could do so an urgent telegram from the Indian community in Natal obliged him to cut short his stay and sail for Durban with his wife and children in November 1896. When the ship reached to Durban, it was put into five day's quarantine. The European community, misled by garbled versions of Gandhi's activities in India and by a rumour that he was bringing shiploads of Indians to settle in Natal, were wild with anger and threatened to drown all the passengers. However, the passengers, including Gandhi's family, were allowed to land unmolested. But when Gandhi came down a little later and his identity was discovered, an infuriated mob fell upon him, stoning, beating and kicking him and would probably have killed him had not a brave English lady came to his rescue.

News of this cowardly assault received wide publicity and Joseph Chamberlain, the British Secretary of States for the Colonies, cabled an order to Natal to prosecute all those who were responsible for the attempted lynching. But Gandhi refused to identify and prosecute his assailants, saying that they were misled and that he was sure that when they came to know the truth they would be sorry for what they had done. Thus spoke the Mahatma in him.

It was during this second period in South Africa that Gandhi's mode of living underwent a change, albeit gradual. Formerly, he was anxious to maintain the standard of an English barrister. Now he began, in his methodical but original fashion, to reduce his wants and his expenses. He "studied the art" of laundering and became his own washerman. He could now iron and starch a stiff white collar. He also learnt to cut his own hair. He not only cleaned his own chamber-pots but often his guests as well. Not satisfied with self-help, he volunteered, despite his busy practice as a lawyer and demand of public work, his free service for two hours a day as compounder in a charitable hospital. He also undertook the education at home of his two sons and a nephew. He read books on nursing and midwifery and in fact served as midwife when his fourth and last son was born.

In 1899 the Boer war broke out. Though Gandhi's sympathies were all with the Boers who were fighting for their independence, he advised the Indian community to support the British cause, on the ground that since they claimed their rights as British subject it was their duty to defend the Empire when it was threatened. He therefore organized and, with the help of Dr. Booth, trained an Indian Ambulance Corps of 1,100 volunteers and offered its services to the Government. The corps under Gandhi's leadership rendered valuable service and was mentioned in dispatches. What pleased Gandhi most was the fact that Indians of all creeds and castes lived and faced danger together. All his life nothing gave him greater happiness than the sight of men working as brothers and rising above the prejudices of creed, caste or race.

In 1901, at the end of the war, Gandhi felt that he must now return to India. His professional success in South Africa might, he feared turn him into a "money-maker". With great difficulty he persuaded his friends to let him go and promised to return should the community need him within a year.

He reached India in time to attend the Calcutta session of the Indian National Congress and had the satisfaction of seeing his resolution on South Africa pass with acclamation. He was however disappointed with the congress. He felt that Indian politicians talked too much but do little. He deplored the importance given to the English language in their discussions and was pained to see the insanitary condition of the latrines in the camp.

After staying for a few days in Calcutta as Gokhale's Guest, when he went out on a tour of India, travelling third class in order to study for himself the habits and difficulties of the poor. He observed that the extreme discomfort of third class travel in India was due to much of the indifference of the railway authorities as to the dirty habits of the passengers themselves and suggested that educated persons should voluntarily travel third so as to reform the people's habits and be in a position to ventilate their legitimate grievances. The diagnosis as well as the remedy suggested were characteristic of his approach to all social and political problems - equal emphasis on obligations as on rights.

Gandhi was not destined to work in India yet. Hardly had he set up in practice in Bombay when a cablegram from the Indian community in Natal recalled him. He had given them his word that he would return if needed. Leaving his family in India he sailed again.

He had been called to put the Indian case before Joseph Chamberlain who was visiting South Africa. But the Colonial Secretary who had come to receive a gift of thirty-five million pounds from South Africa had no mind to alienate the European community. Gandhi failed in his mission to win Chamberlain's sympathy and discovered in the process that the situation in the Transvaal had become ominous for the Indians. He therefore decided to stay on in Johannesburg and enrolled as an advocate of the Supreme court.

Though he stayed on specifically to challenge European arrogance and to resist injustice, he harboured no hatred in his heart and was in fact always ready to help his opponents when they were in distress. It was this rare combination of readiness to resist wrong and capacity to love his opponent which baffled his enemies and compelled their admiration. When the so-called Zulu rebellion broke out, he again offered his help to the Government and raised an Indian Ambulance Corps. He was happy that he and his men had to nurse the sick and dying Zulus whom the white doctors and nurses were unwilling to touch.

It was during these marches through the Zulu country that he pondered deeply over the kind of life he should lead in order to dedicate himself completely to the service of humanity. He realized that absolute continence or brahmacharya was indispensable for the purpose, for one "could not live both after the flesh and the spirit". And so immediately after his return from the Zulu campaign in 1906, he announced his resolution to take a vow of absolute continence to a select group of friends.

This step was taken under the influence of the Bhagvad Gita which he had been reading regularly every morning for some time and committing to memory. Another doctrine of the Gita which influenced him profoundly was "non-possession". As soon as he realized its implications he allowed his insurance policy of Rs.10,000 to lapse. Henceforth he would put his faith in God alone.

Next to the Gita , the book which influenced him most deeply was Ruskin's Unto This Last which his friend Polak had given him to read one day in 1904. What Ruskin preached, or rather what Gandhi understood him to preach, was the moral dignity of manual labour and the beauty of community living on the basis of equality. Since, unlike Ruskin, Gandhi could not appreciate an ideal without wanting to practice it, he immediately set about to buy a farm where such a life could be lived. Thus was founded the famous Phoenix colony, on a hundred acres of land, some fourteen miles from Durban.

But Gandhi could not stay long at Phoenix. Duty called him to Johannesburg where also, later, he found another colony on similar ideals, at a distance of twenty-one miles from the city. He called it the Tolstoy Farm. In both these ashrams, as settlements organized on spiritual ideals are known in India, the inmates did all the work themselves, from cooking to scavenging. Extreme simplicity of the life was observed, reinforced by a strict code of moral and physical hygiene. No medicines were kept, for Gandhi who had earlier read Adolf Just's Return to Nature believed profoundly in nature cure. Every inmate had to practise some handicraft. Gandhi himself learnt to make sandals.

He foresaw that a shadow with the South African Government was sooner or later inevitable and knew from his own individual experience that no brute force could quell the spirit of man ready to defy and willing to suffer. What he could do himself he could train others to do. Individual resistance could be expanded and organized into a mass struggle in the prosecution of a moral equivalent of war. He had read Tolstoy and Thoreau's use of the term "civil disobedience" did not seem to express Gandhi's own concept of ahimsa as a positive force of love, nor did he like the use of the phrase "passive resistance". The concept was now clearly formulated in his mind but the word to describe it was wanting. His cousin Maganlal Gandhi suggested sadagraha, meaning holding fast to truth or firmness in a righteous cause. Gandhi liked the term and changed to Satyagraha. Thus was evolved and formulated Gandhi's most original idea in political action.

The occasion was not long in coming. In 1907, when the Transvaal received responsible government, it passed what came to be known as the Black Act, requiring all Indians, men and women, to register and submit to finger prints. Gandhi advised the Indian community to refuse to submit to this indignity and to court imprisonment by defying the law. In January 1908, he was arrested and sentenced to two months' simple imprisonment. He was followed by other satyagrahis.

Before the prison term was over General smuts sent him an emissary proposing that if the Indians voluntarily registered themselves he promised to repeal the Act. Gandhi agreed to the compromise. He always believed in trusting the opponent. But the other Indians were not so trusting. One burly Pathan even charged Gandhi with having betrayed them and threatened to kill him if he registered. On the day Gandhi went out to register he has waylaid and attacked by this and other Pathans and severely injured. When he recovered consciousness and was told that his assailants had been arrested he insisted on their being released.

Gandhi registered, but his disappointment was great when Smuts went back on his word and refused to repeal the Black Act. The Indians made a bonfire of their registration certificates and decided to defy the ban on immigration to the Transvaal. Jails began to be filled. Gandhi was arrested a second time in September 1908 and sentenced to two months' imprisonment, this time hard labour. The struggle continued. In February 1909 he was arrested a third time and sentenced to three months' hard labour. He made such good use of his time in jail with study and prayer that he was able to declare that "the real road to ultimate happiness lies in going to jail and undergoing sufferings and privations there in the interest of one's own country and religion".

In 1911, a provisional settlement of the Asiatic question in the Transvaal brought about a suspension of the Satyagraha. In the following year, Gokhale visited South Africa and on the eve of his departure assured Gandhi that the Union Government had promised to repeal the Black Act, to remove the racial bar from the immigration law and to abolish the £3 tax. But Gandhi had his fears which were soon borne out. The Union Government went back on its promise, and to this fire was added a very powerful fuel when a judgment of the Supreme Court ruled that only Christian marriages were legal in South Africa, turning at one stroke all Indian marriages in South Africa invalid and all Indian wives into concubines. This provoked Indian women, including, Kasturbai, to join the struggle.

It was illegal for the Indians to cross the border from the Transvaal into Natal, and vice versa, without a permit. Indian women from the Tolstoy Ashram crossed the border without permits and proceeded to Newcastle to persuade the Indian miners there to strike. They succeeded and were arrested. The strike spread and thousands of miners and other Indians prepared, under Gandhi's leadership, to march to the Transvaal border in a concerted act of nonviolent defiance. Gandhi made strict rules for the conduct of the satyagrahis who were to submit patiently and without retaliation to insult, flogging or arrest. He was arrested and sentenced, but the Satyagraha spread. At one time there were about fifty thousand indentured labourers on strike and several thousand other Indians in jail. The Government tried repression and even shooting, and many lives were lost. "In the end", as an American biographer has put it, "General Smuts did what every Government that ever opposed Gandhi had to do - he yielded."

Gandhi was released and, in January 1914, a provisional agreement was arrived at between him and General Smuts and the main Indian demands were conceded. Gandhi's work in South Africa was now over and, in July 1914, he sailed with his wife for England where Gokhale had called him. Before sailing, he sent a pair of sandals he had made in jail to General Smuts as a gift. Recalling the gift twenty-five years later, the General wrote : "I have worn these sandals for many a summer since then even though I may feel that I am not worthy to stand in the shoes of so great a man."

Great Soul in Beggar's Garb

In April 1893, Gandhi had sailed for South Africa, a young and inexperienced barrister in search of fortune. In January 1915 he finally returned to India, a Mahatma, with no possessions and with only one ambition - to serve his people. Though the intelligentsia had heard of his exploits in South Africa, he was not much known in India and Indians in general did not realize that "the Great Soul in beggar's garb", as the poet Tagore called him called him later, had reached her shores. Nor did he know his shores. Nor did he know his India well. He therefore readily promised his "political guru", Gokhale, that he would spend the first year in India studying the country, with "his ears open but his mouth shut".

At the end of his year's wanderings, Gandhi settled down on the bank of the river Sabarmati, on the outskirts of Ahmedabad, where he founded an ashram in May 1915. He called it the Satyagraha Ashram. The inmates about twenty-five men and women, took the vows of truth, ahimsa, celibacy, non-stealing, non-possession and control of the palate, and dedicated themselves to the service of the people .

Gandhi's first public address in India was on the occasion of the opening ceremony of the Benares Hindu University in February 1916, which was distinguished by the presence of many magnets and princes and of the Viceroy himself. Speaking in English he shocked them all by expressing his "deep humiliation and shame" at being compelled "to address my countrymen in a language that is foreign to mc". He shocked them more when turning to the bejewelled princes he said: "There is no salvation for India unless you strip yourselves of this jewellery and hold it in trust for your countrymen in India." Many princes walked out.

His first Satyagraha in India was in Champaran, in Bihar, where he went in 1917 at the request of a poor peasants to inquire into the grievances of the much exploited peasants of that district, who were compelled by British indigo planters to grow indigo on 15 percent of their land and part with the whole crop for rent. The news that a Mahatma had arrived to inquire into their sufferings spread like wild fire and thousands of peasants left their villages to have his darshan and to tell him of their woes. The vested interests were up in arms and the police superintendent ordered Gandhi to leave district. Gandhi refused and was summoned to appear in court the next day. Thousand of peasants followed him there. The embarrassed magistrate postponed the trial and released him without bail, for Gandhi refused to furnish any.

Later, the case was withdrawn and Gandhi proceeded with his inquiry. Along with the inquiry, he educated the peasants in the principles of Satyagraha and taught them that the first condition of freedom was freedom from fear. He sent for volunteers who helped to instruct the illiterate and ignorant peasants in elementary hygiene and ran schools for their children.

This kind of activity was typical of Gandhi. Even as he taught people to fight for their rights, he taught them to fulfil their obligations. A free people must learn to stand on their feet. But the more he worked for the people the less was his presence welcome to the Government who were at last obliged to set up a committee of inquiry. The report of the committee of which Gandhi was a member went in favour of the tenant farmers. The success of his first experiment in Satyagraha in India greatly enhanced Gandhi's reputation in this country.

Hardly had his work in Champaran been done when Gandhi was called to his ashram at Sabarmati by an urgent appeal from the textile workers of Ahmedabad whose dispute with the mill-owners was taking a serious turn. Having satisfied himself that the workers' demands were legitimate and mill-owners' refusal to submit the dispute to arbitration unreasonable, Gandhi asked the workers to strike, on condition that they took a pledge to remain nonviolent. They agreed, but after a few days their zeal began to flag and Gandhi feared that they might break the pledge and resort to violence. Since it was the fear of starvation which drove the workers to desperation, Gandhi decided to starve himself. He declared that he would not touch food until a settlement had been reached. At the end of three days, both parties agreed on an arbitration amid general rejoicing.

Almost immediately after came the agrarian trouble in the Kheda district of Gujarat. The peasants who were on the verge of starvation were being forced by the Government to pay the usual tax. Gandhi advised Satyagraha and persuade all the peasants, the well-to-do as well as the poor, to take a pledge not to pay any tax until those who could not pay were granted remission. The no-tax campaign lasted for about four months at the end of which the Government suspended the assessment for the poor peasants.

Now there took place an event which still baffles the pacifists in the West. In 1917, the Viceroy Lord Chelmsford invited Gandhi to a War conference convened in Delhi to enlist the support of Indian leaders for the recruitment campaign. At that time Gandhi believed that the British Empire was by and large a power for good, and that since India had on the whole benefited by British connection, it was the duty of every Indian to help the Empire in the hour of its need. Gandhi not only supported the resolution of the War Conference but actually toured the Kheda district (where previously he had led the peasants in Satyagraha) to persuade people to enlist.

Mahatma and the Masses

It was the Rowlatt Bill with its denial of civil liberties which finally brought Gandhi into active Indian politics. From 1919 to his death in 1948, he occupied the centre of the Indian stage and was the hero of the great historical drama which culminated in the independence of his country. He changed the entire character of the political scene in India. He only grew. In the thick of the battle he remained a man of God.

Since the Rowlatt Bill was not a local issue and the struggle was to be launched on an all-India scale, Gandhi pondered deeply what shape it should take. He had to rouse the people's enthusiasm and yet keep their passions from breaking into violence. Finally, he hit upon the idea of hartal or a national observance of mourning or protest by the closing of shops and places of business.

The hartal was observed all over India, by Hindus and Muslims alike, with an enthusiasm which surprised every one. Even Gandhi had not realized how great was his hold on the imagination of the Indian masses. The Government's complacency received a rude shock to see the war-time "recruiting sergeant" of the Empire turn a rebel. When Gandhi who was now in demand everywhere left for Delhi and Amritsar, he was served with a notice at Palwal station forbidding him to cross into the Punjab. On his refusal to obey the order, he was arrested and brought back to Bombay. The news of his arrest spread like wild fire and created great excitement among the people. Crowds gathered in cities and some violence took place. When Gandhi came to Ahmedabad and found that a police officer had been killed by the mob, he was horrified and felt that "a rapier run through my body could hardly have pained me more". He suspended the Satyagraha movement and undertook a fast for three days as penance for the violence committed by people.

On the very day, April 13, 1919, when Gandhi announced his three-day fast in Ahmedabad, the British General Dyer ordered the massacre of unarmed and peaceful citizens attending a meeting in Jallianwala Bagh at Amritsar. Later, even the official report admitted that 400 people had been killed and between 1,000 and 2,000 wounded, though the unofficial inquiry conducted by the Gandhi himself estimated 1,200 dead and 3,600 wounded. This cowardly massacre of the innocent was followed by the declaration of martial law in the Punjab, with wholesale arrests, floggings and the inhuman order by which no Indian could pass a certain street except by crawling on his belly. The events of that day which has been called by Sir Valentine Chirol as "that black day in the annals of British India" mark a turning point in the history of the Indian struggle. The moral prestige of Britain received a fatal blow. Henceforth, Gandhi could not keep away from the battlefield of Indian politics.

It was typical of Gandhi that great as was his concern over the happenings in the Punjab, he shared with equal zeal the Indian Muslim's concern at the rate of the defeated Turkish Sultan who was also the Caliph or the religious head of Islam. In fact, it was at a Muslim Conference held in Delhi in November 1919 that he first advocated noncooperation with the British Government.

It is interesting to recall that four years earlier, when he attended the Lucknow session of the Congress, he was more an observer than a participant and had seemed to Jawaharlal Nehru "very distant and different and unpolitical". In 1920, he dominated the political scene. In fact, he recreated the Congress and turned talking politicians into active revolutions and anglicized leaders of society into servants of the people who henceforth wore white homespun. He bridged the gulf between the intelligentsia and the masses and widened the concept of Swaraj to include almost every aspect of social and moral regeneration. From now on, the story of life is the story of how Congress fought for and won India's freedom.

Like a magician, Gandhi roused a storm of enthusiasm in the country with his call to non-cooperate. He began the campaign by returning to the Viceroy the medals and decorations he had received from the Government for his war-services and humanitarian work. "I can retain", he wrote to wrong to defend its immorality." Many Indians renounced their titles and honours, lawyers gave up their practice, students left colleges and schools, and thousand of the city-bred went into the villages to spread the message of nonviolent noncooperation with the "satanic" government and to prepare the masses of defy the law. The somnolent people woke up in a frenzy of courage and self-sacrifice. Bonfires of foreign cloth lit the sky everywhere and the hum of the spinning wheel rose like a sacrificial chant in thousands of homes. Women, secluded for centuries, marched in the streets with men and incidentally freed themselves from age-old shackles. In speech after speech, article after article in his two weeklies, Young India and Navjivan, Gandhi poured forth his passionate utterances which electrified the people. Thousands of people were put in prison and many more thousands were preparing to court arrest.

The anticlimax came suddenly in February 1922. An outbreak of mob violence in Chauri Chaura so shocked and pained Gandhi that he refused to continue the campaign and undertook a fast for five days to atone for a crime committed by others in a state of mob hysteria. Many of his colleagues protested and though Gandhi admitted that "the drastic reversal of practically the whole of the aggressive programme may be politically unsound and unwise", he maintained that "there is no doubt that it is religiously sound". He felt that "it is a million times better to appear untrue before the world than to be untrue to ourselves". Where Gandhi's conscience was concerned he was always ready to stand alone. However, the immediate result was that the British Government found this anticlimax a convenient opportunity to arrest him. He told the English judge at the trial : " I have no personal ill-will against any single administrator, much less can I have any disaffection towards the King's person. But I hold it a virtue to be disaffected towards a government which in its totality has done more harm to Indian than any previous system. India is less manly under British rule than ever before. Holding such a belief I consider it a sin to have any affection for the system.......... The only course open to you, the judge is either to resign your post and thus dissociate yourself from evil, if you feel that the law you are called upon to administer is an evil and that in reality I am innocent; or to inflict on me the severest penalty if you believe that the system and the law you are assisting to administer are good for the people of this country, and that my activity is therefore, injurious to the public weal."

The judge sentenced him to six years' simple imprisonment and expressed the hope that "if the course of events in India should make it possible for the Government to reduce the period and release you, no one will be better pleased than I."

Prison was for Gandhi more a luxury than a punishment. He could devote more time to prayer, study and spinning than he could outside. But in January 1924 he fell seriously ill with acute appendicitis. He was removed to a hospital in Poona where a British surgeon performed the operation. While he was convalescing he was released by the Government.

What he saw of India as a free man greatly pained him. At the time of his arrest he had left his people on the wave of a great moral upsurge which had united Hindus and Muslims as never before. But in the meanwhile the Khilafat issue had been killed by Kamal Ataturk. The Muslims no longer needed Hindu support; the two communities had drifted apart. There were communal riots in several places. Not knowing how to stem this tide of frustration, he undertook a fast if twenty-one days a to atone once again for the sins of his people. "It seems as if God has been dethroned," he said, announcing the fast. "Let us reinstate Him in our hearts." The fast caused considerable heart-searching, and long before it was over, pledges of amity poured in upon him from men of various communities.

For the next five years Gandhi seemingly retired from active agitational politics and devoted himself to the propagation of what he regarded as the basic national needs, namely, Hindu-Muslim unity, removal of untouchability, equality of women, popularization of hand-spinning and the reconstruction of village economy in general. "I am not interested". He wrote in June 1923, "freeing India merely from the English yoke. I am bent upon freeing and social and economic freedom, must go together.

There was also the fact that Gandhi, on his release from prison, had found the Congress divided. By 1929, however, the various groups had once more rallied under his leadership, and when on the last day of that year he himself moved the Resolution in the Congress session declaring complete Independence as the goal of Congress policy, it was obvious that he was again ready to lead the nation in an open challenge which was taken by millions throughout the country on January 26, 1930, which day has been celebrated as Independence as the goal of Congress policy, it was obvious that he was again ready to lead the nation in an open challenge to British rule. He drew up a pledge of "Purna Swaraj" or complete independence which was taken by millions throughout the country on January 26, 1930, which day has been celebrated as Independence Day ever since. All eyes were now turned to Sabarmati. What will the wizard of nonviolence do next?

On March 12, 1930, after having duly informed the Viceroy, Gandhi, followed by seventy-eight members of his ashram, both men and women, began his historic 24-day march to the sea beach at Dandi to break the law which had deprived the poor man of his right to make his own salt.

This seemed a small issue, but the dramatic manner in which he announced and executed the plan, the march on foot of this unarmed man of God for 241 miles, with villagers flocking from miles around to kneel by the roadside, set the imagination of the nation aflame and roused enthusiasm such as no one had anticipated. Early in the morning of April 6, after prayers, he went to the beach and picked up a little lump of salt left by the waves. This simple act was immediately followed by a nationwide defiance of the law. Men and women, simple villagers and sophisticated city folk, marched in thousands to invite arrest, police lathi charges and even shooting in many cases. Gandhi himself was arrested on May 4, soon after midnight. Within a few weeks about a hundred thousand men and women were in jail, throwing mighty machinery of the British Government out of gear.

When the First Round Table Conference met in November 1930, the Labour Government was faced with an embarrassing situation. At the closing session of the Conference, on January 19, 1931, Ramsay MacDonald expressed the hope that the Congress would be represented at the Second Round Table Conference. Gandhi and some other Congress leaders were therefore unconditionally released on January 26, exactly a year after the first independence pledge had been taken.

Soon after, on February 14, the Gandhi-Irwin talks began to the disgust of Winston Churchill, who was scandalized at "the nauseating and humiliating spectacle of this one-time Inner Temple Lawyer, now seditious fakir, striding half-naked up the steps of the Viceroy's palace, there to negotiate a parley on equal terms with the representative of the King-Emperor."

Interlude in England and a Christmas Gift

On March 5 was signed the Gandhi-Irwin Pact and on August 29 Gandhi sailed for London to attend the Second Round Table Conference as the delegate of the Congress. "There is every chance of my returning empty-handed", he said, as he embarked. He was right. But though he returned empty-handed, his visit was not without good results. He had by now become a legend and fantastic stories, some kind some malicious, had spread about him. It was good therefore for the British people to see for themselves how simple, kindly and irresistible was the charm of his personality, how universal his sympathies, how keen his humour and infectious his laughter.

In London, he declined to go to a hotel and stayed at Kingsley Hall, a social service centre in the East End, where he soon won the hearts of the young and old. His kindliness and his humour broke down the barriers of national and race prejudice. When asked why he chose to wear only a loin-cloth, he replied, "You people wear plus-fours, mine are minus-four." He went to Lancashire where his agitation against foreign cloth had caused unemployment. The workers cheered him and one of the unemployed said : "I am one of the unemployed, but if I was in India I would say the same thing that Mr. Gandhi is saying."

On his way back he visited Romain Rolland in Switzerland. It was at a meeting of the pacifists at Lausanne that he explained why rather than say, god is Truth, he would say, Truth is God.

The day he reached Bombay he said: "I am not conscious of a single experience throughout my three months stay in England and Europe that made me feel that after all East is East and West is West. On the contrary, I have been convinced more than ever that human nature is much the same, no matter under what clime it flourishes, and that if you approached people with trust and affection you would have ten-fold trust and thousand-fold affection returned to you."

But the immediate experience that awaited him hardly bore out this optimism. Even before he had reached India, the effect of the Gandhi-Irwin Pact had been destroyed by the repressive policy of the new Viceroy, Lord Willingdon. India was being ruled by Ordinances, and shooting and arrests had become the order of the day. Jawaharlal Nehru who was coming to Bombay to receive Gandhi was arrested on the way. "I take it", said Gandhi when he landed on December 28, 1931, "that these are Christmas gifts from Lord Willingdon, our Christian Viceroy." A week later Gandhi himself was arrested and locked up in Yervada Jail without trial.

Quit India

With the Outbreak of the war in 1939, Gandhi was dragged back into the political arena. He had loyally supported the Empire in the First World War. In the Boer War, even though his moral sympathies were with the Boers who were fighting for their independence, he had offered his services to the Empire out of a sense of loyalty. His feelings were different now, though, as stated, "my sympathies are wholly with the allies." He had came to believe "all war to be wholly wrong". He was also aware of the anomaly in Britain's position in fighting for freedom while denying India her. There were many patriots in India who felt that this was the hour to strike, since Britain's difficulty was India's opportunity. But Gandhi refused to countenance such an attitude. "We do not seek our independence out of Britain's ruin. That is not the way of nonviolence."

The majority of Congress leaders would have welcomed participation in the war effort, provided India could do so as an equal partner with Britain. Gandhi did not believe in conditional nonviolence, but he was realistic enough to know that he could not carry the majority of the Congress leaders, who were at best patriot-politicians, not saints, along the arduous path of absolute nonviolence. Nor was he vain enough to insist on the Congress accepting his terms as the price of his leadership, though he knew that in the impending political crisis the party could not do without him. He therefore effaced himself and advised the nation to accept the Congress stand and pleaded with the British on its behalf.

But the British Government was in no mood to listen and Winston Churchill was frank enough to say that he had not become "the King's First Minister in order to preside at the liquidation of the British Empire." In the meanwhile, the situation rapidly deteriorated. The British were unable to stem the Japanese advance to the Indian border.

The people were becoming increasingly restive and impatient, and Gandhi feared that if this excitement were not given an organized nonviolent expression, it would break out in sporadic disorder and violence. Since the British did not seem able at that time to ensure India's defence and were not willing to let India defend herself, Gandhi called upon them to "Quit India" and prepared to organize Satyagraha. Addressing historic session of the All India Congress Committee on August 7, 1942, he said : Our quarrel is not with the British people; we fight their imperialism. The proposal for the withdrawal of British power did not come out of anger. It came to enable India to play its due part at the present critical juncture." He had not yet formulated any clear plan of action. In any case, he wanted to see the Viceroy before doing so. But the initiative was taken away from his hands, for in the early hours of the morning of August 9, he and other leaders of the Congress were arrested. Disorders broke out immediately all over India, many of them violent. The Government having deprived the people of nonviolent leadership answered violence with greater violence till India virtually became a country under armed occupation.

Gandhi was interned in the Aga Khan Palace near Poona. He was greatly perturbed by the terror reigning in the country and at the British Government's charge that he was responsible for violence. He entered into a long correspondence with the Government which ended in his fasting for twenty-one years. During the fast, which began on February 10, 1943, his condition grew very critical and it was feared that he would not survive. Fortunately he did. This period in prison was one of tribulation and tragedy for Gandhi. Six days after his arrest, Mahadev Desai, his secretary and companion for twenty-four years, died suddenly of heart failure. In December 1943, Kasturbai fell ill and in February of the following year she, too, died.

The mental strain he had gone through his arrest told on Gandhi's health and six weeks after Kasturbai's death he had a severe attack of malaria. On May 3, the doctor's bulletin described his general condition as "giving rise to anxiety." The Government, embarrassed by the public agitation caused by the news of his illness, released him unconditionally on May 6. For a long time after, he was so weak that to conserve his energy he was obliged to observe long periods of silence.

But weak or strong, he could not sit idle and watch the situation in the country rapidly deteriorate. He asked to see the Viceroy but Lord Wavell declined to meet him. He knew that the British were encouraging Muslim demands to keep the Hindus and Muslims divided and were using this difference as an excuse for their continued occupation of India. Although his political career he had worked passionately for Hindu-Muslim accord. In 1919, he had made the Khilafat cause his own and had later fasted to bring about communal harmony. But the more he tried to placate the Muslims the more adamant and extravagant grew their demands until their leader Jinnah would be satisfied with nothing less than a separate state for the Muslims.

Freedom and Martyrdom

The British were unable to control the situation in India which was steadily becoming worse. Famine and disorder had sapped the foundations of imperial prestige. Britain emerged from the war victorious but physically exhausted and morally sober. The general elections of 1945 returned Labour to power and Mr. Attlee, the British Prime Minister, unwilling to lose India altogether by persisting in the Church illian policy of blood and iron, promised "an early realization of self Government in India." In the meanwhile, elections were to be held and a Constituent Assembly convened to frame a constitution for a united India. A Cabinet Mission arrived from England to discuss with Indian leaders the future shape of a free and united India, but failed to bring the Congress and Muslims together. Having encouraged Muslims separatism the British were now unable to control it,

On August 12, 1946, the Viceroy invited Jawaharlal Nehru to form an interim government. Jinnah declared a "Direct Action Day" in Bengal which resulted in an orgy of bloodshed. Shootings and stabbing took place in many places in India. This blood-red prologue to freedom was pure agony for Gandhi. He was staying in the Bhangi colony (untouchable's quarters) in Delhi from where day after day he raised his voice against violence. But his voice seemed a voice in the wilderness.

Then came the news of a large-scale outbreak of violence against the Hindu minority In the Noakhali district of East Bengal. Gandhi could no longer sit quite. He must beard the lion in his own den and teach the two communities to live and let live if necessary at the cost of his life. If he could not do that his message of nonviolence had fallen on deaf at the ears and the freedom to which he had brought India so near was not the freedom he had dream of. And so, against the pleading of his Congress colleagues who did not wish that he should risk his life, he left for Noakhali in Bengal where the Muslim League government was in power. While in Calcutta, he heard that the Hindus of Bihar had retaliated against the Muslims, repeating the outrages of Noakhali. Bitter sorrow filled Gandhi's heart, for he always felt the misdeeds of his co-religionists more acutely than he did of others, and Bihar was the land where he had launched his first Satyagraha in India. As penance, he resolved to keep himself "on the lowest diet possible" which would become "a fast unto death if the erring Biharis have not turned over a new leaf." Fortunately, "the erring Bihari's were restored to sanity by this warning and Gandhi proceeded to Noakhali.

In the noble book of Gandhi's life this chapter is the noblest. Just when political freedom was almost achieved and the State apparatus of power his for the asking, he renounced it and embraced the hazards of a lone pilgrimage to plant the message of love and courage in a wilderness of hatred and terror. In a region were 80 per cent of the people were Muslim, most of whom hostile, where there were hardly any roads and almost no means of modern communication, where hundreds of Hindus had been butchered, their women raped and thousands forcibly converted and where hordes of unruly fanatics still roamed the countryside in search of loot and fresh victims. Gandhi pitched his camp, refusing police protection and keeping only one Bengali interpreter and one stenographer with him. At the age of seventy-seven, he went barefoot from village to village, through a most difficult countryside, where low, marshy patches had to be crossed on precarious, improvised bridges of bamboo poles. He lived on local fruit and vegetables and worked day and night to plant courage in the hearts of the Hindus and love in the hearts of the Muslims. "I have only one object in view and it is a clear one : namely, that God should purify the hearts of Hindus and Muslims and the two communities should be free from suspicion and fear of one another."

Thus he lived and suffered and taught in Noakhali from November 7, 1946, to March 2, 1947, when he had to leave for Bihar in answer to persistent request. In Bihar also, he did what he had done in Noakhali. He went from village to village, mostly on foot, asking to people to make amends for the wrongs they had done to the Muslims. Unlike Noakhali, he was besieged by worshipping crowds wherever he went in Bihar. He collected money for the relief of the injured and homeless Muslims. Many women gave away their jewellery. Harrowing tales were pouring in of the massacre of the Hindus in Rawalpindi in the Punjab and but for Gandhi's presence the Biharis might have again lost their heads in a frenzy of retaliation. "If ever you become mad again, you must destroy me first", he told them.

In May 1947, he was called to Delhi where the new Viceroy, Lord Mountbatten had succeeded in persuading the Congress leaders to accept Jinnah's insistent demand for the partition of India as a condition precedent for British withdrawal. Gandhi was against partition at any cost but he was unable to convince the Congress leaders of the wisdom of his stand.

On August 15, 1947, India was partitioned and became free. Gandhi declined to attend the celebrations in the capital and went to Calcutta where communal riots were still raging. And then on the day of independence a miracle happened. A year-old riot stopped as if by magic and Hindus and Muslims began to fraternize with one another. Gandhi spent a day in fast and prayer.

Unfortunately, the communal frenzy broke loose again on August 31, and while he was staying in a Muslim house, the safety of his own persons was threatened. On the following day he went on a fast which was "to end only if and when sanity returns to Calcutta". The effect was magical. Those who had indulged in loot, arson and murder amid shouts of glee, came and knelt by his beside and begged for forgiveness. On September 4, the leaders of all communities in the city brought him a signed pledge that Calcutta would see no more of such outrages. Then Gandhi broke the fast. Calcutta kept the pledge even when many other cities were plunged in violence in the wake of Partition.

When Gandhi returned to Delhi in September 1947, the city was in the grip of communal hysteria. Ghastly tales of what had happened to Hindus and Sikhs in West Pakistan had kindled passions which burst into a conflagration when the uprooted victims of this tragedy poured into the city. In the frenzy of vengeance Hindu and Sikhs had taken the law into their hands and were looting Muslim houses, seizing mosques and stabbing innocent passer-by. The Government had taken stern measures but it was helpless without public cooperation. Into this chaos of fear and terror came this little man in the loin-cloth to bring courage to the frightened, comfort to the afflicted and sanity to the frenzied.

On his birthday October 2, when messages and greetings poured in from all over the world, he asked: "Where do congratulations come in? Would it not be more appropriate to send condolences? There is nothing but anguish in my heart . . . I cannot live while hatred and killing mar the atmosphere."

His anguish continued and increased. Though his presence had calmed the fury in Delhi, sporadic violence had occurred. The tension was still there and the Muslims could not move about freely in the streets. Gandhi was anxious to go to Pakistan to help the harassed and frightened minorities there but could not leave Delhi until the mood of the people was such as to assure him that the madness would not flare up again. He felt helpless and since, as he put it, "I have never put up with helplessness in all my life", he went on a fast on January 13, 1948. "God sent me the fast", he said. He asked people not to worry about him and to "turn the searchlight inward".

It was turned, although it is difficult to say how deep the light penetrated. On January 18, after a week of painful suspense and anxiety, representatives of various communities and organizations in Delhi including the militant Hindu organization known as R.S.S., came to Birla house where Gandhi lay on a cot, weak but cheerful, and gave him a written pledge that "we shall protect the life, property and faith of the Muslims and that the incidents which have taken place in Delhi will not happen again". Gandhi then broke the fast amid the chanting of passages from the various scriptures of the world.

Though the fast had touched the hearts of millions all over the world, its effect on the Hindu extremists was different. They were incensed at the success of the fast and felt that Gandhi had blackmailed the Hindu conscience to appease

Pakistan. On the second day after the fast while Gandhi was at his usual evening prayers, a bomb was thrown at him. Fortunately it missed the mark. Gandhi sat unmoved and continued his discourse.

It had been practice for many years to pray with the crowd. Every evening, wherever he was, he held his prayers in an open ground, facing a large congregation. No orthodox ritual was followed at these prayers. Verses from the scriptures of various religions were recited and hymns sung. At the end Gandhi would address a few words in Hindi to the congregation, not necessary on a religious theme but on any topic of the day. Whatever the topic, he raised it to a moral and spiritual plane so that even when he talked of a political issue it was as if a religious man were teaching the way of righteousness.

Sometimes these congregations were of a few hundred only and sometimes they ran into hundred of thousands, depending on the place where the prayers were held. Men of all faiths and of all political persuasions were free to come. There was no restriction. Sitting on a raise platform he was always an easy target. So far the only protection he needed was form the unbounded adulation of the adoring crowds anxious to touch his feet as is the Hindu way of showing reverence. But now the times were unhappy. Violent passions had been aroused. Hatred was in the air. Hindu fanatics were impatient with his doctrine of love and looked upon him as the main stumbling block to their lust for vengeance against Muslim atrocities in Pakistan. As in Pakistan, so here, the cry of religion in danger served as a cloak of idealism for the demon of barbaric passions. He had been warned.

The police were nervous. But Gandhi refused any kind of police protection. He care not to live except by the power of love. Forty years earlier when his life was threatened by a Pathan in South Africa, he had replied : "Death is appointed end of all life. To die by the hand of a brother, rather than by disease or in such other way, cannot be for me a matter of sorrow. And if, even in such a case, I am free from the thought of anger or hatred against my assailant, I know that will redound to my eternal welfare."

These sublime words proved to be prophetic. On January 30, 1948, ten days after the bomb incident, Gandhi hurriedly went up the few steps of the prayer ground in the large park of the Birla House. He had been detained by a conference with the Deputy Prime Minister, Sardar Vallabhbhai Patel, and was late by a few minutes. He loved punctuality and was worried that he had kept the congregation waiting. "I am late by ten minutes," he murmured. "I should be here at the stroke of five." He raised his hands and touched the palms together to greet the crowd that was waiting. Every one returned the greeting. Many came forward wanting to touch his feet. They were not allowed to do so, as Gandhi was already late. But a young Hindu from Poona forced his way forward and while seeming to do obeisance fired three point-blank shots from a small automatic pistol aimed at the heart. Gandhi fell, his lips uttering the name of God (He Ram). Before medical aid could arrive the heart had ceased to beat-the heart that had beat only love of man.

Thus died the Mahatma, at the hands of one of his own people, to the eternal glory of what he had lived for and to the eternal shame of those who failed to understand that he was the best representative of the religion for which he suffered martyrdom.

The nation's feeling was best expressed by Prime Minister Nehru when with a trembling voice and a heart full of grief he gave the news to the people on the radio:

> *"The light has gone out of our lives and there is darkness everywhere and I do not quite know what to tell you and how to say it. Our beloved leader, Bapu as we call him, the father of our nation, is no more... The light has gone out, I said, and yet I was wrong. For the light that shone in this country was no ordinary light. The light that has illumined this country for these many years, and the world will see it and it will give solace to innumerable hearts. For that light represented the living truth, and the eternal man was with us with his eternal truth reminding us of the right path, drawing us from error, taking this ancient country to freedom..."*

Such men cannot die, for they live in their achievements. His were many, each one of which, judged by the greatness of its execution or in its results for human welfare, would have made his name immortal anywhere in the world. He brought freedom from foreign subjection to a fifth of the human race. The freedom he wrought for India naturally includes that of Pakistan, for the latter was an offshoot of the former. Of no less importance was what he did for those who were once known as the untouchables. He freed millions of human beings from the shackles of caste tyranny and social indignity by his insistence that freedom was to be measured by the well-being of the millions who were living in the villages, he laid the foundation for a new way of life which may one day well provide an effective alternative to both a regiment and an acquisitive economy. His martyrdom shamed his people out of communal hysteria and helped to establish the secular and democratic character of the Indian State.

The moral influence of his personality and of his gospel and technique of nonviolence cannot be weighed in any material scale. Nor is its value limited to any particular country or generation it is his imperishable gift to humanity.

2

BIOGRAPHY OF GANDHI

CHILDHOOD

Mohandas Gandhi was born on October 2,1869, at Porbandar, on the western coast of India. His grandfather Uttamchand Gandhi and father Karamchand Gandhi occupied the high office of the diwan (Chief Minister) of Porbandar. To be Diwan of one of the princely states was on sinecure. Porbandar was one of some three hundred 'native' states in western India which were ruled by princes whom the accident of birth and the support of the British kept on the throne. To steer one's course safely between wayward Indian princes, the overbearing British 'Political Agent' of the suzerain power and the long-suffering subjects required a high degree of patience, diplomatic skill and commonsense. Both Uttamchand and Karamchand were good administrators. But they were also upright and honourable men. Loyal to their masters, they did not flinch from offering unpalatable advice. They paid the price for the courage of their convictions. Uttamchand Gandhi had his hose besieged and shelled by the ruler's troops and had to flee the State; his son Karamchand also preferred to leave Porbandar, rather than compromise with his principles.

Karamchand Gandhi was, in the words of his son, "a lover of his clan, truthful, brave, generous." The strongest formative influence on young Mohandas, however, was that of his mother Putlibai. She was a capable woman who made herself felt in court circles through her friendship with the ladies of the palace, but her chief interest was in the home. When there was sickness in the family, she wore herself out in days and nights of nursing. She had little of the weaknesses, common to women of her age and class, for finery or jewellery. Her life was an endless chain of fasts and vows through which her frame seemed to be borne only by the strength of her faith.

The children clung to her as she divided her day between the home and the temple. Her fasts and vows puzzled and fascinated them. She was not versed in the scriptures; indeed except for a smattering of Gujarati, she was practically unlettered. But her abounding lover, her endless austerities and her iron will, left a permanent impression upon Mohandas, her youngest son. The image of woman he imbibed from his mother was one of love and sacrifice. Something of her maternal love he came to possess himself, and as he grew, it flowed out in an ever-increasing measure, bursting the bonds of family and community, until it embraced the whole of humanity. To his mother, he owed not only a passion for nursing which later made him wash leper's sores in his ashram, but also an inspiration for his techniques of appealing to the heart through self-suffering-a technique which wives and mothers have practised from time immemorial.

Young Mohandas' school career was undistinguished. He did not shine in the classroom or in the playground. Quiet, shy and retiring, he was tongue-tied in company. He did not mind being rated as a mediocre student, but he was exceedingly jealous of his reputation. He was proud of the fact that he had never told a lie to his teachers or classmates; the slightest aspersion on his character drew his tears. Like most growing children he passed through a rebellious phase, but contrary to the impression fostered by his autobiography, Gandhi's adolescence was no stormier than that of many of his contemporaries. Adventures into the forbidden land of meat-eating and smoking and petty pilfering were, and are not uncommon among boys of his age. What was extraordinary was the way his adventures ended. In every case when he had gone astray, he posed for himself a problem for which he sought a solution by framing a proposition in moral algebra. 'Never again' was his promise to himself after each escapade. And he kept the promise.

OFF TO ENGLAND

Mohan passed the matriculation examination of Bombay University in 1887. His father's death a year earlier had strained the means of the family. Being the only boy in the family who had persevered in his studies, its hopes rested on him and he was sent to Bhavnagar, the nearest town with a college. Unfortunately for Mohan the teaching was in English. He was unable to follow the lectures and despaired of making any progress. Meanwhile, Mavji Dave, a friend of the family, suggested that Mohan should go to English to qualify at the bar. Mohan jumped at the idea of going abroad. His elder brother had no doubt that the proposal was attractive but wondered how they could afford it. His mother was reluctant to let her youngest boy sail to an alien land to face unknown temptations and dangers. The Modh Bania caste to which the Gandhis belonged, threatened to excommunicate the whole family if its injunction against foreign travel was infringed. All these hurdles were, however, successfully overcome by Mohan's determination to go abroad, and in September 1888, at the age of 18, he sailed for England.

From the rural surroundings of Rajkot to the cosmopolitan atmosphere of a steamship was a tremendous change for Mohan. Adaptation to Western food, dress and etiquette was a painful process. Both on board the ship and in London in the first few weeks, Mohan could not help feeling that he was making a fool of himself. He had promised his mother before leaving India that he would not "touch wine, woman or meat". The vegetarian vow became a continual source of embarrassment to him. His friends feared that his food fads would ruin his health, and make of him, socially, a square peg. To disarm his critics and to prove that, vegetarianism apart, he was not impervious to the new environment, he decided to put on a thick veneer of 'English culture'. Having made up his mind to become an 'English Gentleman', he spared neither time nor money. Whatever the cost, the veneer had to be the best in the market. New suits were ordered from the most fashionable tailors in London; the watch was adorned with a double gold chain from India; under expert tuition, lessons began in elocution, dancing and music. Gandhi could not, however, throw himself into this experiment with complete self-abandon. The habit of introspection had never deserted him. English dancing and music did nit come easy to him. He began to see that drapers and dance halls could turn him into an English gentleman, but only an English gentleman about town. After a brief three months' excursion, the introvert returned to his shell. There was a rebound from extreme extravagance to meticulous economy. He began to keep an account of every farthing he spent. He changed his rooms, cooked his own breakfast and, to save bus fares, walked eight to ten miles daily. He was able to pare down his expenses to £2 a month. He began to feel keenly the obligations to his family and was glad that he had reduced the calls on his brother for funds. Simplicity harmonized his inward and outward life; the dandyism of the first three months had been only a defensive armour against those who considered him a misfit in English society.

Vegetarianism, which had been a source of embarrassment to him, soon became an asset. He came across a book entitled Plea for Vegetarianism by Henry S. Salt, whose arguments went home. A meatless diet had been hitherto a matter of sentiment to him; henceforth, it was one of reasoned conviction. Vegetarianism was no longer an inconvenient obligation to his parents; it became a mission, the starting point of a discipline of body and mind which was to transform his life. With the zeal of a new convert, Gandhi devoured books on developed an interest in cooking, outgrew the taste for condiments, and came to the sensible conclusion that the seat of taste is not in the tongue but in the mind. The control of the palate was one of the first steps in that discipline which was to culminate many years later in total sublimation.

The immediate effect of vegetarianism was to give a new poise to young Gandhi, and to draw him out of his shell. He made his first venture into journalism by contributing nine articles to the Vegetarian. These articles, largely descriptive, and had occasional flashes of humour.

That he should have sent these articles for publication at all is a notable achievement, if we recall that back home in

Bhavnagar College he had been unable to follow lectures in English. He became a member of the Executive committee of the London Vegetarian Society. In Bays water where he stayed for a short time, he formed a vegetarian club. He came into contact with at least one eminent vegetarian, Sir Edwin Arnold, the author of the Light of Asia and The song Celestial, the two books which moved him deeply. He was stirred by the life if the Buddha and the message of the Gita. In the vegetarian restaurants and boarding houses of London he came across not only food faddists but also a few devout men of religion. He owed his introduction to the Bible to one such contact.

The New Testament, particularly the Sermon on the Mount went straight to his heart. The verses, "But I say unto you that ye resist not evil; but whosoever shall thee at the law and take away thy coat, let him have thy cloak also" reminded him of the lines of the Gujarati poet, Shamal Bhatt, which he used to hum as a child:

For a bowl of water give a goodly meal;

For a kindly greeting bow thou down with zeal;

For a single penny pay thou back with gold;

If the life be rescued, life do not withhold.

Thus the words and actions of the wise regard;

Every little service tenfold they reward.

But the truly noble know all men as one,

And return with gladness good for evil done.

The teachings of the Bible, the Buddha and Bhatt fused in his mind. The idea of returning love for hatred, and good for evil, captivated him; he did not yet comprehend it full, but it continued to ferment in his impressionable mind.

BRIEFLESS BARRISTER

In 1891 Gandhi passed the law examination successfully, but was assailed by doubts and anxieties. He had read the law, but could he practise it? He found it hard enough to speak to strangers in a small party. How would he be able to cross swords with his rivals in the courtroom? He had hard of legal luminaries like Sir Pherozeshah Mehta of Bombay and could well imagine the sorry figure he would cut in comparison. It was thus "with just a little leaven of hope mixed with despair" that he sailed for India.

A great shock lay in store for him when he landed at Bombay. His mother had died while he was in England. It was only natural that he should have been anxious to justify the hopes of his family which had invested so much on his foreign education. His elder brother frankly expected rich dividends in the form of "wealth, and name and fame". The barrister's degree, however, was not an open sesame to the top of the bar. Gandhi noticed that the home-bred Vakils of Rajkot knew more of Indian law and charged lower fees than England sure ridicule; Gandhi, therefore, accepted the advice of friends to go to Bombay to study India law and to secure what briefs he could.

His experience in Bombay was no happier than in Rajkot. After waiting unconscionably, he got his first brief for the modest fee of thirty rupees. As he rose to cross-examine a witness, he was unable to collect his thoughts, collapsed into his chair and refunded the fee to his client. This was a disgraceful debut, which filled the young barrister with black despair as to his future in a profession he had entered at such a heavy cost.

The straits to which he had been reduced may be surmised from the fact that he applied and was turned down for a part time job as a teacher in a Bombay high school with the modest salary of seventy rupees (£5 1/2) a month. It was with some relief that he discovered that he had a flair for drafting memorials and petitions. He wound up his little establishment in Bombay and returned to Rajkot where petition-writing brought him an income of three hundred rupees a month. He might have settled down as a barrister scribe if he had not incurred the displeasure of the British Political Agent in Rajkot in whose court most of his work lay. So, when an offer of a job came to him from South Africa, he gladly accepted it. The contract was for a year in connection with a civil suit; the remuneration was £105, a first-class return fare and actual expenses. The fee was modest and it was not quite clear whether he was engaged as counsel or as a clerk, but he was in no position to pick and choose. He could hardly have imagined the new vistas of maturity and public service which the South African adventure was to open to him.

IN THE 'DARK CONTINENT'

Gandhi landed at Durban in May 1893. His employer Dada Abdulla, one of the wealthiest Indian merchants in Natal, took him to see the Durban court. When the European magistrate ordered Gandhi to take off his turban, he refused, left the courtroom and wrote a letter of protest in the local press in which he was mentioned "as an unwelcome visitor". The experience in Durban, however, was nothing compared with what befell him in the course of his journey from Durban to Pretoria. When his train reached Maritzburg late in the evening, he was ordered to leave the first class compartment and shift to the van compartment. He refused, but was unceremoniously turned out of the carriage. It was a bitterly cold night as he crept into the unlit waiting-room of Maritzburg station and brooded over what had happened. His client had given him no warning of the humiliating conditions under which Indians lived in South Africa. Should he not call off the contract and return to India? Should he accept these affronts as part of the bargain? So far Gandhi had not been conspicuous for assertiveness; on the contrary he had been pathologically shy and retiring. But something happened to him in that windswept waiting-room of Maritzburg railway station as he smarted under the insult inflicted on him. The iron entered his soul. In retrospect, this incident seemed to him as one of the most creative experiences of his life. From that hour, he refused to accept injustice as a part of the natural-or unnatural-order in South Africa. He would reason, he would plead; he would appeal to the better judgment and the latent humanity of the ruling race; he would resist, but he would never be a willing victim of racial arrogance. It was not so much a question of redeeming his own self-respect as that of his community, his country, even of humanity.

The helpless resignation of the mass of Indian settlers, the fact that they were illiterate, had few rights and did not know how to assert the rights they had. All this had the miraculous effect of dissipating young Gandhi's own diffidence. The feeling of inferiority which had dogged him as a student in England and as a budding lawyer in India vanished. In Bombay he had been unable to face a small cause court but one of the first things he did on arrival at Pretoria was to convene a meeting of the Indian residents "to present to them a picture of their condition in Transvaal".

During the next twelve months, Gandhi was busy with the civil suit which had brought him to Pretoria. In June 1894, he returned to Durban to sail for India. At the farewell party which his grateful client Dada Abdulla gave him at Sydenham, a pleasant suburb of Durban, Gandhi happened to glance through the pages of the Natal Mercury, and learnt that a bill was being introduced into the Natal Legislature to disfranchise India settlers. Gandhi's host and other Indian merchants present at the party were unable to throw any light on this measure. They knew enough English to be able to converse with their white customers, but few of them could read newspapers, much less follow the proceedings of the Natal Legislature. They had come to Natal for trade, and politics did not interest them. They had not yet realized that politics could affect their trade. "This is the first nail into our coffin", was Gandhi's comment. The Indian merchants pleaded with him to stay on in Natal to take up the fight on their behalf. Gandhi agreed to defer his stay for a month.

Gandhi lost no time in settling down to work; the farewell party converted itself into a political committee to plan Indian opposition to the bill. A sound instinct seems to have guided the young barrister in organizing his first political campaign. He infused a spirit of solidarity into the heterogeneous elements composing the Indian community, and brought home the implications of the disfranchising measures not only to his own people, but to the saner section of the European public opinion and the Natal Government Most important of all, he gave the widest publicity to his campaign to quicken the conscience of the peoples and Governments of India and Great Britain; through petitions to the legislatures, statements in newspapers, letters to prominent persons in Natal, Britain and India, and through public meeting, Gandhi stressed the justice of the Indians, case. All this created a great stir but the disfranchising bill was nevertheless passed by the Natal Legislature. On the insistence of his Indian friends in Durban, Gandhi agreed to prolong his stay in Natal, and was enrolled as an advocate to the Supreme Court. Since he retaining fees to produce a minimum 300 a year which he reckoned enough to pay his way in Durban.

THE YOUNG POLITICIAN

The first experience of political agitation into which Gandhi had been pitch forked cured him of what once had seemed an incorrigible self-consciousness. Not that he had a sudden attack of egotism; he was conscious of his limitations, and in a letter dated July 5, 1894 to Dadabhai Nauroji, the eminent leader of the Indian National Congress, wrote: "A word for myself and I have done. I am inexperienced and young and, therefore, quite liable to make mistakes. The responsibility undertaken is quite out of proportion to my ability. So, you will see that I have not taken the matter up, which is beyond my ability, in order to enrich myself at the expense of the Indians. I am the only available person who can handle the question." The concept of inferiority is a relative one; in a community looking to him for leadership, Gandhi forgot his own limitations. As the only available person, he undertook a task from which elsewhere he would have shrunk. Gandhi had come to South Africa in 1893 for a year. He could hardly have imagined that he would have to stay on for the best part of two decades. The struggle of the Indian immigrants for elementary civic rights was to be long and hard The disfranchising of the Indians which had been the immediate cause of Gandhi's intervention in the politics of Natal was only a symptom of the racial malaise that had begun to afflict the Dark Continent.

"The Asiatics", wrote Lord Milner, "are strangers forcing themselves upon a community reluctant to receive them." In fact, the Indian emigration to South Africa in the eighteen-sixties started at the instance of the European settlers who were in possession of vast virgin lands ideal for tea, coffee and sugar plantations, but lacked manpower. The Negro could not be compelled to work after the abolition of slavery. Recruiting agents of the European planters toured some of the poorest and most congested districts of India and painted rosy prospects of work in Natal. Free passage, board and lodging; a wage of ten shillings a month for the first year rising by one shilling every year; and the right to a free return passage to India after five years' 'indenture' (or alternatively, the option to settle in the land of their adoption) drew thousands of poor and illiterate Indians to distant Natal.

The European planters and merchants did not relish the idea of Indian Labourers settling down as free citizens at the end of the five year' 'indenture'. A tax of £3 was therefore levied on every member of the family of an ex-indentured labourer even though he was merely exercising his right to settle in Natal in terms of the agreement which had governed his emigration from India. It was a crippling tax for the poor wretches whose wages ranged between ten and twelve shillings month.

The Indian merchant who had followed the Indian labourer to Natal had disabilities of his own. No one could trade without a licence, which a European could have for the asking and Indian only after much effort and expense, if at all. And since an educational test in a European language was made a sine quanon for an immigrant from India, except of course the semi-slave indentured labourers who continued to be imported.

The legal disabilities on Indians were bad enough, but the daily humiliations they suffered were worse. They were commonly described as "Asian dirt to be heartily curse, chokeful of vice, that live upon rice and the black vermin". They were not allowed to walk on footpaths. First and second class tickets were not issued to them. If a white passenger objected, they could be unceremoniously bundled out of a railway compartment; they had sometimes to travel on footboards of trains. European hotels would not admit them.

Gandhi realized that what the India urgently needed was a permanent organization to look after their interests. Out of deference to Dadabhai Naµroji, Who had presided over the Indian National Congress in 1893, he called the new organization Natal Indian Congress. He was not conversant with the constitution and functions of the Indian National Congress. This ignorance proved an asset, as he fashioned the Natal Congress in his own way to suit the needs of the Natal Indians, as a live body functioning throughout the year and dedicated not only to politics but to the moral and social uplift of its members. Though it served a community which had very little political experience, it was not a one-man show. An indefatigable secretary though he was, Gandhi enlisted popular interest and enthusiasm at every step. He made the enrolment of members and the collection of subscriptions into something more than a routine. He employed a gently but irresistible technique for exerting moral pressure on halfhearted supporters. Once in a small village, he sat through the night and refused to take his dinner until at dawn his host, an Indian merchant, agreed to raise his subscription for thc Natal Indian Congress from three to six pounds.

In these early years of his politics apprenticeship, Gandhi formulated his own code of conduct for a politician. He did not accept the popular view that in politics one must fight for one's; arty, right or wrong. He avoided exaggeration and discouraged it in his colleagues. The Natal Indian Congress was not merely an instrument for the defence of political and economic rights for the Indian minority, but also a lever for its internal reform and unity. He did not spare his own people and roundly criticized them for their shortcomings. He was not only the stoutest champion of the Natal Indians, but also their severest critic.

Under his leadership, the Indian community in Natal endeavoured to secure the repeal of discriminatory laws and vexatious regulations and stave off further oppressive measures. Gandhi was in touch with Nauroji and other members of the British committee of the Indian National Congress in London. He sought their advice and support in representing the South African Indian Indian's case to the Secretary of State for India, and British Colonial Secretary. He was an indefatigable correspondent, bombarding his friends, opponents, newspaper editors and men in authority in three continents, with telegrams, letters and memoranda on the grievances of the India in South Africa. It is a measure of Gandhi's success as a publicist that the Indian National Congress Recorded its protest against the disabilities imposed upon the Indian settlers in South Africa, and the London Times devoted several leading articles to this problem. In 1896 he paid a brief visit to India to canvass public support for the cause he had made his own. On return to Natal from this trip on January 10,1897, he was nearly lynched in the streets Durban by a mob of Europeans who had been infuriated by Press reports of Gandhi's advocacy of the Indian cause in his native land.

On the outbreak of the Boer War in 1899, Gandhi organized an Indian Ambulance Corps of 1100 men. Vere Stent, the editor of the Pretoria News, has left a fascinating pen-portrait of Gandhi in the battlefield: "After a night's work which had shattered men with much bigger frames, I came across Gandhi in the early morning sitting by the roadside-eating a regulation biscuit. Every man in (General) Buller's force was dull and depressed, and damnation was heartily invoked on everything. But Gandhi was stoic in his bearing, cheerful and confident in his conversation and had a kindly eye." It must be recognised that Gandhi's ideas on nonviolence had not yet fully matured. His argument at this time was that Indian settlers in British colonies, while demanding all the privileges of citizenship must also accept all its obligations, which included participation in the defence of the country of adoption. Gandhi's gesture in raising an ambulance corps on behalf of a minority which was denied elementary rights was a fine one, but it was wasted. The end of the Boer War brought no relief to the Indians. Their grievances remained unredressed. Indeed, new chains were forged for them in the former Boer Colonies.

THE MAKING OF MAHATMA

In 1914 Gandhi left South Africa. He had gone there as a junior counsel of a commercial firm for £105 a year; he had stayed on to command, and then voluntarily to give up a peak practice of £5000 a year. In Bombay as a young lawyer he had a nervous breakdown while cross-examining witnesses in a petty civil suit; in the South Africa, he had founded a new political organization with the sure touch of a seasoned politician. The hostility of the European politicians and officials and the helplessness of the Indian merchants and labourers had put him on his mettle. No glittering rewards for him; the perils ranged from professional pinpricks to lynching. Nevertheless, it was a piece of good fortune that he began his professional and political career in South Africa. Dwarfed as he had felt by the great lawyers and leader of India, it is unlikely that he would have developed much initiative in his homeland. When he founded the Natal Indian Congress at the age of twenty-five, he was writing on a tabula rasa: he could try out ideas which in an established political organization would have been laughed out court.

What had truth and vows to do with politics? It was a question which often recurred in Indian politics, and if Gandhi was not confounded by it, it was because, far back in South Africa, he had observed and confirmed the connection. For a man who was no doctrinaire, and whose theory often lagged behind practice, it was a decided advantage that the scene of his early activities should have been one where he was unfettered by political precedents or professionals. Natal and Transvaal were no bigger than some of the smallest provinces of India. The struggle for Indian independence was conducted Gandhi on much larger scale and on much bigger issues, but there were not a few occasions when he derived inspiration from his experience in South Africa.

Not only his politics, but his personality took shape in South Africa. The most formative years of his life had been spent there. His interest in moral and religious questions dated back to his early childhood. But it was only in South Africa that he had an opportunity of studying them systematically. His Quaker friends in Pretoria failed to convert him to Christianity, but they whetted his innate appetite for religious studies. He delved deep into Christianity and other religions, including his own. In his first year in South Africa he read 'quite eighty books', most of them on religion. One of these was Tolstoy's Kingdom of God is Within You. Tolstoy became his favourite author and in the coming years he read the Gospels in Brief, What to do? The Slavery of Our Times, How Shall We Escape? Letters to a Hindu and The First Step. Tolstoy's bold idealism and fearless candour gripped him, his Christian anarchism dissipated the spell of institutional religion. Tolstoy's emphasis on the necessity of an accord between moral principles and daily life confirmed his own strivings for self-improvement.

Few men read so little to so much profit as Gandhi did. A book was for Gandhi not a mere diversion for the hour, it was embodied experience, which had to be accepted or rejected. Ruskin's Unto The Last drove him with compelling urgency from the capital of Natal to the wilderness of Zululand to practise a life of voluntary poverty, and literally to live by the sweat of his brow. It was in Tolstoy's books that we may seek one of the strongest influences on Gandhi. He was, of course, not given to indiscriminate imitation. But in Tolstoy he found a writer whose views elaborated his own inchoate beliefs. It was not only on the organized or covert violence of the modern state and the right of the citizen to civil disobedience that Gandhi found support in Tolstoy.

RETURN TO INDIA

A hero's welcome awaited Gandhi when he landed on January 9, 1915, at the Apollo Bunder in Bombay. Three days later he was honoured by the people of Bombay at a magnificent reception in the palatial house of a Bombay magnate Jehangir Petit. The Government of India joined with the people of India in showering honours on Gandhi. He received a "Kaiser-I-Hind" gold medal in the King's birthday honours list of 1915. His association with Gokhale was guarantee enough of his being a safe politician.

Of course, he had led an extra-constitutional movement in South Africa, defied laws and filled goals, but the cause for which he had fought appeared as much humanitarian as political, dear to all Indian as and all Englishmen whose sense of humanity had not been blunted by racial arrogance or political expediency. Lord Hardinge's open support of the Satyagraha movement had in any case removed the stigma of rebellion from South Africa's Indian movement.

Gandhi was in no hurry to plunge into politics. His political mentor on the Indian scene was Gokhale. One of the first things Gokhale did was to extract a promise from Gandhi that he would not express himself upon public questions for a year, which was to be a "year of probation". Gokhale was very keen that Gandhi should join the Servants of India Society in Poona. Gandhi was only too willing to fall in with the wishes of Gokhale, but several members of the Society feared that there was too great a gap between the ideals and methods of the Society and those of Gandhi. While the question of his admission as a 'Servant of India' was being debated, Gandhi visited his home towns of Porbandar and Rajkot and went on to Shantiniketan in West Bengal, the cosmopolitan University of the Poet Rabindranath Tagore.

GANDHI'S ASHRAM

While his political views were yet unformed, Gandhi's immediate problem was to settle the small band of relatives and associates in the South African struggle who had cast their lot in with him. He decided to found an ashram and locate it at Kochrab, a village near Ahmedabad. Later the ashram was shifted to a more permanent site on the bank of the river Sabarmati. Gandhi once defined an ashram as "group life lived in a religious spirit".

The word "religious" was used here in the widest sense. The ashram did not enforce on its inmates any theology or ritual, but only a few simple rules of personal conduct. Some of the vows administered in the ashram, such as those to truth, nonviolence and chastity, were of universal application; others, such as those to eradicate untouchability, to do physical labour and to practise fearlessness were intended to meet the peculiar conditions of the Indian society, which was caste-ridden, discounted dignity of labour and was dominated by an alien government. All these vows were to be observed in an intelligent and creative way. They were not intended to be mechanical formulae, but as practical aids to moral and spiritual growth. They may appear to be platitudes, but nevertheless they embodied ancient truths which were none the less valid for not having been realized by the common run of mankind in workaday life.

A mere enumeration of the vows is enough to indicate that life in the ashram was austere. It was also busy. Everyone had to put in some manual work. There was a spinning and weaving department, a cowshed and a large farm. Every inmate of the ashram cleaned his own plates and washed his own clothes. There were no servants. The atmosphere was, however, not so much of a monastery but that of a large family under a kindly but exacting patriarch. Gandhi was Bapu, the father of the household, Kasturba was Ba, the mother. It was a motley group including little children and octogenarians, graduates of American and European universities and Sanskrit scholars, devout whole-hoggers, and thinly disguised sceptics.

It was a human laboratory where Gandhi tested his moral and spiritual hypotheses. It was also to him what the family is to most people, a haven from the dust and din of the world. It was a family linked not by blood or property, but by allegiance to common ideals. Gandhi ruled the ashram but his authority in the ashram, as well as in the rest of the country, was moral. When things went wrong or a member of the ashram was guilty of a serious lapse, Gandhi would take the blame upon himself and atone for it by undertaking a fast.

WORLD WAR I

When World War I broke out, Gandhi was on the high seas, he was homeward bound, though he hoped to spend a few weeks in England. On August 6, 1914, he landed on English soil and lost no time in calling a meeting of his Indian friends to raise an ambulance unit. The argument that the Empire's crisis was India's chance did not impress him: "I knew the difference of status between an Indian and an Englishman," he wrote later, "but I did not believe that we had been quite reduced to slavery. I felt then that it was more the fault of individual officials than of the British system, and that we could convert them by love. If we would improve our status through the help and cooperation of the British, it was our duty to win their help by standing by them in their hour of need."

Were it not for an attack of pleurisy, Gandhi may have continued to serve in the ambulance unit he had raised, and his return to India may have been indefinitely delayed.

When he arrived in India he found that nationalist opinion was opposed to unconditional support for the war effort. Only those who were politically backward or flourished on official patronage were for loyalty at all costs. Gandhi did not favour a bargain with the government by offering cooperation at a price and said: "That we have been loyal at a time of stress is no test of fitness for Swaraj (self-government). Loyalty is no merit. It is a necessity of citizenship all the world over."

During the years 1916-18, Gandhi did not take active part in politics. His ideals and methods did not quite fit in with those of the two dominant groups in the Indian National Congress. The Moderates did not like his extra-constitutional methods of Satyagraha, the Extremists did not like his studied tenderness to the British Government during the war. He did not participate in the Home Rule agitation nor in the negotiations which led to the Lucknow pact between the Indian National Congress and the All India Muslim League. He seemed to be isolated from the main currents of Indian politics. It was not Gandhi, but the Annie Besant-Tilak combination which dominated the national scene and impressed the Government. Edwin Montague, a member of the British Cabinet, who visited India in 1917, recorded in his diary that Tilak was "at the moment probably the most powerful man in India." Gandhi seemed to Montague "a social reformer with a real desire to find grievances and to cure them not for any reasons of self advertisement, but to improve the conditions of his fellowmen. He dresses like a coolie, forswears all personal advancement, lives practically on the air and is a pure visionary."

The fact that he was committed to abstention from political agitation during the war did not prevent Gandhi from championing just grievances which could not brook delay. In the summer of 1917, he went to the indigo-growing district of

Champaran and took up the cause of the tenants against the European planters. The same year he led the textile workers of Ahmedabad in a strike against the mill-owners. The following year, he agitated for reduction of land tax in Kaira district where crops had suffered from the failure of rains. The local officers were perturbed by Gandhi's activities but the Government was anxious not to precipitate a showdown. Gandhi himself took care to localize these conflicts and sought solutions which secured a modicum of justice to the workers and peasants without creating a national crisis.

Early in 1918, the war seemed to be going badly for the Allies; a German thrust was expected on the western front, and the Viceroy summoned prominent leaders of Indian opinion to a War Conference in Delhi. Gandhi supported the resolution on recruitment with a single sentence in Hindi: "With a full sense of my responsibility, I beg to support the resolution."

After the War Conference, Gandhi threw himself heart and soul into a recruiting campaign There was something comic in this votary of nonviolence touring the villages of his home province of Gujarat to secure recruits for the British Indian army to fight in the battle fronts of Europe. Not infrequently, unable to get bullock-carts for their journeys in the interior of the Gujarat countryside, Gandhi and his colleagues had to march on foot twenty miles a day. The strain was too much for him and at last a severe attack of dysentery laid him low.

Meanwhile the war came to end, and Gandhi learnt that the Sedition Committee Report had been published and the Government of India proposed to introduce legislation to curb civil liberties. He had been almost alone among Indian leaders who had argued for unconditional support to Britain in her hour of need in the hope of a worthy gesture at the end of he war. He felt that he had received stone for bread. He had done his best to keep out of political agitation during the war. Now he felt an irresistible call to fight a wrong perpetrated in peace.

ROWLATT BILLS

The Government of India rushed the Rowlatt Bills, through the Imperial Legislative Council in March 1919 in the teeth of the opposition of all the elected Indian members. Gandhi heard the debate in the Imperial Legislative Council and saw how the eloquent logic of Indian councillors had been wasted on the official benches. "You can wake a man," he wrote later, "only if he is really asleep; no effort that you may make will produce any effect upon him if he is merely pretending sleep". The conviction grew upon him that the Government of India was impervious to popular feeling. A Government which really cared for public opinion would not have enacted a measure-whatever its merits-which had been opposed by every shade of public opinion.

NONVIOLENT NON-COOPERATION

The programme of "nonviolent noncooperation" included the boycott of councils, courts and schools, set up by the British and of all foreign cloth. With some naivete Gandhi claimed that his movement was not unconstitutional: In his dictionary, constitutional and moral were synonymous terms. The British saw that the success of "noncooperation" would paralyse their administration. Lord Chelmsford, the Viceroy, tried to kill with ridicule "the most foolish of all foolish schemes", which would "bring ruin to those who had any stake in the country". A number of eminent "moderate" politicians joined official critics in underlining the risks of mass noncooperation as proposed by Gandhi.

That a political programme had no chance of success without an adequate organization to implement it, Gandhi had realized at the age of twenty-five, when he had founded the Natal Indian Congress to fight for the rights of Indians in Natal. The Indian National Congress, had, therefore, to be refashioned, if it was to prove an efficient instrument of nonviolent noncooperation. Gandhi saw that what the country needed was not a forum for an annual pageant and feast of oratory, but a militant organization in touch with the masses. Under the new constitution, the Congress was given a broad-based pyramidal structure by formation of village, taluka, district and provincial committees, with the All India Congress Committee and the Working Committee at the apex. The

Congress was thus reorganized not only on a more representative basis, but in such a way that it could function efficiently between its annual sessions. It ceased to be a preserve of the upper and middle classes; its doors were opened to the masses in the small towns and villages whose political consciousness Gandhi himself was quickening.

Gandhi was swept to the top of Indian politics in 1919-20 because he had caught the imagination of the people. He was loved and respected as the Mahatma, the great soul; with voluntary poverty, simplicity, humility and saintliness, he seemed a rishi (sage) of old who had stepped from the pages of an ancient epic to bring about the liberation of his country. Nay, to millions he was the incarnation of God. It was not only for his message that people came to him, but for the merit of seeing him. The sacred sight of the Mahatma-his darshan-was almost equivalent to a pilgrimage to holy Benares. The unthinking adoration of the multitude sometimes made Gandhi feel sick. "The woes of the Mahatma", he wrote, "are known only to the Mahatma". But this adoration was the mainspring from which was drawn the immense influence he exercised over Indian public life.

Gandhi had struck some of the inner chords of Indian humanity; his appeal for courage and sacrifice evoked a ready response because he was himself the epitome of these qualities. It was because he was, to use Churchill's epithet, a "naked fakir", because his life was one of austerity and self-sacrifice that a great emotional bond grew between him and the Indian people. The number of such "fakirs" was to multiply fast. Among those who gave up their lucrative careers and queued up for prison under Gandhi's leadership were Motilal Nehru, Rajendra Prasad, C.R. Das, Vallabhbhai Patel, and C. Rajagopalachari. Life acquired a new meaning for them. Abbas Tyabji, a former Chief Justice of Baroda, wrote from a village that he was feeling twenty years younger. "God?" he exclaimed, "what an experience ! I have so much love and affection for the common folk to whom it is now an honour to belong. It is the fakir's dress that has broken down all barriers." It is of this period that Jawaharlal Nehru has written in his autobiography that the movement absorbed him so wholly that he "gave up all other associations and contacts, old friends, books, even newspapers except in so far as they dealt with the work in hand.... I almost forgot my family, my wife, my daughter."

From the autumn of 1920, the noncooperation movement gathered momentum. The attitude of the Government at first was one of caution. It was reluctant to launch a drastic repression, as it did not want to alienate moderate Indian opinion. Soon after his arrival in India in April, 1921, Lord Reading, the new Viceroy, met Gandhi. In a private letter to his son, the Viceroy confessed to a feeling of excitement, almost a thrill, in meeting his unusual visitor and described his religious and moral views as admirable, though he found it difficult to understand his practice of them in politics.

Throughout 1921, the tension between the Congress and the Government was steadily mounting. There was no meeting of minds between Gandhi and Reading. The Ali Brothers, the principal leaders of the Khilafat, were arrested in September 1921 on a charge of inciting the army to disloyalty; their offence was repeated by a number of Indian leaders including Gandhi. This was a challenge which was difficult for the Government not to accept. The official optimism that the movement would melt away by internal differences or popular apathy proved to be misplaced. Nearly thirty thousand non-cooperators were arrested. The Government was reluctant to touch Gandhi until a favourable opportunity came. Indeed as late as December 1921, Lord Reading seemed willing to hold a round table conference with Gandhi and other Indian leaders to reach an understanding and to avoid unseemly scenes during the visit to India of the Prince of Wales. Lord Reading was, however, hardly in a position to make any substantial political concessions. Meanwhile, Gandhi was under increasing pressure from his adherents to launch a civil disobedience campaign. The Ahmedabad Congress in December 1921 invested him with authority to launch a mass movement. Mass civil disobedience was, in the words of Gandhi, "an earthquake, a sort of general upheaval on the political plane-the Government ceases to function... the police stations, the courts, offices, etc., all cease to be Government property and shall be taken charge of by the people." He proposed to proceed cautiously. His plan was to launch civil disobedience in one district; if it succeeded he proposed to extend it to the adjacent districts, and so on, until the whole of India was liberated. But he gave a clear warning that if violence broke out in any form in any part of the country, the movement would lose its character as a movement of peace, "even as a lute would begin to emit notes of discord the moment a single string snaps."

A riot which disfigured Bombay during the visit of Prince of Wales in November 1921 had led Gandhi to postpone civil disobedience. Nevertheless, two months later, under growing pressure from his colleagues, he decided to launch a no-tax campaign in Bardoli taluka in Gujarat. He communicated the step he contemplated, with his reasons for it, in a letter to the Viceroy. This was taken by the Government of India as an ultimatum. A head-on collision between the Government on the one hand and the nationalist forces on the other seemed imminent. Gandhi's letter to the Viceroy was dated February 1,1922. Three days later, there was a clash between a procession and the police at Chauri Chaura, a small village in the United Province, in which the police station was set on fire and 22 policemen were killed.

Gandhi viewed the Chauri Chaura tragedy as a red signal, a warning that the atmosphere in the country was.too explosive for a mass movement. He decided to retrace his steps, to cancel the plans for civil disobedience in Bardoli, to suspend the aggressive part of the noncooperation campaign, and to shift the emphasis to the 'constructive' programme of hand-spinning, communal unity, abolition of untouchability, etc. His action shocked and bewildered his closest colleagues. Their reaction is best expressed in Romain Rolland's words: "It was dangerous to assemble all the forces of a nation and to hold the nation panting before a prescribed movement, to lift one's arm to give the final command, then at the last moment, let one's arm drop and thrice call a halt just as the formidable machinery has been set in motion. One risks ruining the brakes and paralysing the impetus." The Viceroy, Lord Reading, cheerfully confided to his son that Gandhi "had pretty well run himself to the last ditch as a politician by extraordinary manifestation in the last month or six weeks before his arrest".

ARREST AND IMPRISONMENT

The Government seized the opportunity for which it was waiting. On the evening of March 10, 1922, Gandhi was arrested in his ashram. The trial was held before Broomfield, District and Sessions Judge of Ahmedabad. The British judge behaved with great consideration, nodding respectfully to the accused in the dock before taking his seat. He acknowledged that Gandhi was in a different category from any person that he had ever tried or was likely to try. Gandhi made his task easy by pleading guilty. He was sentenced to six years' imprisonment.

An observer noted that Gandhi was not only serene but 'festively joyful' during the 100-minute trial. "So far as the sentence is concerned," he told the judge "I certainly consider that it is as light as any judge would inflict on me; and so far as the whole proceedings are concerned, I must say that I could not have expected greater courtesy." He was lodged in the Yeravda prison in Poona. He was not allowed to sleep in the open. He was denied a pillow but he devised one with books and spare clothes. Among the 150 and odd books he read during this term were Henry James' The Varieties of Religious Experience, Bernard Shaw's Man and Superman, Buckle's History of Civilization, Wells' Outline of History, Goethe's Faust and Kipling's Barrack Room Ballads. He kept up his daily routine of morning and evening prayers, and spinning. His literary and religious studies which had been neglected in the midst of other activities were resumed. There is no doubt that in spite of occasional pinpricks, prison life proved for Gandhi, as Tagore once put it, "arrest cure".

REACTION AND RECOVERY

Soon after Gandhi's imprisonment, signs of a serious rift appeared among his followers. Some prominent Congressmen including Motilal Nehru and C.R. Das declared themselves in favour of lifting the boycott of the councils. They formed the

Swaraj Party to contest elections to the provincial and central legislative councils and to "carry the fight into the enemy's camp". Vallabhbhai Patel, Rajagopalachari and others who were opposed to any change in the original non cooperation programme came to be known as 'No-Changers'. During the whole of 1923, Congress politics were extremely fluid. There were a number of resignations from the Working Committee and the All India Congress Committee, bona fides were questioned; 'points of order' were raised, and the constitution of Congress discussed threadbare. In September 1923, at a special session of the Congress, it was decided that the Swarajists should be allowed to put up candidates at the election, which were scheduled in November. The Swarajists had barely two months to fight the elections, but they succeeded in capturing a solid bloc of seats in the Central Legislative Assembly, a substantial representation in provincial legislatures and even a majority in the Central Provinces Council. Motilal Nehru led the party in the Central Assembly, while C. R. Das took up the leadership of the party in Bengal Council.

In February, after he had served only two years in jail, Gandhi, after an operation for appendicitis, was released. He did not, as his faithful No-Changers hoped, throw his weight in their favour. On the contrary, he did everything to avoid a split in the party. He made a series of gestures to the "rebels"-the Swarajists-and let them dominate the political stage. The Viceroy wrote home: "Gandhi is now attached to the tail of Das and Nehru, although they try their utmost to make him and his supporters think that he is one of the heads, if not the head."

If the rift in the Congress ranks on Council entry was one disappointment to Gandhi, after his release from jail, the division between Hindus and Muslims was another and greater. The Hindu-Muslim unity of the heyday of noncooperation movement was now a mere memory. Trust had given way to distrust,. Apart from the riots which periodically disfigured several towns, there was a new bitterness in politics and in the press. There were not a few who put down the new tension to the noncooperation movement and its alliance with the 'Khilafat" cause, and blamed Gandhi for having played with the masses and roused them prematurely. "The awakening of the masses," wrote Gandhi, "was a necessary part of the training. I would do nothing to put the people to sleep again." However, he wanted this awakening to be diverted into constructive channels. The two communities had to be educated out of the mental morass into which they had slipped. His doctrine of nonviolence held the key not only to the political freedom of the country but also to peace between the communities. Hearts could never be united by breaking heads. A civilized society which had given up violence as a means of settling individual disputes could also eschew violence for reconciling differences between groups. Disagreements could be resolved by mutual tolerance and compromise.

In September 1924, Gandhi went on a twenty-one day fast to "purify" himself and " to recover the power to react on the people." The fast had a soothing effect, but only for a while; India had not yet seen the last of communal wrangles. The problem had really been reduced to the struggle for fruits of political power between the professional classes of the two communities. It was a scramble for crumbs which the British offered to political India. Gandhi had declared that "majorities must set the example of self-sacrifice." The blank cheque which he later offered to the Muslims was ridiculed by them and resented by the Hindus, but it epitomized his approach to this squabble for seats in legislatures and jobs under the Government. Unfortunately in the course of the negotiations, the Hindus tended to deal with Muslims as the British Government dealt with nationalist India: they made concessions but it was often a case of too little and too late.

During the next three years, while national politics were dominated by communal issues and controversies in legislatures, Gandhi retired from the political scene; to be precise, he retired only from the political controversies of the day to devote his time to the less spectacular but more important task of nation-building "from the bottom up". He toured the country extensively from one end to the other, using every mode of transport from railway trains to bullock-carts. He exhorted the people to shake off the age-old social evils such as child-marriage and untouchability, and to ply the spinning wheel. Primarily advocated as a solution of the chronic underemployment in the villages, the spinning-wheel in Gandhi's hands became something more than a simple tool of a cottage industry. In his efforts to "sell" the spinning wheel to the people, he romanticized it. He put in forward not only as a panacea for economic ills but also for national unity and freedom. It became a symbol of defiance of foreign rule; Khadi, the cloth made from yarn spun on the spinning wheel, became the nationalist garment, the 'livery of freedom', as Jawaharlal Nehru once picturesquely described it.

By 1928 Indian politics began to recover from the malaise which had affected them after the collapse of the noncooperation movement seven years before. This recovery was assisted by discontent among industrial workers, peasants and middle class youth. The trade unions became militant bodies. The peasantry was in distress because of an unprecedented economic depression; there was a dramatic no-tax campaign in Bardoli in Gujarat, Gandhi's home province, under his able lieutenant, Vallabhbhai Patel. The Swaraj Party which had professed an alternative to the Gandhian programme was deeply disillusioned by 1928; dissensions and defections had emasculated it.

In November 1927, the British Government announced the appointment of a royal Commission headed by Sir John Simon, to report on the working of the

Constitutional reforms of 1919, and on the possibilities of further advance towards self-government. The commission included representatives of the British political parties, but no Indian. The "all-white" commission came to be looked upon in India as an inquisition by foreigners into India's fitness for self-government. The Indian National Congress decided to boycott the commission "at every stage and in every form". Even moderate and Muslim politicians, whose cooperation the Government had taken for granted, were unanimous in denouncing the commission.

A challenge from Birkenhead, the Conservative Secretary of State, stung Indian leaders to seek an agreed solution of the constitutional problem. An All-Party committee headed by Motilal Nehru drafted a constitution for a self-governing India. The "Nehru Report" adopted Dominion Status as he basis of its recommendations: it represented the lowest measure of agreement among the Congress, the "Liberals" and the other political groups. The younger wing of the Congress led by Subhash Chandra Bose, the brilliant young leader from Bengal, and Motilal Nehru's own son, Jawaharlal, repudiated Dominion Status. A rift was avoided at the Calcutta Congress in December 1928 by a compromise formula framed by Gandhi. A resolution was passed endorsing the Nehru Report on the condition that, if by December 31, 1929, it was not accepted by the Government, the Congress would fight for complete independence, if necessary, by resorting to nonviolent noncooperation.

The Calcutta Congress opened the way for Gandhi's return to politics. If the British Government did not concede that demand of the Congress-and there was little prospect of their doing so-the Congress was committed to a noncooperation movement and it was obvious to all that Gandhi alone could conduct it.

In May 1929, as the result of the British General Election, a Labour Government headed by Ramsay Mac Donald came into office. The Viceroy, Lord Irwin, visited England and, on return to India towards the end of October 1929, issued a statement that it "is implied in the declaration of 1917 that the natural issue of India's constitutional progress, as there contemplated, is the attainment of Dominion Status". The statement had a favourable reception in India, but a storm broke over Irwin and the Labour Government in England. The British press and Parliament subjected the announcement to a protracted postmortem. The official spokesmen were on the defensive, explained away the statement, and asserted that there had been no radical departure from past policy. The breach between the Government and the Congress thus remained unhealed. No more success attended an eleventh-hour effort at an understanding between Gandhi and the Viceroy through an interview arranged at Delhi on December 23, just before the Congress session at Lahore.

DECLARATION OF COMPLETE INDEPENDENCE

The Lahore session proved a momentous one. At Gandhi's instance, the All India Congress Committee had elected Jawaharlal Nehru as its president. The Congress, instinct with new hope and energy, needed a young man at the helm. The forty-year-old Jawaharlal whom Gandhi described "pure as crystal.... truthful beyond suspicion... a knight sans peur et sans reproche" was to be in fullness of time the Mahatma's political heir. There was a bond of deep affection between the two men in spite of the twenty years and widely differing intellectual backgrounds which separated them.

The year of grace which the Calcutta Congress had granted had drawn to a close. Dominion Status had not been conceded; the offer of the minimum national demand embodied in the Nehru Report lapsed. At midnight on December 31, 1929, as the new year dawned, the Indian National Congress unfurled the flag of independence on the bank of the river Ravi. The Congress called upon its members in central and provincial legislatures to resign their seats and authorized the launching of a civil disobedience campaign.

In January 1930, Gandhi wrote that he was "furiously thinking night and day" The first step he took was to call for the celebration of an "Independence Day" on January 26. On that day, in the towns and villages of India, hundreds of thousands of people took a pledge that "it was a crime against man and God to submit to British rule." Gandhi was encouraged by the latent enthusiasm in the country revealed by the observance of the Independence Day; he felt the country was ripe for a mass movement. He suggested the inauguration of the movement with the breach of Salt Laws.

The salt tax, though relatively light in incidence, hit the poorest in the land. But salt did not quite seem to fit into the plan of a national struggle for liberation. And when Gandhi announced that he would walk the 241 miles from his ashram in Ahmedabad to Dandi on the Arabian Sea, the first impulse of the Government, as of the Congress intellectual, was to ridicule the "kindergarten stage of political revolution", and to laugh away the idea that the King-Emperor could be unseated by boiling sea-water in a kettle. Events were to show that those who had scoffed at Salt Satyagraha and failed to see any connection between salt and Swaraj (independence) had underrated Gandhi's knack for organizing the Indian masses for corporate action. Gandhi was arrested on May 5. Just before his arrest he had planned a more "aggressive" phase of his nonviolent rebellion by raiding and taking possession of the salt depots at Dharasana. The raid took place a fortnight after Gandhi's arrest. There were 2500 volunteers. Before they advanced, Sarojini Naidu, the poetess, led them in prayer and appealed to them to be true to Gandhi's teaching and to abstain from violence. Round the depot, a barrier of barbed wire had been erected and a ditch dug. As the first column of volunteers advanced, police officers ordered them to disperse. The volunteers advanced in silence even though scores of policemen fell on them and rained blows upon them. Not one man so much as raised his arm to fend off the blows. Webb Miller, an American correspondent, who witnessed the scene, wrote: "In eighteen years of reporting in twenty two countries, FI have never witnessed such harrowing scenes as at Dharasana. Sometimes the scenes were so painful that I had to turn away momentarily. One surprising feature was the discipline of volunteers. It seemed they were thoroughly imbued with Gandhi's nonviolent creed."

The Satyagraha campaign was extended by the Congress to include breach of salt as well as forest laws, the non-payment of taxes and the boycott of foreign cloth, banks and shipping. The Government replied by issuing "ordinances" which conferred extraordinary powers on the executive authority for arrest and prosecution of Congress workers.

GANDHI-IRWIN PACT

The Viceroy, Lord Irwin, was at this time directing the sternest repression which Indian nationalism had known, but he did not really relish the role. The British civil service and the commercial community were in favour of even harsher measures. But Premier Ramsay MacDonald and Secretary of State Benn were eager for peace, if they could secure it without weakening the position of the Labour Government; they wanted to make a success of the Round Table Conference and they knew that this body without the presence of Gandhi and the Congress could not carry much weight. In January 1931, at the closing session of the Round Table Conference, Ramsay MacDonald went so far as to express the hope that the Congress would be represented at the next session. The Viceroy took the hint and promptly ordered the unconditional release of Gandhi and all members of the Congress Working Committee. To this gesture Gandhi responded by agreeing to meet the Viceroy.

"The Two Mahatmas"-as Sarojini Naidu described Gandhi and Irwin-had eight meetings which lasted for a total of 24 hours. Gandhi was impressed by Irwin's sincerity. The terms of the "Gandhi-Irwin Pact" fell manifestly short of those which Gandhi had prescribed as the minimum for a truce. Some of his colleagues considered the Gandhi-Irwin Pact a clever manoeuvre, and Suspected that Irwin had led the Mahatma upon the garden path of the Viceroy's House.

On the other hand, it is fair to record that British officials in India, and Tory politicians in England, were outraged by the idea of a pact with a party whose avowed purpose was the destruction of the British Raj. Winston Churchill publicly expressed his disgust "at the nauseating and humiliating spectacle of this one-time Inner Temple lawyer, now seditious fakir, striding half-naked up the steps of the Viceroy's palace, there to negotiate and parley on equal terms with the representative of the King Emperor".

Gandhi's motives in concluding a pact with the Viceroy can be best understood in terms of his technique. The Satyagraha movements were commonly described as "struggles", "rebellions" and "wars without violence". Owing, however, to the common connotation of these words, they seemed to lay a disproportionate emphasis on the negative aspect of the movements, namely, opposition and conflict. The object of Satyagraha was, however, not to achieve the physical elimination or moral breakdown of an adversary, but, through suffering at his hands, to initiate those psychological processes which could make it possible for minds and hearts to meet. In such a struggle a compromise with an opponent was neither heresy nor treason, but a natural and necessary step. And if it turned out that the compromise was premature and the adversary was unrepentant, there was nothing to prevent the Satyagrahi from returning to nonviolent battle.

ROUND TABLE CONFERENCE

On August 29, 1931, Gandhi sailed for England in the SS Rajputana to attend the Second Round Table Conference, He went as the sole representative of the Indian National Congress. All the delegates were nominees of the British Government; they had a sprinkling of able individuals, but most of them were drawn from the princely order, the landlords, the titled gentry and the leaders of communal groups and vested interests.

What with its composition and what with its procedure, which the British Government controlled, the conference side-tracked its energies into secondary issues and particularly the communal problem. Gandhi was prepared to give a "blank cheque" to Muslims and other minorities to remove their legitimate fears, provided they were willing to press the national demand for freedom. Most of the Hindu delegates were not ready for this gesture, and the Muslim nationalists were not represented at the conference.

Gandhi pleaded for an honourable and equal partnership between Britain and India, held not by force but "by the silken cord of love" He found the odds against him. There was a financial crisis and a change of government in Britain; in the new Ministry, the Conservatives were heavily represented. The British public was preoccupied with domestic issues; for it, the financial crisis was a more urgent issue than the niceties of an Indian Constitution. Inevitably, even if imperceptibly, there was a change in emphasis. Sir Samuel Hoare, the new Secretary of State, told Gandhi that he sincerely believed that Indians were unfit for complete self-government.

IN LONDON

Meanwhile Gandhi was, as he put it, "doing the real round table work, getting to know the people of England". He had accepted Muriel Lester's invitation to stay in Kingsley Hall in the East end, in order to be "among the same sort of people to whom I have given my life" Every morning the light appeared in his room at four for the morning prayer. He had his morning walk in the main streets of the East End; he visited his neighbours in Bow; he made friends with the children. "Uncle Gandhi" became a popular figure. He explained to the children why he had chosen to stay in the East End and why he wore his meagre dress. He advised them to return good for evil. There was an interesting sequel to this advice, when the father of a four-year-old girl told the Mahatma that he had a bone to pick with him. "And what is it?" asked Gandhi. "Well my little Jane comes every morning to me, hits me and wakes me up and says: Now, don't you hit back, for Gandhi told us not to hit back". On October 2, Gandhi's birth day, the children presented him with 'two woolly dogs, three pink birthday candles, a tin plate, a blue pencil and some jelly sweets'-gifts which he especially treasured and took to India.

One of the most pleasant surprises of the tour was the courtesy and even affection Gandhi received from the cotton operatives of Lancashire, which had been hit the hardest by the boycott of British goods in India. He listened with obvious attention and sympathy to the tale of woe of those who were jobless. Many of them saw the background of the boycott which he had sponsored, when he told them: "You have three million unemployed, but we have 200 million unemployed for half the year. Your average unemployment dole is seventy shillings. Our average income is 7s. 6d. a month."

Gandhi's homely logic and transparent sincerity left an indelible impression on some of those whom he met. They formed clearer impressions of him than the loin cloth and goat's milk version with which the popular press regaled them. While his opinions might appear utopian or revolutionary, he could no longer be dismissed as "humbug", the appellation with which Truth had heralded his arrival in England.

Meanwhile, the news from India had been far from reassuring. The compromise which had been patched up between the Congress and the Government before Gandhi's departure for England had virtually broken down. Gandhi was anxious to return home; he declined invitations to prolong his itinerary in Europe and to visit America, but he decided to spend a few days in Switzerland with his biographer, Romain Rolland. In Rome, where he spent a day, he walked through the Vatican galleries; in the Sistine Chapel he was spell-bound: "I saw a figure of Christ there. It was wonderful. I could not tear myself away. The tears sprang to my eyes as I gazed."

RESUMPTION OF STRUGGLE

On December 28, 1931, Gandhi landed at Bombay. Within a week he was in jail and civil disobedience was resumed; the Indian National Congress was out-lawed and the Gandhi-Irwin Pact had gone to pieces.

While Gandhi was on the high seas, the arrests of Jawaharlal Nehru and Abdul Ghaffar Khan, two of his ablest lieutenants, had created a crisis. Most of the British officers in India had really been unhappy at the rapprochement which Irwin had attempted with Gandhi; they won over his successor Lord Willingdon to a tougher policy towards the Mahatma. Gandhi sought an interview with the Viceroy to smooth away difficulties but was rebuffed. The Government of India was not in a conciliatory mood. Indeed it struck with lightning speed to deprive the Indian National Congress of its leaders, organization and resources. Despite the suddenness and severity of the repression, 61,551 persons came forward and were convicted for civil disobedience in the first nine months of the movement in 1932; this figure was a little higher than that of the earlier campaign in 1930-31.

CAMPAIGN AGAINST UNTOUCHABILITY

A new twist to the civil disobedience movement came in September 1932 when Gandhi, who was in Yeravda Jail, went on a fast as a protest against the segregation of the so-called "untouchables" in the electoral arrangement planned for the new Indian constitution. Uncharitable critics described the fast as a form of coercion, a political blackmail. Gandhi was aware that his fast did exercise a moral pressure, but the pressure was directed not against those who disagreed with him, but against those who loved him and believed in him. He did not expect his critics to react in the same way as his friends and co-workers, but if his self-crucifixion could demonstrate his sincerity to them, the battle would be more than half-won. He sought to prick the conscience of the people and to convey to them something of his own inner anguish at a monstrous social tyranny. The fast dramatized the issues at stake; ostensibly it suppressed reason, but in fact it was designed to free reason from that mixture of inertia and prejudice which had permitted the evil of untouchability, which condemned millions of Hindus to humiliation, discrimination and hardship.

The news that Gandhi was about to fast shook India from one end to the other. September 20, 1932, when the fast began, was observed as a day of fasting and prayer. At Shantiniketan, poet Tagore, dressed in black, spoke to a large gathering on the significance of the fast and the urgency of fighting an age-old evil. There was a spontaneous upsurge of feeling; temples, wells and public places were thrown open to the "untouchables". A number of Hindu leaders met the representatives of the untouchables; an alternative electoral arrangement was agreed upon, and received the approval of the British Government before Gandhi broke his fast.

More important than the new electoral arrangement was the emotional catharsis through which the Hindu community had passed. The fast was intended by Gandhi "to sting the conscience of the Hindu community into right religious action". The scrapping of separate electorates was only the beginning of the end of untouchability. Under Gandhi's inspiration, while he was still in prison, a new organization, Harijan Sevak Sangh was founded to combat untouchability and a new weekly paper, the Harijan, was started. Harijan means "children of God"; it was Gandhi's name for the "untouchables"

After his release Gandhi devoted himself almost wholly to the campaign against untouchability. On November 7, 1933, he embarked on a country-wide tour which covered 12,500 miles and lasted for nine months. The tour evoked great enthusiasm for the breaking down of the barriers which divided the untouchables from the rest of the Hindu community, but it also provoked the militancy of the orthodox Hindus. On June 25, while Gandhi was on his way to the municipal hall in Poona, a bomb was thrown at his party. Seven persons were injured, but Gandhi was unhurt. He expressed his "deep pity" for the unknown thrower of the bomb. "I am not aching for martyrdom," he said, "but if it comes in my way in the prosecution of what I consider to be the supreme duty in defence of the faith I hold in common with millions of Hindus, I shall have well earned it."

Gandhi's fast had aroused public enthusiasm, but diverted it from political to social issues. In May 1933, he suspended civil disobedience for six weeks. He revived it later, but confined it to himself. A year later he discontinued it: this was a recognition of the fact that the country was fatigued and in no mood to continue a campaign of defiance. These decisions disconcerted many of his adherents, who did not relish his moral and religious approach to political issues, and chafed at his self-imposed restraints. Gandhi sensed the critical mood in the Congress party and in October 1934, announced his retirement from it. For the next three years, not politics but village economics was his dominant interest.

A NEW DEAL FOR THE VILLAGE

Ever since Gandhi had entered Indian public life in 1915, he had been pleading for a new deal for the village. The acute pressure on land and the absence of supplementary industries had caused chronic unemployment and underemployment among the peasants whose appalling poverty never ceased to weigh upon Gandhi's mind. His advocacy of the spinning wheel really derived from its immediate value as a palliative. Since eighty-five per cent of the population of India lived in villages, their economic and social resuscitation seemed to Gandhi to be a sine qua non for freedom from foreign rule. The growing gap in economic standards and social amenities between the village and the town had to be bridged. This could best be done by volunteers from the towns who spread themselves in the countryside to help revive dead or dying village industries, and to improve standards of nutrition, education and sanitation.

It was not Gandhi's habit to preach what he did not practise; he decided to settle in a village. His choice fell upon Segaon which was situated near Wardha. It had a population of six hundred, and lacked such bare amenities as a pucca road, a shop and a post office. Here, on land owned by his friend and disciple Jamnalal Bajaj, Gandhi occupied a one-room hut. Those who came to see him during the rains had to wade through ankle-deep mud. The climate was inhospitable; there was not an inhabitant of this village who had not suffered from dysentery or malaria. Gandhi himself fell sick but was resolved not to leave Segaon. He hoped he would draw his team for village uplift from Segaon itself, but could not prevent his disciples, old and new, from collecting around him. When Dr. John Mott interviewed him in 1937, Gandhi's was the solitary hut; before long a colony of mud and bamboo grew up. Among its residents were Prof. Bhansali, who had roamed in forests naked and with sealed lips, subsisting on neem leaves; Maurice Frydman, a Pole, who became a convert to the Gandhian of a handicraft civilization based on nonviolence; a Sanskrit scholar who was a leper and was housed next to Gandhi's hut so that he could tend him; a Japanese monk who (in the words of Mahadev Desai, Gandhi's Secretary) worked like a horse and lived like a hermit.

Sevagram (as Segaon came to be known) was not planned as an ashram. Gandhi never conceived it as such and did not impose any formal discipline upon it. It became a centre of the Gandhian scheme of village welfare. A number of institutions grew up in and around it to take up he various strands of economic and social uplift. The All India Village Industries Association supported and developed such industries as could easily be fostered, required little capital and did not need help from outside the village. The Association set up a school for training village workers and published its own periodical, the Gram Udyog Patrika. There were other organizations such as the Goseva Sangh, which sought to improve the condition and breed of the Hindustani Talimi Sangh, which experimented in Gandhi's ideas on education. The educational system in India had always struck Gandhi as inadequate and wasteful. The vast majority of the population could not get the rudiments of education, but even those who went to village primary schools soon unlearnt what was taught to them because it had little to do with their daily lives and environment. Gandhi suggested that elementary education suited to the Indian village could best be imparted through handicrafts so as to substitute a coordinated training in the use of the hand and the eye for a notoriously bookish and volatile learning. His ideas found an expression in the scheme of "Basic Education" which stirred the stagnant pools of the Indian educational system and stimulated administrators and educationists along new lines.

Work in the village was an arduous and slow affair; it was plodder's work, as Gandhi once put it. It did not earn banner headlines in the press and did not seem to embarrass the Government. Many of Gandhi's colleagues did not see how this innocuous activity could help India in advancing to the real goal-that of political freedom. On the other hand, the first official reaction to Gandhi's village uplift work was to consider it a well-laid plan to spread sedition among the rural masses; the government of India warned the provincial governments to be on their guard and to start counter-propaganda in the villages.

THE NEW CONSTITUTION

Indian politics were in the doldrums during the years 1934-35, but as the time came for elections to the provincial legislatures in accordance with the Act of 1935, political excitement rose to a high pitch. From the point of view of the Indian National Congress, the new Constitution was the inadequate and unsatisfactory. The scheme of the Indian Federation gave a sizeable representation to the princely states, and since their representatives, because of the absence of elective bodies, were likely to be the nominees of the princes, (who in turn were dependant for their very existence on the British Government) Indian nationalists viewed the new Constitution with a feeling bordering on dismay. In the provinces a wider field was permitted to Ministers responsible to elected legislatures, but even here the Governors had been invested with over-riding and preventive authority.

Because of these limitations, there was a large and vocal section in the Congress led by Jawaharlal Nehru which did not want to have anything to do with the new Constitution. Nevertheless, the Congress decided to contest the elections, which were held early in 1937. It acquitted itself very well indeed, and was in a position to form ministries in six out of eleven provinces.

A section of the Congress even favoured acceptance of office and its hands were strengthened by the moral support it received from Gandhi. The Mahatma felt that with all its deficiencies, the new Constitution could promote the programme of village uplift. He saw no reason why Congress ministries in the provinces could not encourage village industries, introduce prohibition, reduce the burden on the peasantry, promote the use of hand-spun cloth, extend education and combat untouchability.

The acceptance of office by the Congress party was facilitated by a statement issued by the Viceroy, Lord Linlithgow, which did not change the legal position or the powers of the Governors, but breathed a spirit of conciliation to which the Congress responded by deciding to form ministries.

For a political party which had remained so long in opposition, to get into the seat of power was a novel, and even a hazardous experience. The left wing in the Congress, which opposed formation of ministries, had in fact stressed the possibilities of internal dissensions and scramble for loaves and fishes among Congressmen. Gandhi found himself inundated with requests for jobs and minister ships; he expressed his surprise and distress at this trend, because to him the legislatures and ministerships were only one and a limited medium of serving the country.

He felt that for the majority of Congressmen the work lay in the villages in the constructive fields of social and economic reform. The caucus system, the struggle for power and pressure politics, which are accepted as part of political democracy, were repellent to Gandhi. As an 'experienced servant and general', he deprecated the struggle for "the spoils of office", and the dissipation of energy in factional rivalries.

HINDU-MUSLIM ANTAGONISM

During these years Gandhi was also much distressed by the rise in communal tension. To some extent this increased tension was attributable to the elections to the legislatures. The religious minorities were allowed to elect their representatives only from a purely communal electorate, from which adherents of all other religions were excluded. It was only natural that Muslim candidates should raise religious issues which could make the widest and easiest appeal to a largely illiterate electorate. It so happened that from 1937 onwards it suited the All India Muslim League, under the leadership of M.A. Jinnah, to whip up religious feeling. The League had done badly in the elections, but it sought to retrieve its position by launching a tirade against the Congress and Gandhi. Gandhi was alleged to be 'Enemy Number One' of the Muslim community and the British Governors were accused of conniving at a systematic oppression of the Muslim minority by the Hindus. Vague and exaggerated accusations were made about "atrocities" on the Muslims.

The Muslim League's antagonism to the Congress acquired a progressively sharper edge. Jinnah began even to question the suitability of a democratic system of government for India, in 1940 came out with the theory that Hindus and Muslims were two separate nations and the Muslim nation needed a 'homeland' of its own in the northwest and northeast of the sub-continent.

Gandhi's reaction to the two-nation theory and the demand for Pakistan was one of bewilderment, almost of incredulity. Was it the function of religion to separate men or to unite them? He described the two-nation theory as an "untruth"; in his dictionary there was no stronger word. He discussed the attributes of nationality. A change of religion did not change nationality; the religious divisions did not coincide with cultural differences. A Bengali Muslim, He wrote, "speaks the same tongue that a Bengali Hindu does, cats the same food, has the same amusements as his Hindu neighbour. They dress alike. His (Jinnah's) name could be that of any Hindu. When I first met him, I did not know he was a Muslim."

To divide India was to undo the centuries of work done by Hindus and Muslims. Gandhi's soul rebelled against the idea that Hinduism and Islam represented antagonistic cultures and doctrines, and that eighty million of Muslims had really nothing in common with their Hindu neighbours. And even if there were religious and cultural differences, what clash of interests could there be on such matters as revenue, industry, sanitation or justice? The differences could only be in religious usage and observances with which a secular state should have no concern.

NONVIOLENCE IN VIOLENT WORLD

The separatist ideology was to receive a fillip from the outbreak of the Second by Nehru in international affairs, Gandhi sympathized with the victims of Fascist and Nazi aggression. Gandhi's own life had been one long struggle against the forces of violence. For more then thirty years he had been experimenting with technique-Satyagraha-which, while eschewing violence, was designed to resolve conflicts.

Gandhi's ideas on nonviolence had matured over many years. In the Boer War and the Fist World War he had raised ambulance units and enlisted soldiers for the British Empire. The fact that he not handled a gun himself did not, in his opinion, make a material difference. As he confessed later: "There is no defence for my conduct only in the scales of nonviolence (ahimsa). I draw no distinction between those who wield weapons of destruction and those who do Red Cross work. Both participate in war and advance its cause. Both are guilty of the crime of war. But even after introspection during all these years, I feel that in the circumstances in which I found myself I was bound to adopt the course I did."

The Indians whom Gandhi led in the battle fronts of the Boer War or exhorted to join the British Indian army in 1914-18 did not believe in nonviolence; it was not repugnance to violence, but indifference or cowardice which had kept them from bearing arms. Believing as he did in those days in the British Empire, as a benign institution, Gandhi also thought that as citizens of the Empire, Indians had duties as well as rights; one of these duties was to participate in the defence of the Empire.

In the twenty years which spanned the First and Second World Wars, Gandhi's faith in the British Empire had been irrevocably shaken. At the same time his own belief in the power of nonviolence had grown. As the threat of war grew and the forces of violence gathered momentum in the late thirties, he felt more strongly than ever that at that moment of crisis in world history, he had a message for India and India had a message for the bewildered humanity. Through the pages of Harijan, his weekly paper, he expounded the nonviolent approach to military aggression and political tyranny He advised the weaker nations to defend themselves not by seeking protection from better armed states, but by nonviolent resistance to the aggressor. A nonviolent Abyssinia, he explained, needed no arms and succour from the League of Nations; if every Abyssinian man, woman and child refused cooperation, willing or forced, with the Italians, the aggressor would have to walk over the dead bodies of their victims and to occupy the country without the people.

It may be argued that Gandhi was making a heavy overdraft upon human endurance. It required supreme courage for a whole people to die to the last man, woman and child, rather than surrender to the enemy. Gandhi's nonviolent resistance was thus not a soft doctrine-a convenient refuge from a dangerous situation. Nor was it an offer on a silver platter to the dictators of what they plotted to wrest by force. Those who offered nonviolent resistance had to be prepared for the extreme sacrifice.

CRIPPS MISSION

Gandhi was thus firmly anchored to pacifism when the war broke out in 1939, but many of his closest colleagues and the rank and file in the Indian National Congress could not bring themselves to accept the feasibility of defending the country against aggression without resort to arms. Twice during the war-after the fall of France in 1940, and the collapse of the British position in South East Asia in 1941-when there was a possibility of a rapprochement between the Congress and the Government for a united war effort, Gandhi stepped aside rather than be a party to organized violence. The rapprochement did not come. The only serious British effort for a compromise was made in the Spring of 1942 with the dispatch of the Cripps Mission to India; it proved abortive.

For nearly two and a half years, Gandhi had resisted pressure from a section of his following for the launching of a mass movement. It became clear that the British Government first under Chamberlain, and then under Churchill, was reluctant to assure Indian freedom in the future, or to offer a practical token of it in the present Gandhi had endeavoured to restrain the radical wing of the Congress party, and diverted its discontent into "individual Satyagraha", a subdued form of civil resistance confined to "selected individuals"

After the failure of the Cripps Mission, Gandhi noted with concern that in the face of grave peril posed by the Japanese advance in South East Asia, the mood of the people of India was not one of resolute defiance, but of panic, frustration and helplessness. If India was not to go the way of Malaya and Burma, something had to be done, and done quickly. He came to the conclusion that only an immediate declaration of Indian independence by the British Government could give the people of India a stake in the defence of their country.

QUIT INDIA

The "Quit India" resolution passed by the All-India Congress Committee brought it into a head-on collision with the Government in August 1942. The Viceroy, with the strong backing of the British Cabinet, struck hard. Gandhi, Nehru and almost all the Congress leaders were imprisoned; the severest repression was launched against the Congress-its funds were frozen offices sealed and publicity media plugged. This "blitzkrieg" had violent repercussions. In the last speech before the All-India Congress Committee before his arrest, Gandhi had made nonviolence the basic premise of the struggle which he proposed to launch; this advice remained unheeded between the frenzy of the people and the hammer blows of the

Government. In several parts of the country, in Bihar, in U. P., in Bengal and in Bombay, the fury of the people burst the dykes and turned on the instruments and symbols of British rule. "The Congress Party", Churchill told the House of Commons, "has now abandoned the policy which Mr. Gandhi had so long inculcated in theory and has come into the open as a revolutionary movement." In India and abroad official propaganda attributed violence to a plot carefully laid by Congress leaders. Gandhi was even accused of being pro-Axis, and assisting a Japanese conquest of India. Official propaganda held the field for a time, but not for long. "It is sheer nonsense," Smuts, Gandhi's old antagonist in South Africa, told a press conference in London in November 1942, "to talk of Mahatma Gandhi as a fifth columnist. He is a great man. He is one of the great men of the world."

Mahadev Desai, who had served as Gandhi's secretary for 25 years, died of a heart attack within a week of his imprisonment and Kasturba, the Mahatma's wife, passed away in 1944 after a long illness. Early in 1944, his health began to cause concern to the Government. He had contracted malaria and had been running a high temperature. The tide of the war had already turned in favour off the Allies, and the risks of his release seemed to the Government immeasurably less than those of his possible death in jail. After his release in May 1944, Gandhi tried to break the political deadlock. Neither Churchill, who still headed the British Cabinet, nor Jinnah, who had the commanding voice in the counsels of the Muslim League, seemed eager for a political detente. The British seemed reluctant to part with power, and the Muslim League evidently was waiting for an opportunity for driving a harder bargain. A formula suggested by C. Rajagopalachari, which Gandhi discussed with Jinnah, conceded the substance of the Muslim League's demand for Pakistan, but the offer was turned down by the League leader.

SIMLA CONFERENCE

In the summer of 1945, a conference was convened at Simla by the Viceroy, Lord Wavell, who had recently returned from England with the approval of the Newspaper report of the outcome of the Simla Conference British Cabinet to a proposal for reconstituting the Executive Council in consultation with Indian leaders. Gandhi was not a delegate to the conference, though he was consulted by the Viceroy and the Congress working committee.

The conference broke down on the insistence of Jinnah that his party should have an exclusive right to nominate Muslim members of the Viceroy's Executive Council. This was something which the Congress could not concede without repudiating its national composition.

The Simla Conference failed to break the deadlock, but two important events took place in the wake of the conference which made a new initiative possible. With the surrender of Japan on August 15, 1945, the Second World War came to an end, and the Labour Party came to power in Britain. Lord Wavell visited London, and on return to India, announced on September 19, 1942, that the British Government was still working "in the spirit of he Cripps Offer of 1942" and intended to convene a constitution-making body. Elections to the central and provincial legislatures, which were in any case overdue, were announced. Indian politics were again deeply stirred and entered a period of intense excitement, interminable negotiations and bitter controversy.

CABINET MISSION

Early in 1946, the Labour Government dispatched an all-party parliamentary delegation to India to meet Indian leaders and convince them of the British desire for an early settlement of the Indian constitutional issue. However, it was only in March 1946 that with the arrival of three Cabinet Ministers, Lord Pethick-Lawrence, Sir Stafford Cripps and Mr. A. V. Alexander, a crucial stage was reached in the negotiations between the British Government and the Indian political parties. The negotiations were conducted on behalf of the Congress by Abul Kalam Azad who was assisted by Nehru and Patel. Gandhi was, however, frequently consulted. The negotiations were bogged down on the basic question whether India was to remain united or to be split up to satisfy the Muslim League's demand for Pakistan. The Congress opposed to the partition of the country, but was prepared to go to the farthest limit in conceding cultural, economic and regional autonomy to various regions. A conference at Simla failed to resolve the Congress-League differences.

The Cabinet Mission then offered a compromise plan in their statement of May 16,1946. They sketched a three-tier constitutional structure for India. On the top was to be a Union of India embracing British India as well as the Indian States, but dealing only with foreign affairs, defence and communications. The bottom tier was to consist of Provinces and States in which were to vest all residuary powers. The intermediate tier was to comprise "groups" to be formed by Provinces (if they chose) to deal with certain common subjects. The Muslim League avowed its acceptance of the Cabinet Mission Plan, but this acceptance was more apparent than real, The League and its leaders made no secret of their hope and design that the new constitution would be used to effect a partition of the country. "Let me tell you," Jinnah told the Muslim League Council on June 5, 1946 "that Muslim India will not rest content until we have established full, complete and sovereign Pakistan." It was this apparent contradiction in the League's stand, which made Gandhi and his colleagues in the Congress uneasy about the "grouping of provinces", which the League wanted to make compulsory and a stepping-stone to Pakistan. The controversy on this issue wrecked the Cabinet Mission Plan.

The three-tier constitution was a delicate mechanism with numerous checks and balances. Without the fullest cooperation between the major parties it was impossible to draft a new constitution, much less to work it. This cooperation was, however, lacking. The Cabinet Mission Plan was a compromise but it did not really bring the two parties together. The result was that questions presumed to have been settled by the Cabinet Mission were reopened soon after the return of its three members to England. Controversy rose to a fever pitch on two crucial issues, that of the "grouping" of provinces and the composition of the "interim government".

COMMUNAL CONFLAGRATION

At a time when tension was mounting, it was imperative that the country should have a strong and stable government at the centre. The Cabinet Mission had failed in the formation of a national interim government. In July 1946, the Viceroy, Lord Wavell, once again took the initiative and called upon Jawaharlal Nehru to form the Government. Jinnah, who was approached by Nehru, refused to cooperate, was bitterly critical and announced that August 16 would be observed by the Muslim League as "the Direct Action Day". On that day Calcutta witnessed a communal riot, the scale and intensity of which had never been known in living memory. "The Great Calcutta Killing" touched off a chain reaction of violent communal explosions in East Bengal, Bihar and the Punjab,

As the news of disturbances in Bengal came through, Gandhi cancelled all his plans and decided to leave for the riot-affected areas. In East Bengal he noticed how fear, hatred and violence had come to pervade the countryside. He toured the villages, saw things at first hand, and tried to lift the issue of peace from the plane of politics to that of humanity. Whatever the political map of the future, he pleaded, it should be common ground among all parties that standards of civilized life would not be thrown overboard. Gandhi's presence acted as a soothing balm on the villages of East Bengal; he eased tensions, assuaged anger and softened. In March 1947, he left for Bihar where the Hindu peasants had wreaked a terrible vengeance on the Muslim minority for the misdeeds of the Muslim majority in East Bengal. In Bihar, Gandhi's refrain was the same as in East Bengal: the majority community must repent and make amends; the minority must forgive and make a fresh start. He would not accept any apology for what had happened, and chided those who sought in the misdeeds. Of the rioters in East Bengal, a justification for what had happened in Bihar. Civilized conduct, he argued, was the duty of every individual and every community irrespective of what others did.

Alarmed by the increasing lawlessness, Lord Wavell brought the Muslim League into the Interim Government. The formation of the coalition between the Congress and the League fanned political controversy instead of putting it out. The Constituent Assembly had been summoned to meet on December 9, 1946, but the Muslim League refused to participate in its deliberations. The constitutional impasse looked complete when in the last week on November in an eleventh hour bid to bring the parties together, the British Government invited Wavell, Nehru, Jinnah, Liaquat Ali and Baldev Singh to London. The discussion proved

Abortive, but the British Government issued a statement to clarify the points at dispute. Though this clarification largely met its objections, the Muslim League did not lift its boycott of the Constituent Assembly.

The year 1947 dawned with the darkest possible prospects on the political horizon. To check the drift to chaos, Clement Attlee, the British Premier, came to the conclusion that what was needed was a new policy and a new Viceroy to carry it out. He announced in the House of Commons on February 20, 1947 that the British Government definitely intended to quit India by June 1948, and if by that date the Indian parties did not agree on an all-India constitution, power would be transferred to "some form of Central Government in British India or in some areas to the existing Provincial Governments." Simultaneously it was announced that Lord Mountbatten would succeed Lord Wavell as Viceroy.

The British withdrawal had been decided and dated by the February 20th statement. Lord Mountbatten arrived in India in March and one of his first acts as Viceroy was to invite Gandhi for a discussion. The Mahatma interrupted his peace mission in Bihar and travelled to New Delhi. During the next few weeks it became evident that a solution of the political deadlock would be sought through the division of India. The Muslim League led by Jinnah was adamant, but there was also a re-orientation of the Congress attitude towards partition. Hitherto the Congress had insisted that partition should, if at all, follow and not precede political liberation, that there could be "no divorce before marriage". But the few months of stormy courtship in the Interim Government had cured Nehru, Patel and other Congress leaders of the desire for a closer union with the Muslim League. In the spring of 1947, the choice seemed to them to be between anarchy and partition; they resigned themselves to the latter in order to salvage three-fourths of India from the chaos which threatened the whole.

PARTITION OF INDIA

The stage was thus set for the June 3 Plan under which power was to be transferred by the British to two successor states on August 15, 1947. What Gandhi has feared had come to pass. India was to be divided, but partition was not being imposed; it had been accepted by Nehru, Patel and a majority of the Congress leaders. Gandhi had serious doubts on the wisdom of this decision. The very violence, which in the opinion of his Congress colleagues and that of the British Government provided a compelling motive for partition was, for him an irresistible argument against it; to accept partition because of the fear of civil war was to acknowledge that "everything was to be got if mad violence was perpetrated in sufficient measure"

Partitions having become a fait accompli, Gandhi's efforts from now on were directed to mitigating its risks. He paid brief visits to Kashmir, the Punjab and Bengal. In Calcutta, just before the transfer of power, his presence had a magical effect; the communal tensions and hatreds of the preceding twelve months vanished almost overnight. When there was a recrudescence of trouble a fortnight later, he went on a fast which electrified the town, moved the Muslims and shamed the Hindus. The leaders of all communities pledged themselves to peace and begged Gandhi to break the fast. The Calcutta fast was rightly acclaimed as a miracle; in the of-quoted words of the London Times, it did what several divisions of troops could not have done.

Gandhi now felt free to turn to Punjab which was witnessing one of the major migrations of population in history. Seized with fantastic hopes and fears, the villages and town of the Punjab had been dreading, and at the same time, preparing for a battle of the barricades. The administrative paralysis caused by the reshuffling of administrative cadres on a communal basis, and the infection of the police and military with communal virus had, by the end of August, led to a situation in which it was impossible for the Hindu minority to stay in West Punjab and the Muslim minority to stay in the East Punjab.

As the interminable caravans of refugees with their tales of woes crawled to their destinations, violence spread. When Gandhi arrived in Delhi early in September, he found it paralysed by communal tension. The Government, led by Nehru, had acted energetically and impartially. Gandhi was not content with a peace imposed by the police and the military; he wanted violence to be purged form the hearts of Hindus and Muslims. It was an uphill task. Delhi had a number of refugee camps, some of which housed Hindus and Sikhs from West Pakistan, while others sheltered Muslims fleeing from Delhi for a passage across the border.

MISSION OF PEACE

The tales of woe that Gandhi heard burned themselves into his soul, but he did not falter in his conviction that only nonviolence and love could end this spiral of hate and violence. In his prayer speech every evening, he touched on this problem. He stressed the futility of retaliation. He wore himself out in an effort to re-educate the people; he heard grievances, suggested solutions, encouraged or admonished his numerous interviewers, visited refugee camps, remained in touch with local officials.

On January 13, 1948, he began a fast; "my greatest fast," he wrote to Miraben, his English disciple. It was also to be his last. The fast was not to be broken until Delhi became peaceful. The fast had a refreshing impact upon Pakistan. In India there was an emotional shake-up. The fast compelled people to think afresh on the problem on the solution of which he had staked his life. On January 18, representatives of various communities and parties in Delhi signed a pledge in Gandhi's presence that they would guarantee peace in Delhi.

After this fast the tide of violence showed definite signs of ebbing. Gandhi felt free to make his plans for the future. He thought he should visit Pakistan to promote the process of reconciliation between the two countries and the two communities. Even as he had grappled with communal violence, the real problems of India, the social and economic uplift of her people, had never been absent from his mind. Political freedom having become a fact, Gandhi's mind was switching more and more to constructive work, and to the refurbishing of his nonviolent technique.

THE END

However, he was not destined to pick up the threads of his constructive Programme. He had a narrow escape on January 20, 1948, when a bomb exploded in Birla House in New Delhi where he was addressing his prayer meeting. He took no notice of the explosion. Next day he referred to the congratulations which he had received for remaining unruffled after the explosion. He would deserve them, he said, if he fell as a result of such an explosion and yet retained a smile on his face and no malice against the assailant. He described the bomb-thrower as a misguided youth and advised the police not to "molest" him but to convert him with persuasion and affection. "The misguided youth" was Madan Lal, a refugee from West Punjab, who was a member of a gang which had plotted Gandhi's death. These highly-strung Youngman saw Hinduism menaced by Islam from without and by Gandhi from within. Madan Lal having missed his aim, a fellow conspirator from Poona, Nathu Ram Godse, came to Gandhi's prayer meeting on the evening of January 30, whipped out his pistol and fired three shots. Gandhi fell instantly with the words 'He Rama' (Oh! God).

GANDHI AND NONVIOLENCE

Gandhi did not claim to be a prophet or even a philosopher. "There is no such thing as Gandhism," he warned, "and I do not want to leave any sect after me." There was only one Gandhian, he said, an imperfect one at that: himself.

The real significance of the Indian freedom movement in Gandhi's eyes was that it was waged non-violently. He would have had no interest in it if the Indian National Congress had adopted Satyagraha and subscribed to nonviolence. He objected to violence not only because an unarmed people had little chance of success in an armed rebellion, but because he considered violence a clumsy weapon which created more problems than it solved, and left a trail of hatred and bitterness in which genuine reconciliation was almost impossible.

This emphasis on nonviolence jarred alike on Gandhi's British and Indian critics, though for different reasons. To the former, nonviolence was a camouflage; to the latter, it was sheer sentimentalism. To the British who tended to see the Indian struggle through the prism of European history, the professions of nonviolence rather than on the remarkably peaceful nature of Gandhi's campaigns. To the radical Indian politicians, who had browsed on the history of the French and Russian revolutions or the Italian and Irish nationalist struggles, it was patent that force would only yield to force, and that it was foolish to miss opportunities and sacrifice tactical gains for reasons more relevant to ethics than to politics.

Gandhi's total allegiance to nonviolence created a gulf between him and the educated elite in India which was temporarily bridged only during periods of intense political excitement. Even among his closest colleagues there were few who were prepared to follow his doctrine of nonviolence to its logical conclusion: the adoption of unilateral disarmament in a world armed to the teeth, the scrapping of the police and the armed forces, and the decentralization of administration to the point where the state would "wither away". Nehru, Patel and others on whom fell the task of organizing the administration of independent India did not question the superiority of the principle of nonviolence as enunciated by their leader, but they did not cope rider it practical politics. The Indian Constituent Assembly include a majority of members owing allegiance to Gandhi or at least holding him in high esteem, but the constitution which emerged from their labours in 1949 was based more on the Western parliamentary than on he Gandhian model. The development of the Indian economy during the last four decades cannot be said to have conformed to Gandhi's conception of "self-reliant village republics". On the other hand, it bears the marks of a conscious effort to launch an Indian industrial revolution.

Jawaharlal Nehru-Gandhi's "political heir"-was thoroughly imbued with the humane values inculcated by the Mahatma. But the man who spoke Gandhi's language, after his death, was Vinoba Bhave, the "Walking Saint", who kept out of politics and government, Bhave's Bhoodan (land gift) Movement was designed as much as a measure of land reform as that of a spiritual renewal. Though more than five million acres of land were distributed to the landless, the movement, despite its early promise, never really spiralled into a social revolution by consent. This was partly because Vinoba Bhave did not command Gandhi's extraordinary genius for organizing the masses for a national crusade, and partly because in independent India the tendency grew for the people to look up to the government rather than to rely on voluntary and cooperative effort for effecting reforms in society.

Soon after Gandhi's death in 1948, a delegate speaking at the United Nations predicted that "the greatest achievements of the Indian sage were yet to come" "Gandhi's times," said Vinoba Bhave, "were the first pale dawn of the sun of Satyagraha." Forty years after Gandhi's death, this optimism would seem to have been too high-pitched. The manner in which Gandhi's techniques have sometimes been invoked even in the land of his birth in recent years would appear to be a travesty of his principles. And the world has been in the grip of a series of crises in Korea, the Congo, the Vietnam, the Middle East, and South Africa with a never-ending trail of blood and bitterness. The shadow of a thermo-nuclear war with its incalculable hazards continues to hang over mankind. From this predicament, Gandhi's ideas and techniques may suggest a way out. Unfortunately, his motives and methods are often misunderstood, and not only by mobs in the street, Not long ago, Arthur Koestler described Gandhi's attitude as one "of passive submission to bayonetting and raping, to villages without sewage, septic childhood's and trachoma." Such a judgement is of course completely with the same tenacity with which he battled with the British Raj. He advocated nonviolence not because it offered an easy way out, but because he considered violence a crude and in the long run, an ineffective weapon.

His rejection of violence stemmed from choice, not from necessity.

Horace Alexander, who knew Gandhi and saw him in action, graphically describes the attitude of the nonviolent resister to his opponent: "On your side you have all the mighty forces of the modern State, arms, money, a controlled press, and all the rest. On my side, I have nothing but my conviction of right and truth, the unquenchable spirit of man, who is prepared to die for his convictions than submit to your brute force. I have my comrades in armlessness. Here we stand; and here if need be, we fall." Far from being a craven retreat from difficulty and danger, nonviolent resistance demands courage of a high order, the courage to resist injustice without rancour, to unite the utmost firmness with the utmost gentleness, to invite suffering but not to inflict it, to die but not to kill.

Gandhi did not make the facile division of mankind into "good" and "bad". He was convinced that every human being-even the "enemy"-had a kernel of decency: there were only evil acts, no wholly evil men. His technique of Satyagraha was designed not to coerce the opponent, but to set into motion forces which could lead to his conversion. Relying as it did on persuasion and compromise, Gandhi's method was not always quick in producing results, but the results were likely to be the more durable for having been brought about peacefully. "It is my firm conviction," Gandhi affirmed, "that nothing enduring can be built upon violence. " The rate of social change through the nonviolent technique was not in fact likely to be much slower than that achieved by violent methods; it was definitely faster than that expected from the normal functioning of institutions which tended to fossilize and preserve the status quo.

Gandhi did not think it possible to bring about radical changes in the structure of society overnight. Nor did he succumb to the illusion that the road to a new order could be paved merely with pious wishes and fine words. It was not enough to blame the opponent or bewail the times in which one's lot was cast. However heavy the odds, it was the Satyagrahi's duty never to feel helpless. The least he could do was to make a beginning with himself. If he was crusading for a new deal for peasantry, he could go to a village and live there, If he wanted to bring peace to a disturbed district, he could walk through it, entering into the minds and hearts of those who were going through the ordeal, If an age-old evil like untouchability was to be fought, what could be a more effective symbol of defiance for a reformer than to adopt an untouchable child? If the object was to challenge foreign rule, why not act on the assumption that the country was already free, ignore the alien government and build alternative institutions to harness the spontaneous, constructive and cooperative effort of the people? If the goal was world peace, why not begin today by acting peacefully towards the immediate neighbour, going more than half way to understand and win him over?

Though he may have appeared a starry-eyed idealist to so me, Gandhi's attitude to social and political problems was severely practical. There was a deep mystical streak in him, but even his mysticism seemed to have little of the ethereal about it. He did not dream heavenly dreams nor see things unutterable in trance; when "the still small voice" spoke to him, it was often to tell how he could fight a social evil or heal a rift between two warring communities. Far from distracting him from his role in public affairs, Gandhi's religious quest gave him the stamina to play it more effectively. To him true religion was not merely the reading of scriptures, the dissection of ancient texts, or even the practice of cloistered virtue: it had to be lived in the challenging context of political and social life.

Gandhi used his nonviolent technique on behalf of his fellow-countrymen in South Africa and India, but he did not conceive it only as a weapon in the armoury of Indian nationalism. On the other hand, he fashioned it as an instrument for righting wrongs and resolving conflicts between opposing groups, races and nations. It is a strange paradox that though the stoutest and perhaps the most successful champion of the revolt against colonialism in our time, Gandhi was frees from the taint of narrow nationalism. As early as 1924, he had declared that "the better mind of the world desires today, not absolutely independent states, warring one against another, but a federation of independent, of friendly interdependent states".

Even before the First World War had revealed the disastrous results of the combination of industrialism and nationalism, he had become a convert to the idea that violence between nation-states must be completely abjured.

In 1931, during his visit to England, a cartoon in the Star depicted him in a loin cloth besides Mussolini, Hitler, de Valera and Stalin, who were clad in black, brown, green and red shirts respectively. The caption, "And he ain't wearing any blooming' shirt at all" was not only literally but figuratively true. For a man of nonviolence, who believed in the brotherhood of man, there was no superficial division of nations into good and bad, allies and adversaries. This did not, however, mean that Gandhi did not distinguish between the countries which inflicted and the countries which suffered violence. His own life had been one struggle against the forces of violence, and Satyagraha was designed at once to eschew violence and to fight injustice.

In the years immediately preceding the Second Word war, when the tide of Nazi and Fascist aggression was relentlessly rolling forward, Gandhi had reasserted his faith in nonviolence and commanded it to the smaller nation which were living in daily dread of being overwhelmed by superior force. Through the pages of his weekly paper the Harijan, he expounded the nonviolent approach to military aggression and political tyranny. He advised the weaker nations to defend themselves not by increasing their fighting potential, but by nonviolent resistance to the aggressor. When Czechoslovakia was black-mailed into submission in September 1938, Gandhi suggested to the unfortunate Czechs: "There is no bravery greater than a resolute refusal

To bend the knee to an earthly power, no matter how great, and that without bitterness of spirit, and in the fullness of faith that the spirit alone lives, nothing else does."

Seven years later when the first atomic bombs exploded over Hiroshima and Nagasaki, Gandhi's reaction was characteristic: "I did not move a muscle. On the contrary, I said to myself that unless now the adopts nonviolence, it will spell certain suicide for mankind." The irony of the very perfection of the weapons of war rendering them useless as arbiters between nations has become increasingly clear during the last forty years. The atomic stockpiles which the major nuclear powers have already built up are capable of destroying civilization, as we know it several time over and peace has been precariously preserved by, what has been grimly termed, "the balance of atomic terror." The fact is that with the weapons of mass destruction, which are at hand now, to attack another nation is tantamount to attacking oneself. This is a bitter truth which old habits of thought have prevented from going home. "This splitting of the atoms has changed everything" bewailed Einstein, "save our modes of thinking and thus we drift towards unparalleled catastrophe."

Nonviolence, as Gandhi expounded it, has ceased to be a pious exhortation, and become a necessity. The advice he gave to the unfortunate Abyssinians and Czechs during the twilight years before the Second Word War, may have seemed utopian thirty years ago. Today, it sounds commonsense. Even some hardheaded military strategists such as Sir Stephen King-Hall have begun to see in Gandhi's method a possible alternative to suicidal violence.

Gandhi would have been the first to deny that his method offered an instant or universal panacea for world peace. His method is capable of almost infinite evolution to suit new situations in a changing world. It is possible that "applied nonviolence" is at present at the same

Stage of development "as the invention of electricity was in the days of Edison and Marconi." The lives-and deaths-of Chief Lithuli and Dr. Martin Luther King have proved that there is nothing esoteric about nonviolence, limiting it to a particular country or a particular period.

Indeed Tagore, the great contemporary and friend of Gandhi, prophesies that the West would accept Gandhi before the East "for the West has gone through the cycle of dependence on force and material things of life and has become disillusioned. They want a return to the spirit. The East has not yet gone through materialism and hence has not become so disillusioned."

3

GANDHI AND HIS MIND

I think that the word 'saint' should be ruled out of present life. It is too sacred a word to be lightly applied to anybody, much less to one like myself who claims only to be a humble searcher after Truth, knows his limitations, makes mistakes, never hesitates to admit them when he makes them, and frankly confesses that he, like a scientist, is making experiments about some 'of the eternal varieties' of life, but cannot even claim to be a scientist because he can show no tangible proof of scientific accuracy in his methods or such tangible results of his experiments as modern science demands. (YI, 12-5-1920, p2)

To clothe me with sainthood is too early even if it is possible. I myself do not feel a saint in any shape or form. But I do feel I am a votary of Truth in spite of all my errors of unconscious omission and commission.

POLICY OF TRUTH

I am not a 'statesman in the garb of a saint'. But since Truth is the highest wisdom, sometimes my acts appear to be consistent with the highest statesmanship. But, I hope I have no policy in me save the policy of Truth and ahimsa. I will not sacrifice Truth and ahimsa even for the deliverance of my country or religion. That is as much as to say that neither can be so delivered. (YI, 20-1-1927, p21)

I see neither contradiction nor insanity in my life. It is true that, as a man cannot see his back, so can he not see his errors or insanity. But the sages have often likened a man of religion to a lunatic. I therefore hug the belief that I may not be insane and may be truly religious. Which of the two I am in truth can only be decided after my death. (YI, 14-8-1924, p267)

It seems to me that I understand the ideal of truth better than that of ahimsa, and my experience tells me that if I let go my hold of truth, I shall never be able to solve the riddle of ahimsa.....

In other words, perhaps, I have not the courage to follow the straight course. Both at bottom mean one and the same thing, for doubt is invariably the result of want or weakness offaith. 'Lord, give me faith' is, therefore, my prayer day and night. (A, p336)

I claim to be a votary of truth from my childhood. It was the most natural thing to me. My prayerful search gave me the revealing maxim 'Truth is God', instead of the usual one 'God is Truth'. That maxim enables me to see God face to face as it were. I feel Him pervade every fibre of my being. (H, 9-8-1942, p264)

Faith in Right

I remain an optimist, not that there is any evidence that I can give that right is going to prosper, but because of my unflinching faith that right must prosper in the end..... Our inspiration can come only from our faith that right must ultimately prevail. (H, 10-12-1938, p372)

Somehow I am able to draw the noblest in mankind, and that is what enables me to maintain my faith in God and human nature. (H, 15-4-1939, p86)

No Ascetic

I have never described myself as a sannyasi. Sannyas is made of sterner stuff. I regard myself as a house-holder, leading a humble life of service and, in common with my fellow-workers, living upon the charity of friends..... The life I am living is entirely very easy and very comfortable, if ease and comfort are a mental state. I have all I need without the slightest care of having to keep any personal treasures. (YI, 1-10-1925, p338)

My loin cloth is an organic evolution in my life. It came naturally, without effort, without premeditation. (YI, 9-7-931, p175)

I hate privilege and monopoly. Whatever cannot be shared with the masses is taboo to me. (H, 2-11-1934, p303)

It is wrong to call me an ascetic. The ideals that regulate my life are presented for acceptance by mankind in general. I have arrived at them by gradual evolution. Every step was thought out, well considered, and taken with greatest deliberation.

Both my continence and nonviolence were derived from personal experience and became necessary in response to the calls of public duty. The isolated life I had to lead in South Africa, whether as a householder, legal practitioner, social reformer or politician, required for the due fulfilment of these duties the strictest regulation of sexual life and a rigid practice of nonviolence and truth in human relations, whether with my own countrymen or with Europeans. (H, 3-10-1936, p268)

Mine is a life full of joy in the midst of incessant work. In not wanting to think of what tomorrow will bring for me, I feel as free as a bird..... The thought that I am ceaselessly and honestly struggling against the requirements of the flesh sustains me. (YI, 1-10-1925, p338)

Work without faith is like an attempt to reach the bottom of a bottomless pit. (H, 3-10-1936, pp268-9)

Shedding the Ego

I know that I have still before me a difficult path to traverse. I must reduce myself to zero. So long as man does not of his own free will put himself last among his fellow-creatures, there is no salvation for him. Ahimsa is the farthest limit of humility. (A, p371)

If we could erase the 'It's' and the 'Mine's' from religion, politics, economics, etc., we shall soon be free and bring heaven upon earth. (YI, 3-9-1926, p336)

A drop in the ocean partakes of the greatness of its parent, although it is unconscious of it. But it is dried up as soon as it enters upon an existence independent of the ocean. We do not exaggerate when we say that life is a mere bubble.

A seeker after truth cannot afford to be an egotist. One who would sacrifice his life for others has hardly time to reserve for himself a place in the sun. (YI, 16-10-1930, p2)

There are limits to the capacity of an individual, and the moment he flatters himself that he can undertake all tasks, God is there to humble his pride. For myself, I am gifted with enough humility to look even to babes and suckling for help. (YI, 12-3-1931, p32)

Fates decide my undertakings for me. I never go to see them. They come to me almost in spite of me. That has been my lot all my life long, in South Africa as well as ever since my return to India. (YI, 7-5-1925, p163)

Little Book Knowledge

I admit my limitations. I have no university education worth the name. My high school career was never above the average. I was thankful if I could pass my examinations. Distinction in the school was beyond my aspiration. (H, 9-7-1938, p176)

During the days of my education I had read practically nothing outside textbooks, and after I launched into active life, I had very little time left me for reading. I cannot, therefore, claim much book knowledge. However, I believe I have not lost much because of this enforced restraint. On the contrary, the limited reading may be said to have enabled me thoroughly to digest what I did read.

Of these books, the one that brought about an instantaneous and practical transformation in my life was Unto This Last. I translated it later into Gujarati, entitling it Sarvodaya (the welfare of all). I believe that I discovered some of my deepest convictions reflected in this great book of Ruskin, and that is why it so captivated me and made me transform my life. (A, p220)

I was living in South Africa then. It was the reading of Unto This Last on a railway journey to Durban, in 1904, when I was thirty-five, that made me decide to change my whole outward life. There is no other word for it, Ruskin's words captivated me. I read the book in one go and lay awake all the following night, and I there and then decided to change my whole plan of life. Tolstoy I had read much earlier. He affected the inner being. (ICS, p245)

Service of the Poor

The heart's earnest and pure desire is always fulfilled. In my own experience, I have often seen this rule being verified. Service of the poor has been my heart's desire and it has always thrown me amongst the poor and enabled me to identify myself with them. (A, p110)

I have always had a love for the poor all my life and in abundance. I could cite illustrations after illustrations from my past life that it was something innate in me. I have never felt that there was any difference between the poor and me. I have always felt towards them as my own kith and kin. (H, 11-5-1935, p99)

I have no desire for the perishable kingdom of earth. I am striving for the Kingdom of Heaven which is moksha. To attain my end it is not necessary for me to seek the shelter of a cave. I carry one about me, if I would but know it.

A cave-dweller can build castles in the air whereas a dweller in a palace, like Janak, has no castles to build. The cave-dweller who hovers round the world on the wings of thought has no peace. A Janak, though living in the midst of 'pomp and circumstance', may have peace that passeth understanding.

For me the road to salvation lies through incessant toil in the service of my country and therethrough of humanity. I want to identify myself with everything that lives. (YI, 3-4-1924, p114)

My life is an indivisible whole, and all my activities run into one another; and they all have their rise in my insatiable love of mankind. (H, 2-3-1934, p24)

I am used to misrepresentation all my life. It is the lot of every public worker. He has to have a tough hide. Life would be burdensome if every misrepresentation had to be answered and cleared. It is a rule of life with me never to explain misrepresentations except when the cause requires correction. This rule has saved much time and worry. (YI, 27-5-1926, p193)

I have been known as a crank, faddist, mad man. Evidently the reputation is well deserved. For wherever I go, I draw to myself cranks, faddists and mad man. (YI, 13-6-1929, p193)

Practical Dreamer

I believe in absolute oneness of God and, therefore, also of humanity. What though we have many bodies? We have but one soul. The rays of the sun are many through refraction. But they have the same source. I cannot, therefore, detach myself from the wickedest soul (nor may I be denied identity with the most virtuous). Whether, therefore, I will or not, I must involve in my experiment the whole of my kind. Nor can I do without experiment. Life is but an endless series of experiments. (YI, 25-9-1924, p313)

I must be taken with all my faults. I am a searcher after truth. My experiments I hold to be infinitely more important than the best-equipped Himalayan expeditions. (YI, 3-12-1925, p422)

It has been my misfortune or good fortune to take the world by surprise. New experiments, or old experiments in new style, must sometimes engender misunderstanding. (EF, p132)

I am indeed a practical dreamer. My dreams are not airy nothings. I want to convert my dreams into realities as far as possible. (H, 17-11-1933, p6)

If any action of mine claimed to be spiritual is proved to be unpractical, it must be pronounced to be a failure. I do believe that the most spiritual act is the most practical in the true sense of the term. (H, 1-7-1939, p181)

My Fallibility

I claim to be a simple individual liable to err like any other fellow-mortal. I own, however, that I have humility enough in me to confess my errors and to retrace my steps. I own that I have an immovable faith in God and His goodness, and unconsumable passion for truth and love. But, is that not what every person has latent in him? (YI, 6-5-1926, p164)

Those who have at all followed my humble career even superficially cannot have failed to observe that not a single act of my life has been done to the injury of any individual or nation..... I claim no infallibility. I am conscious of having made Himalayan blunders, but I am not conscious of having made them intentionally or having even harboured enmity towards any person or nation, or any life, human or sub-human. (EF, p133)

I have made the frankest admission of my many sins. But I do not carry their burden on my shoulders. If I am journeying Godward, as I feel I am, it is safe with me. For I feel the warmth of the sunshine of His presence.

My austerities, fastings and prayers are, I know, of no value if I rely upon them for reforming me. But they have an inestimable value, if they represent, as I hope they do, the yearnings of a soul striving to lay his weary head in the lap of his Maker. (H, 18-4-1936, p77)

Kinship with All

Whenever I see an erring man, I say to myself I have also erred; when I see a lustful man, I say to myself so was I once; and in this way, I feel kinship with every one in the world and feel that I cannot be happy without the humblest of us being happy. (YI, 10-2-1927, p44)

I shall have to answer my God and my Maker if I give any one less than his due, but I am sure that He will bless me if He knows that I gave someone more than his due. (YI, 10-3-1927, p80)

I am too conscious of the imperfections of the species to which I belong to be irritated against any single member thereof. My remedy is to deal with the wrong wherever I see it, not to hurt the wrongdoer, even as I would not like to be hurt for the wrongs I continually do. (YI, 12-3-1930, pp89-90)

I can truthfully say that I am slow to see the blemishes of fellow-beings, being myself full of them and, therefore, being in need of their charity, I have learnt not to judge any one harshly and to make allowances for defects that I may detect. (H, 11-3-1939, p47)

Regard for Opponents

Differences of opinion should never mean hostility. If they did,-my wife and I should be sworn enemies of one another. I do not know two persons in the world who had no difference of opinion, and as I am a follower of the Gita, I have always attempted to regard those who differ from me with the same affection as I have for my nearest and dearest. (YI, 17-3-1927, p82)

It is to me a matter of perennial satisfaction that I retain generally the affection and trust of those whose principles and policies I oppose. The South Africans gave me personally their confidence and extended their friendship.

In spite of my denunciation of British policy and system, I enjoy the affection of thousands of Englishmen and women, and in spite of unqualified condemnation of modern materialistic civilization, the circle of European and American friends is ever widening. It is again a triumph of nonviolence. (ibid, p86)

I cannot intentionally hurt anything that lives, much less fellow-human beings, even though they may do the greatest wrong to me and mine. (YI, 12-3-1930, p93)

It would be impossible for any person to point to a single act of mine during the past 50 years which could be proved to have been antagonistic to any person or community. I have never believed anyone to be my enemy. My faith demands that I should consider no one as such. I may not wish ill to anything that lives. (H, 17-11-1933, p4)

MY MAHATMASHIP

No Mahatma

I DO not feel like being one [a Mahatma]. But I do know that I am among the humblest of God's creatures. (YI, 27-10-1921, p.342)

Often the title has deeply pained me; and there is not a moment I can recall when it may be said to have tickled me. (A, p. xiv)

My Mahatma ship is worthless. It is due to my outward activities, due to my politics which is the least part of me and is, therefore, evanescent. What is of abiding worth is my insistence on truth, nonviolence and brahmacharya which is the real part of me. That part of me, however small, is not to be despised. It is my all. I prize even the failures and disillusionment's which are but steps towards success. (YI, 25-12-1926, pp78-79)

The world knows so little of how much my so-called greatness depends upon the incessant toil and drudgery of silent, devoted, able and pure workers, men as well as women. (YI, 26-4-1928, p130)

Truth to me is infinitely dearer than the 'mahatmaship', which is purely a burden. It is my knowledge of my limitations and my nothingness which has so far saved me from the oppressiveness of the 'mahatmaship'. (YI, 1-11-1928, p361)

Sick of Adoration

I have become literally sick of the adoration of the unthinking multitude. I would feel certain of my ground if I was spat upon by them. Then there would be no need for confession of Himalayan and other miscalculations, no retracing, no re-arranging. (YI, 2-3-1922, p135)

In the majority of cases, addresses presented to me contain adjectives which I am ill able to carry. Their use can do good neither to the writers nor to me. They unnecessary humiliate me, for I have to confess that I do not deserve them. When they are deserved, their use is superfluous. It cannot add to the strength of the qualities possessed by me. They may, if I am not on my guard, easily turn my head. The good that a man does is more often than not better left unsaid. Imitation is the sincerest flattery. (YI, 21-5-1925, p176)

The Mahatma I must leave to his fate. Though a non-co-operator, I shall gladly subscribe to a Bill to make it criminal for anybody to call me Mahatma and to touch my feet. Where I can impose the law myself, i.e., at the Ashram, the practice is criminal. (YI, 17-3-1927, p86)

True Honour

The highest honour that my friends can do me is to enforce in their own lives the programme that I stand for or to resist me to their utmost if they do not believe in it. (YI, 12-6-1924, p197)

It will be waste of good money to spend . . . on erecting a clay or metallic statue of the figure of a man who is himself made of clay and is more fragile than a bangle which can keep by preservation for a thousand years, whereas the human body disintegrates daily and undergoes final disintegration after the usual span of life. I have learnt from my Muslim friends, among whom I have passed the best part of my life, my dislike of statues and photographs of my figure. . . .

Let these lines serve as a warning to those who want to honour me by erecting statues and having portraits of my figure, that I heartily dislike these exhibitions. I shall deem it ample honour if those who believe in me will be good enough to promote the activities I stand for. (H, 11-12-1939, p1)

No 'Avatar'

I hold it to be a blasphemy to represent me as Shri Krishna. I claim to be a humble worker and no more among many in a great cause, which can only be injured rather than advanced by glorification of its leaders. A cause has the best chance of success when it is examined and followed on its own merits. Measures must always, in a progressive society, be held superior to men, who are after all imperfect instruments, working for their fulfilment. (YI, 13-7-1921, p224)

The only virtue I want to claim is Truth and Nonviolence. I lay no claim to superhuman powers. I want none. I wear the same corruptible flesh that the weakest of my fellow-beings wears, and am, therefore, as liable to err as any. My services have many limitations, but God has up to now blessed them in spite of the imperfections. (YI, 16-2-1922, p102)

I lay claim to nothing exclusively divine in me. I do not claim prophetship. I am but a humble seeker after Truth and bent upon finding It. I count no sacrifice too great for the sake of seeing God face to face. The whole of my activity, whether it may be called social, political, humanitarian or ethical, is directed to that end. And as I know that God is found more often in the lowliest of His creatures than in the high and mighty, I am struggling to reach the status of these. I cannot do so without their service. Hence my passion for the service of the suppressed classes. And as I cannot render this service without entering politics, I find myself in them. Thus I am no master. I am but a struggling, erring, humble servant of India and there through of humanity. (H, 11-9-1924, pp298)

It is curious how we delude ourselves. We fancy that one can make the perishable body impregnable and we think it impossible to evoke the hidden powers of the soul. Well, I am engaged in trying to show, if I have any of these powers, that I am as frail a mortal as any of us and that I never had anything extraordinary about me nor have any now. (YI, 6-5-1926, p164)

I do not consider myself worthy to be mentioned in the same breath with the race of prophets. I am a humble seeker after truth. I am impatient to realize myself, to attain moksha in this very existence. My national service is part of my training for freeing my soul from the bondage of flesh. Thus considered, my service may be regarded as purely selfish. I have no desire for the perishable kingdom of earth. I am striving for the Kingdom of Heaven, which is moksha. (YI, 3-4-1924, p114)

I claim to be no more than an average man with less than average ability. Nor can I claim any special merit for such nonviolence or continence as I have been able to reach with laborious research. I have not the shadow of a doubt that any man or woman can achieve what I have, if he or she would make the same effort and cultivate the same hope and faith. (H, 3-10-1936, p269)

Some of my correspondents seem to think that I can work wonders. Let me say as a devotee of truth that I have no such gift... All the power I may have comes from God. But He does not work directly. He works through His numberless agencies. (H, 8-10-1938, p285)

Awareness of Limitations

I consider myself to be a sagacious worker and my sagacity means no more and no less than a fine perception of my limitations. I hope I never travel beyond my limits. Certainly,

I have never done so consciously. (YI, 23-6-1920, p3) I am conscious of my own limitations. That consciousness is my only strength. Whatever I might have been able to do in my life has proceeded more than anything else out of the realization of my own limitations. (YI, 13-11-1924, p378)

If I was what I want to be, the fast would not have been necessary. I would not then need to argue with anyone. My word would go straight home. Indeed, I would not even need to utter the word. The mere will on my part would suffice to produce the required effect. But I am painfully aware of my limitations. (H, 15-4-1939, p86)

I shall continue to confess blunders each time the people commit them. The only tyrant I accept in this world is the 'still small voice' within. And even though I have to face the prospect of a minority of one, I humbly believe I have the courage to be in such a hopeless minority. (YI, 2-3-1922, p135)

I claim to be a fairly accurate student of human nature and vivisector of my own failings. I have discovered that man is superior to the system he propounds. (MGI, p241)

I hope there is no pride in me. I feel I recognize fully my weakness. But my faith in God and His strength and love is unshakable. I am like clay in the Potter's hand. (YI, 26-1-1922, p49)

I have no desire for prestige anywhere. It is furniture required in courts of Kings. I am a servant of Mussalmans, Christians, Parsis and Jews as I am of Hindus. And a servant is in need of love, not prestige. That is assured to me so long as I remain a faithful servant. (YI, 26-3-1925, p112)

Readiness for Martyrdom

There are certain things which you cannot escape all at once, even whilst you are avoiding them. This earthly case in which I am locked up is the bane of my life, but I am obliged to put up with it and even indulge it. (YI, 27-10-1921, p342)

I implicitly believe in the truth of the saying that not a blade of grass moves but by His will. He will save it [my life] if He needs it for further service in this body. None can save it against His will. (EF, p114)

Do not seek to protect me. The Most High is always there to protect us all. You may be sure that when my time is up, no one, not even the most renowned in the world, can stand between Him and me. (YI, 2-4-1931, p64-55)

I must be true to my Maker, and the moment I feel that life is insupportable for me, I hope not to be found wanting. What better reparation can I do than willing surrender of the body that has ceased to evoke response and may be a hindrance to the discovery of the true way? (ibid, p60)

I am not aching for martyrdom, but if it comes in my way in the prosecution of what I consider to be the supreme duty in defense of the faith I hold. . . I shall have earned it. (H, 29-6-1934, p156)

Whilst I prize the unbounded affection of the people, let them realize that my life is not worth keeping if anxiety to save it deflects the attention of the nation from the main purpose. (H, 11-3-1939, p44)

Assaults have been made on my life in the past, but God has spared me till now, and the assailants have repented for their action. But if someone were to shoot me in the belief that he was getting rid of a rascal, he would kill not the real Gandhi, but the one that appeared to him a rascal. (BC, 9-8-1942)

God alone is my protector. How can puny man, who is not sure even of his own tomorrow, presume to protect another? I am content to be under God's care. He may protect or destroy. I know He sometimes even destroys to protect. (H, 9-6-1946, p170)

I do not want to die . . . of a creeping paralysis of my faculties-a defeated man. An assassin's bullet may put an end to my life. I would welcome it. But I would love, above all, to fade out doing my duty with my last breath. (MGMLP, I, p562)

I am not afraid to die in my mission, if that is to be my fate. (H, 27-4-1947, p127)

Avoidance of Anger

I have learnt through bitter experience the one supreme lesson to conserve my anger, and as heat conserved is transmuted into energy, even so our anger controlled can be transmuted into a power which can move the world. (YI, 15-9-1920, p6)

I spare neither friend nor foe when it is a question of departing from the code of honour. (YI, 2-3-1922, p140)

It is not that I do not get angry. I do not give vent to anger. I cultivate the quality of patience as angerlessness, and, generally speaking, I succeed. But I only control my anger when it comes. How I find it possible to control it would be a useless question, for it is a habit that everyone must cultivate and must succeed in forming by constant practice. (H, 11-5-1935, p98)

If I had no sense of humour, I should long ago have committed suicide. (YI, 18-8-1921, p238)

I am an irrepressible optimist, because I believe in myself. That sounds very arrogant, doesn't it? But I say it from the depths of my humility. I believe in the supreme power of God. I believe in Truth and, therefore, I have no doubt in the future of this country or the future of humanity.

I am an optimist because I expect many things from myself. I have not got them, I know, as I am not yet a perfect being. If I was one, I should not even need to reason with you. When I am a perfect being, I have simply to say the word and the nation will listen. I want to attain that perfection by service. (YI, 13-8-1925, pp.279-80)

My philosophy, if I can be said to have any, excludes the possibility of harm to one's cause by outside agencies. The harm comes deservedly and only when the cause itself is bad or, being good, its champions are untrue, fainthearted or unclean. (H, 25-7-1936, p185)

I KNOW THE PATH

I know the path. It is straight and narrow. It is like the edge of a sword. I rejoice to walk on it. I weep when I slip. God's word is: 'He who strives never perishes.' I have implicit faith in that promise. Though, therefore, from my weakness I fail a thousand times, I will not lose faith, but hope that I shall see the Light when the flesh has been brought under perfect subjection, as some day it must. (YI, 17-6-1926, p215)

My soul refuses to be satisfied so long as it is a helpless witness of a single wrong or a single misery. But it is not possible for me, a weak, frail, miserable being, to mend every wrong or to hold myself free of blame for all the wrong I see.

The spirit in me pulls one way, the flesh in me pulls in the opposite direction. There is freedom from the action of these two forces, but that freedom is attainable only by slow and painful stages.

I cannot attain freedom by a mechanical refusal to act, but only by intelligent action in a detached manner. This struggle resolves itself into an incessant crucifixion of the flesh so that the spirit may become entirely free. (YI, 17-11-1921, p368)

Search for Truth

I am but a seeker after Truth. I claim to have found a way to it. I claim to be making a ceaseless effort to find it. But I admit that I have not yet found it. To find Truth completely is to realize oneself and one's destiny, i.e., to become perfect. I am painfully conscious of my imperfections, and therein lies all the strength I posses, because it is a rare thing for a man to know his own limitations.

If I was a perfect man, I own I should not feel the miseries of neighbours as I do. As a perfect man I should take note of them, prescribe a remedy, and compel adoption by the force of unchallengeable Truth in me. But as yet I only see as through a glass darkly and, therefore, have to carry conviction by slow and laborious processes, and then, too, not always with success.

That being so, I would be less than human if, with all my knowledge of avoidable misery pervading the land and of the sight of mere skeletons under the very shadow of the Lord of the Universe, I did not feel with and for all the suffering but dumb millions of India. (ibid, p377)

Trust in God

I am in the world feeling my way to light 'amid the encircling gloom'. I often err and miscalculate... My trust is solely in God.

And I trust men only because I trust God. If I had no God to rely upon, I should be like Timon, a hater of my species. (YI, 4-12-1924, p398)

I will not be a traitor to God to please the whole world. (H, 18-2-1933, p4)

Whatever striking things I have done in life, I have not done prompted by reason but prompted by instinct, I would say, God. (H, 14-5-1938, p110)

I am a man of faith. My reliance is solely on God. One step is enough for me. The next step He will make clear to me when the time for it comes. (H, 20-10-1940, p330)

No Secrecy

I have no secret methods. I know no diplomacy save that of truth. I have no weapon but nonviolence. I may be unconsciously led astray for a while, but not for all time. (YI, 11-12-1924, p406)

My life has been an open book. I have no secrets and I encourage no secrets. (YI, 19-3-1931, p43)

I am but a poor struggling soul yearning to be wholly good-wholly truthful and wholly nonviolent in thought, word and deed, but ever failing to reach the ideal which I know to be true. I admit it is a painful climb, but the pain of it is a positive pleasure for me. Each step upward makes me feel stronger and fit for the next. (YI, 9-4-1924, p126)

When I think of my littleness and my limitations on the one hand and of the expectations raised about me on the other, I become dazed for the moment, but I come to myself as soon as I realize that these expectations are a tribute not to me, a curious mixture of Jekyll and Hyde, but to the incarnation, however imperfect but comparatively great in me, of the two priceless qualities of truth and nonviolence. I must, therefore, not shirk the responsibility of giving what aid I can to fellow-seekers after truth from the West. (YI, 3-10-1925, p344)

Guidance

I claim to have no infallible guidance or inspiration. So far as my experience goes, the claim to infallibility on the part of a human being would be untenable, seeing that inspiration too can come only to one who is free from the action of opposites, and it will be difficult to judge on a given occasion whether the claim to freedom from pairs of opposites is justified. The claim to infallibility would thus always be a most dangerous claim to make. This, however, does not leave us without any guidance whatsoever. The sum-total of the experience of the sages of the world is available to us and would be for all time to come.

Moreover, there are not many fundamental truths, but there is only one fundamental truth which is Truth itself, otherwise known as Nonviolence. Finite human being shall never know in its fullness Truth and love which is in itself infinite. But we do know enough for our guidance. We shall err, and sometimes grievously, in our application. But man is a self-governing being, and self-government necessarily includes the power as much to commit errors as to set them right as often as they are made. (YI, 21-4-1927, p128)

I deny being a visionary. I do not accept the claim of saintliness. I am of the earth, earthly . . . I am prone to as many weakness as you are. But I have seen the world. I have lived in the world with my eyes open. I have gone through the most fiery ordeals that have fallen to the lot of man. I have gone through this discipline. (SW, p531)

Self-sacrifice

I am asking my countrymen in India to follow no other gospel than the gospel of self-sacrifice which precedes every battle. Whether you belong to the school of violence or nonviolence, you will still have to go through the fire of sacrifice and of discipline. (ibid, p532)

I want to declare to the world, although I have forfeited the regard of many friends in the West - and I must bow my head low; but even for their friendship or love, I must not suppress the voice of conscience, - the promptings of my inner basic nature today. There is something within me impelling me to cry out my agony. I have known humanity. I have studied something of psychology. Such a man knows exactly what it is. I do not mind how you describe it. That voice within tells me, "You have to stand against the whole world although you may have to stand alone. You have to stare in the face the whole world although the world may look at you with blood-shot eyes. Do not fear. Trust the little voice residing within your heart." It says: "Forsake friends, wife and all; but testify to that for which you have lived and for which you have to die." (MN, pp201-2)

No Defeatism

Defeat cannot dishearten me. It can only chasten me..... I know that God will guide me. Truth is superior to man's wisdom. (YI, 3-7-1924, p218)

I have never lost my optimism. In seemingly darkest hours hope has burnt bright within me. I cannot kill the hope myself. I must say I cannot give an ocular demonstration to justify the hope. But there is no defeat in me. (H, 25-1-1935, p399)

I do not want to foresee the future. I am concerned with taking care of the present. God has given me no control over the moment following...

Trust

It is true that I have often been let down. Many have deceived me and many have been found wanting. But I do not repent of my association with them. For I know how to non-co-operate, as I know how to co-operate. The most practical, the most dignified way of going on in the world is to take people at their word, when you have no positive reason to the contrary. (YI, 26-12-1924, p430)

I believe in trusting. Trust begets trust. Suspicion is fetid and only stinks. He who trusts has never yet lost in the world. (YI, 4-6-1925, p193)

A breach of promise shakes me to my root, especially when I am in any way connected with the author of the breach. And if it cost my life which, after all, at the age of seventy has no insurance value, I should most willingly give it in order to secure due performance of a sacred and solemn promise. (H, 11-3-1939, p46)

To my knowledge, throughout my public and private career, I have never broken a promise. (H, 22-4-1939, p100)

My Leadership

They say I claim to understand human nature as no one else does. I believe I am certainly right, but if I do not believe in my rightness and my methods, I would be unfit to be at the helm of affairs. (YI, 1-1-1925, p8)

As for my leadership, if I have it, it has not come for any seeking, it is a fruit of faithful service. A man can as little discard such leadership as he can the color of his skin. And since I have become an integral part of the nation, it has to keep me with all my faults and shortcomings, of some of which I am painfully conscious and of many others of which candid critics, thanks be to them, never fail to remind me. (YI, 13-2-1930, p52)

It is a bad carpenter who quarrels with his tools. It is a bad general who blames his men for faulty workmanship. I know I am not a bad general. I have wisdom enough to know my limitations. God will give me strength enough to declare my bankruptcy if such is to be my lot. He will perhaps take me away when I am no longer wanted for the work which I have been permitted to do for nearly half a century.

But I do entertain the hope that there is yet work for me to do, that the darkness that seems to have enveloped me will disappear, and that, whether with another battle more brilliant than the Dandi March or without, India will come to her own demonstrably through nonviolent means. I am praying for the light that will dispel the darkness. Let those who have a living faith in nonviolence join me in the prayer. (H, 23-7-1938, p193)

My Work

I am content with the doing of the task in front of me. I do not worry about the why and wherefore of things... Reason helps us to see that we should not dabble in things we cannot fathom. (H, 7-9-1935, p234)

My work will be finished if I succeed in carrying conviction to the human family, that every man or woman, however weak in body, is the guardian of his or her self-respect and liberty. This defense avails, though the whole world may be against the individual resister. (Hst, 6-8-1944)

It will be time enough to pronounce a verdict upon my work after my eyes are closed and this tabernacle is consigned to the flames. (YI, 4-4-1929, p107)

My Mission

I AM not a visionary. I claim to be a practical idealist. The religion of nonviolence is not meant merely for the rishis and saints. It is meant for the common people as well. Nonviolence is the law of our species as violence is the law of the brute. The spirit lies dormant in the brute and he knows no law but that of physical might. The dignity of man requires obedience to a higher law-to the strength of the spirit. (YI, 11-8-1920, p3)

There are more instances than one in my public life when, with the ability to retaliate, I have refrained from doing so and advised friends to do likewise. My life is dedicated to the spread of that doctrine. I read it in the teachings of all the greatest teachers of the world-Zoroaster, Mahavir, Daniel, Jesus, Muhammad, Nanak and a host of others. (YI, 9-2-1922, p85)

Nonviolence is the first article of my faith. It is also the last article of my creed. (YI, 23-3-1922, p166)

I am but an humble explorer of the science of nonviolence. Its hidden depths sometimes stagger me just as much as they stagger fellow-workers. (YI, 20-11-1924, p382)

Mission of Satyagraha

My mission is to teach by example and precept under sever restraint the use of the matchless weapon of Satyagraha; which is a direct corollary of nonviolence and truth. I am anxious, indeed I am impatient, to demonstrate that there is no remedy for the many ills of life save that of nonviolence....

When I have become incapable of evil and when nothing harsh or haughty occupies, be it momentarily, my thought-world, then, and not till then, my nonviolence will move all the hearts of all the world. I have placed before me and the reader no impossible ideal or ordeal. It is man's prerogative and birthright.

We have lost the paradise only to regain it. If it takes time, then it is but a speck in the complete time-circle. The Divine

Teacher of the Gita knew when he said that millions of our days are equal to only a day of Brahma. (YI, 2-7-1925, p232)

Ahimsa is my God, and Truth is my God. When I look for ahimsa, Truth says 'Find it out through me'. When I look for Truth, ahimsa says 'Find it out through me'. (YI, 4-6-1925, p191)

I believe myself to be saturated with ahimsa - nonviolence. Ahimsa and Truth are as my two lungs. I cannot live without them. But I see every moment with more and more clearness the immense power of ahimsa and the littleness of man. Even the forest-dweller cannot be entirely free from violence, in spite of his limitless compassion. With every breath he commits a certain amount of violence.

The body itself is a house of slaughter, and, therefore, moksha and Eternal Bliss consist in perfect deliverance from the body, and therefore, all pleasure, save the joy of moksha, is evanescent, imperfect. That being the case, we have to drink, in daily life, many a bitter draught of violence. (YI, 21-10-1926, p364)

Application of Nonviolence

We have to make truth and nonviolence not matters for mere individual practice but for practice by groups and communities and nations. That, at any rate, is my dream. I shall live and die in trying to realize it.

My faith helps me to discover new truths every day. Ahimsa is the attribute of the soul, and therefore, to be practiced by everybody in all the affairs of life. If it cannot be practiced in all departments, it has no practical value. (H, 2-3-1940, p23)

My faith in truth and nonviolence is ever growing, and as I am ever trying to follow them in my life, I too am growing every moment. I see new implications about them. I see them in a newer light every day and read in them a newer meaning. (H, 1-5-1934, p94)

I have not conceived my mission to be that of a knight-errant wandering everywhere to deliver people from difficult situations. My humble occupation has been to show people how they can solve their own difficulties. (H, 28-6-1942, p201)

My imperfections and failures are as much a blessing from God as my successes and my talents, and I lay them both at His feet. Why should He have chosen me, an imperfect instrument, for such a mighty experiment? I think He deliberately did so. He had to serve the poor, dumb, ignorant millions. A perfect man might have been their despair. When they found that one with their failings was marching on towards ahimsa, they too had confidence in their own capacity. We should not have recognized a perfect man if he had come as our leader, and we might have driven him to a cave. May be he who follows me will be more perfect and you will be able to receive his message. (H, 21-7-1940, p211)

No Gandhian Sect

I claim to be a humble servant of India and humanity, and would like to die in the discharge of such service. I have no desire to found a sect. I am really too ambitious to be satisfied with a sect for a following. For I represent no new truths. I endeavour to follow and represent Truth, as I know it. I do claim to throw a new light on many an old truth. (YI, 25-8-1921, p267)

I have presented no new principles, but tried to restate old principles. (YI, 2-12-1926, p419)

There is no such thing as 'Gandhism', and I do not want to leave any sect after me. I do not claim to have originated any new principle or doctrine. I have simply tried in my own way to apply the eternal truths to our daily life and problems....

I have nothing new to teach the world. Truth and Nonviolence are as old as the hills. All I have done is to try experiments in both on as vast a scale as I could do. In doing so I have sometimes erred and learnt by my errors. Life and its problems have thus become to me so many experiments in the practice of truth and nonviolence.

By instinct I have been truthful, but not nonviolent. As a Jain muni once rightly said, I was not so much a votary of ahimsa as I was of truth, and I put the latter in the first place and the former in the second. For, as he put it, I was capable of sacrificing nonviolence for the sake of truth. In fact, it was in the course of my pursuit of truth that I discovered nonviolence. (H, 28-3-1936, p49)

I myself do not know what is the Gandhian hue. I am sailing on an uncharted sea.. I have to take frequent soundings. (H, 17-12-1938, p385)

Gandhi-ites is no name worth having. Rather than that, why not ahimsa-ites? For Gandhi is a mixture of good and evil, weakness and strength, violence and nonviolence, but ahimsa has no adulteration. (H, 13-5-1939, p121)

I come now to what is called the 'Gandhian' ideology and the means of propagating it. The propagation of truth and nonviolence can be done less by books than by actually living those principles. Life truly lived is more than books. (ibid, p122)

There is always a saving clause about all my advice. No one need follow it unless it appeals to his head and heart. No one who has honestly the inner call need be deterred from obeying it because of my advice. In other words, it applies only to those who are not conscious of any inner call and who have faith in my riper experience and soundness of judgment. (H, 15-7-1939, p197)

Let Gandhism be destroyed if it stands for error. Truth and ahimsa will never be destroyed, but if Gandhism is another name for sectarianism, it deserves to be destroyed. If I were to know, after my death, that what I stood for had degenerated into sectarianism, I should be deeply pained...

Let no one say that he is a follower of Gandhi. It is enough that I should be my own follower. I know what an inadequate follower I am of myself, for I cannot live up to the convictions I stand for. You are no followers but fellow-students, fellow-pilgrims, fellow-seekers, fellow-workers. (H, 2-3-1940, p23)

If there is one Gandhi-ite, it must be me. I hope, however, that I am humble enough not to arrogate any such claim. Gandhi-ite means a worshipper of Gandhi. There must be a God to worship. But I have never arrogated to myself any such claim. Hence there can be no devotee of mine. (H, 2-11-1947, p389)

Law of Suffering

I....have ventured to place before India the ancient law of self-sacrifice.-For Satyagraha and its off-shoots, noncooperation and civil resistance are nothing but new names for the law of suffering. The rishis, who discovered the law of nonviolence in the midst of violence, were greater geniuses than Newton. They were themselves greater warriors than Wellington. Having themselves known the use of arms, they realized their uselessness, and taught a weary world that its salvation lay not through violence but through nonviolence.

Nonviolence in its dynamic condition means conscious suffering. It does not mean meek submission of the will of the evildoer, but it means putting of one's whole soul against the will of the tyrant. Working under this law of our being, it is possible for a single individual to defy the whole might of an unjust empire to save his honor, his religion, his soul, and lay the foundation for that empire's fall or its regeneration.

India's Role

And so I am not pleading for India to practice nonviolence because it is weak. I want her to practice nonviolence being conscious of her strength and power. No training in arms is required for realization of her strength. We seem to need it, because we seem to think that we are but a lump of flesh. I want India to recognize that she has a soul that cannot perish and that can rise triumphant above every physical weakness and defy the physical combination of a whole world. (YI, 11-8-1920, pp3-4)

If I can say so without arrogance and with due humility, my message and methods are, indeed, in their essentials for the whole world and it gives me keen satisfaction to know that it has already received a wonderful response in the hearts of a large and daily growing number of men and women of the West. (YI, 17-9-1925 p320)

Brotherhood of Man

My mission is not merely brotherhood of Indian humanity. My mission is not merely freedom of India, though today it undoubtedly engrosses practically the whole of my life and whole of my time. But, through realization of freedom of India, I hope to realize and carry on the mission of brotherhood of man.

My patriotism is not an exclusive thing. It is all embracing and I should reject that patriotism which sought to mount upon the distress or exploitation of other nationalities. The conception of my patriotism is nothing if it is not always, in every case without exception, consistent with the broadest good of humanity at large.

Not only that, but my religion and my patriotism derived from my religion embrace all life. I want to realize brotherhood or identity not merely with the beings called human, but I want to realize identity with all life, even with such things as crawl upon earth....because we claim descent from the same God, and that being so, all life in whatever form it appears must be essentially one. (YI, 4-4-1929, p107)

I have that implicit faith in my mission that, if it succeeds - as it will succeed, it is bound to succeed—history will record it as a movement designed to knit all people in the world together, not as hostile to one another but as parts of one whole. (H, 26-1-1934, p8)

Nonviolent Way

My aspiration is limited. God has not given me the power to guide the world on the path of nonviolence. But I have imagined that He has chosen me as His instrument for presenting nonviolence to India for dealing with her many ills. The progress already made is great. But much more remains to be done. (H, 23-7-1938, p193)

Fraud and untruth today are stalking the world. I cannot sit as a helpless witness to such a situation.....If today I sit quiet and inactive, God will take me to task for not using up the treasure He had given me, in the midst of the conflagration that is enveloping the whole world. (BC, 9-8-1942)

I cannot impose my personal faith on others, never on a national organization. I can but try to convince the nation of its beauty and usefulness...

It would be a calamity if by obstinacy I stand in the way of the country's progress by other means, so long as they are not positively mischievous and harmful. I should, for instance, rise, even if I was alone, against methods of actual violence. But I have recognized that the nation has the right, if it so wills, to vindicate her freedom even by actual violence. Only, then India ceases to be the land of my love even though she be the land of my birth, even as I should take no pride in my mother if she went astray. (YI, 20-11-1924, p382)

I have not the capacity for preaching universal nonviolence. I preach, therefore, nonviolence restricted strictly to the purpose of winning our freedom and, therefore, perhaps for preaching the regulation of international relations by nonviolent means. Before I can preach universal nonviolence, I must be wholly free from passions, I must be wholly incapable of sin. (H, 25-1-1942, p15)

My preaching and teaching are not emotional or unpractical, for I teach what is ancient and strive to practice what I preach. And I claim that what I practice is capable of being practiced by all, because I am a very ordinary mortal open to the same temptations and liable to the same weaknesses as the least among us. (YI, 15-12-1927, p424)

While I prate about Universal Nonviolence, my experiment is confined to India. If it succeeds, the world will accept it without effort. There is, however, a bit BUT. The pause does not worry me. My faith is brightest in the midst of impenetrable darkness. (H, 11-2-1939, p8)

Somehow or other, I dread a visit to Europe and America. Not that I distrust the peoples of these great continents any more than I distrust my own, but I distrust myself. I have no desire to go to the West in search of health or for sightseeing. I have no desire to deliver public speeches. I detest being lionized. I wonder if I shall ever again have the health to stand the awful strain of public speaking and public demonstrations.

If God ever sent me to the West, I should go there to penetrate the hearts of the masses, to have quiet talks with the youth of the West and have the privilege of meeting kindred spirits—lovers of peace at any price save that of truth.

But I feel that I have as yet no message to deliver personally to the West. I believe my message to be universal, but as yet I feel that I can best deliver it through my work in my own country. If I can show visible success in India, the delivery of the message becomes complete. If I came to the conclusion that India had no use for my message, I should not care to go elsewhere in search of listeners even though I still retained faith in it. If I ventured out of India, I should do so because I have faith, though I cannot demonstrate it to the satisfaction of all, that the message is being received by India, be it ever so slowly. (M, II, p417)

When I have become incapable of evil and when nothing harsh or haughty occupies, be it momentarily, my thought-world, then, and not till then, my nonviolence, will move all the hearts of all the world. (YI, 2-7-1925, p232). Millions like me may fail to prove the truth in their own lives, that would be their failure, never of the eternal law. (M, VIII, p23)

THE INNER VOICE

There come to us moments in life when about some things we need no proof from without. A little voice within us tells us, 'You are on the right track, move neither to your left nor right, but keep to the straight and narrow way. (L, 25-12-1916)

There are moments in your life when you must act, even though you cannot carry your best friends with you. The 'still small voice' within you must always be the final arbiter when there is a conflict of duty. (YI, 4-8-1920, p3)

Having made a ceaseless effort to attain self-purification, I have developed some little capacity to hear correctly and clearly the 'still small voice within'. (EF, p34)

I shall lose my usefulness the moment I stifle the still small voice within. (YI, 3-12-1925, p422)

Penances with me are no mechanical acts. They are done in obedience to the inner voice. (YI, 2-4-1931, p60)

No False Claim

A person falsely claiming to act under divine inspiration or the promptings of the inner voice without having any such, will fare worse than the one falsely claiming to act under the authority of an earthly sovereign. Whereas the latter on being exposed will escape with injury to his body, the former may perish body and soul together.

Charitable critics impute no fraud to me, but suggest that I am highly likely to be acting under some hallucination. The result for me, even then, will not be far different from what it would be if I was laying a false claim. A humble seeker that I claim to be has need to be most cautious and, to preserve the balance of mind, he has to reduce himself to zero before God will guide him. Let me not labour this point.

There is no question of hallucination. I have stated a simple scientific truth, thus to be tested by all who have the will and the patience to acquire the necessary qualifications, which are again incredibly simple to understand and easy enough to acquire where there is determination. (BC, 18-11-1932)

You have to believe no one but yourselves. You must try to listen to the inner voice, but if you will not have the expression "inner voice", you may use the expression "dictates of reason", which you should obey, and if you will not parade God, I have no doubt you will parade something else which in the end will prove to be God, for, fortunately, there is no one and nothing else but God in this universe.

I would also submit that it is not everyone claiming to act on the urge of the inner voice [who] has that urge. Like every other faculty, this faculty for listening to the still small noise within requires previous effort and training, perhaps much greater than what is required for the acquisition of any other faculty, and even if out of thousands of claimants only a few succeed in establishing their claim, it is well worth running the risk of having and tolerating doubtful claimants. (M, III, p229)

Nobody has to my knowledge questioned the possibility of the inner voice speaking to some, and it is a gain to the world even if one person's claim to speak under the authority of the inner voice can be really sustained. Many may make the claim, but not all will be able to substantiate it. But it cannot and ought not to be suppressed for the sake of preventing false claimants.

There is no danger whatsoever if many people could truthfully represent the inner voice. But, unfortunately, there is no remedy against hypocrisy. Virtue must not be suppressed because many will feign it. Men have always been found throughout the world claiming to speak for the inner voice. But no harm has yet overtaken the world through their short-lived activities.

Before one is able to listen to that voice, one has to go through a long and fairly serve course of training, and when it is the inner voice that speaks, it is unmistakable. The world cannot be successfully fooled for all time. There is, therefore, no danger of anarchy setting in because a humble man like me will not be suppressed and will dare to claim the authority of the inner voice, when he believes that he has heard it. (H, 18-3-1933, p8)

My claim to hear the voice of God is no new claim. Unfortunately, there is no way that I know of proving the claim except through results. God will not be God if He allowed Himself to be an object of proof by His creatures. But He does give His willing slave power to pass through the fiercest of ordeals.

I have been a willing slave to this most exacting Master for more than half a century. His voice has been increasingly audible, as years have rolled by. He has never forsaken me even in my darkest hour. He has saved me often against myself and left me not a vestige of independence. The greater the surrender to Him, the greater has been my joy. (H, 6-5-1933, p4)

Voice of God

For me the Voice of God, of Conscience, of Truth, or the Inner Voice or 'the Still Small Voice' mean one and the same thing. I saw no form. I have never tried, for I have always believed God to be without form. But what I did hear was like a Voice from afar and yet quite near. It was as unmistakable as some human voice definitely speaking to me, and irresistible. I was not dreaming at the time I heard the Voice. The hearing of the Voice was preceded by a terrific struggle within me.

Suddenly the Voice came upon me. I listened, made certain it was the Voice, and the struggle ceased. I was calm. The determination was made accordingly, the date and the hour of the fast were fixed...

Could I give any further evidence that it was truly the Voice that I heard and that it was not an echo of my own heated imagination? I have no further evidence to convince the skeptic. He is free to say that it was all self-delusion or hallucination. It may well have been so. I can offer no proof to the contrary. But I can say this, that not the unanimous verdict of the whole world against me could shake me from the belief that what I heard was the true Voice of God.

But some think that God himself is a creation of our own imagination. If that view holds good, then nothing is real, everything is of our own imagination. Even so, whilst my imagination dominates, me I can only act under its spell. Realest things are only relatively so. For me the Voice was more real than my own existence. It has never failed me, or for that matter, anyone else. And everyone who wills can hear the Voice. It is within everyone. But like everything else, it requires previous and definite preparation. (H, 8-7-1933, p4)

Rightly or wrongly, I know that I have no other resource as a satyagrahi than the assistance of God in every conceivable difficulty, and I would like it to be believed that what may appear to be inexplicable actions of mine are really due to inner promptings.

It may be a product of my heated imagination. If it is so, I prize that imagination as it has served me for a chequered life extending over a period of now nearly over fifty-five years, because I learned to rely consciously upon God before I was fifteen years old. (H, 11-3-1939, p46)

MY FASTS

My Religion teaches me that, whenever there is distress which one cannot remove, one must fast and pray. (YI, 25-9-1924, p. 319)

They [fasts] are a part of my being. I can as well do without my eyes, for instance, as I can without fasts. What the eyes are for the outer world, fasts are for the inner. (YI, 3-12-1925, p. 422)

Higher Dictate

I am not responsible for these fasts. I do not undertake them for my amusement. I would not torture the flesh for the love of fame. Though I bear joyfully the pangs of hunger and many other discomforts of fasting, let no one imagine that I do not suffer. These fasts are bearable only because they are imposed upon me by a higher Power and the capacity to bear the pain also comes from that Power. (H, 24-8-1934, p. 223)

I cannot fast at the dictation of anyone. Such fasts [unto death] cannot be lightly undertaken. They can conceivably be wholly undesirable. They cannot be undertaken out of anger. Anger is a short madness. I must, therefore, undertake the fast only when the still small voice within me calls for it. (H, 15-6-1947, p. 194)

Fasting and Prayer

A genuine fast cleanses the body, mind and soul. It crucifies the flesh and to that extent sets the soul free. A sincere prayer can work wonders. It is an intense longing of the soul for its even greater purity. Purity thus gained, when it is utilized for a noble purpose, becomes a prayer. (YI, 24-3-1920, p. 1)

I believe that there is no prayer without fasting, and there is no real fast without prayer. (H, 16-2-1933, p. 2)

A complete fast is a complete and literal denial of self. It is the truest prayer. 'Take my life and let it be, always, only, all for Thee' is not, should not be, a mere lip or figurative expression. It has to be reckless and joyous giving without the least reservation. Abstention from food and even water is but the mere beginning, the least part of the surrender. (H, 15-4-1933, p. 4)

Subduing the Flesh

Fasting, unless it is the result of God's grace, is useless starvation, if not much worse. (H, 11-4-1939, p. 46)

I know that the mental attitude is everything. Just as prayer may be merely a mechanical intonation as of a bird, so may a fast be a mere mechanical torture of the flesh..... Neither will touch the soul within. (YI, 16-2-1922, p. 103)

It is my own firm belief that the strength of the soul grows in proportion as you subdue the flesh. (YI, 23-10-1924, p. 354)

Mortification of the flesh is a necessity when the flesh rebels against one; it is a sin when the flesh has come under subjection and can be used as an instrument of service. In other words, there is no inherent merit in mortification of the flesh. (H, 2-11-1936, p. 299)

There is something in denying satisfaction of the flesh. It is not possible to see God face to face unless you crucify the flesh. It is one thing to do what belongs to it as a temple of God, and it is another to deny it what belongs to it as the body of flesh. (H, 10-12-1938, p. 373)

Out of the fullness of my own experience and that of fellow cranks, I say without hesitation, fast (1) if you are constipated, (2) if you are anemic, (3) if you are feverish, (4) if you have indigestion, (5) if you have a headache, (6) if you are rheumatic, (7) if you are gouty, (8) if you are fretting and fuming, (9) if you are depressed, (10) if you are overjoyed; and you will avoid medical prescriptions and patent medicines. (YI, 17-12-1925, p. 442)

Coercive Fasts

Fasting can only be resorted to against a lover, not to extort rights but to reform him, as when a son fasts for a father who drinks. My fast at Bombay and then at Bardoli was of that character. I fasted to reform, say, General Dyer, who not only does not love me, but who regards himself as my enemy. (YI, 1-5-1924, p. 145)

It is not to be denied that fasting can be really coercive. Such are fasts to attain a selfish object. A fast undertaken to wring money from a person or for fulfilling some such personal end would amount to the exercise of coercion or undue influence. I would unhesitatingly advocate resistance of such undue influence.

I have myself successfully resisted it in the fasts that have been undertaken or threatened against me. And, if it is argued that the dividing line between a selfish and an unselfish end is often very thin, I would urge that a person who regards the end of a fast to be selfish or otherwise base should resolutely refuse to yield to it, even though the refusal may result in the death of the fasting person. If people will cultivate the habit of disregarding fasts which, in their opinion, are taken for unworthy ends, such fasts will be robbed of the taint of coercion and undue influence. Like all human institutions, fasting can be both legitimately and illegitimately used. But as a great weapon in the armoury of Satyagraha, it cannot be given up because of its possible abuse. (H, 9-9-1933, p. 5)

The weapon of fasting, I know, cannot be lightly wielded. It can easily savour of violence unless it is used by one skilled in the art. I claim to be such an artist in this subject. (H, 11-3-1939, p. 46)

MY INCONSISTENCIES

I decline to be slave to precedents or practice I cannot understand or defend on a moral basis. (YI, 21-7-1921, p228)

I must admit my many inconsistencies. But since I am called 'Mahatma', I might well endorse Emerson's saying that 'Foolish consistency is the hobgoblin of little minds.' There is, I fancy, a method in my inconsistencies. In my opinion, there is a consistency running through my seeming inconsistencies, as in Nature there is unity running through seeming diversity. (YI, 13-2-1930, p52)

Friends who know me have certified that I am as much a moderate as I am an extremist and as much a conservative as I am a radical. Hence, perhaps, my good fortune to have friends among these extreme types of men. The mixture is due, I believe, to my view of ahimsa. Inconsistency is only apparent. It appears so to many friends because of my responsiveness to varying circumstances. Seeming consistency may really be sheer obstinacy. (YI, 16-4-1931, p77)

Fetish of Consistency

I am not at all concerned with appearing to be consistent. In my pursuit after Truth I have discarded many ideas and learnt many new things. Old as I am in age, I have no feeling that I have ceased to grow inwardly or that my growth will stop with the dissolution of the flesh. What I am concerned with is my readiness to obey the call of Truth, my God, from moment to moment. (H, 29-4-1933, p2)

I have never made a fetish of consistency. I am a votary of Truth and I must say what I feel and think at a given moment on the question, without regard to what I may have said before on it. ... As my vision gets clearer, my views must grow clearer with daily practice. Where I have deliberately altered an opinion, the change should be obvious, only, a careful eye would notice a gradual and imperceptible evolution. (H, 28-9-1934, p. 260)

My aim is not to be consistent with my previous statements on a given question, but to be consistent with truth as it may present itself to me at a given moment. The result has been that I have grown from truth to truth. (H, 30-9-1939, p288)

No Expedience

I have sacrificed no principle to gain a political advantage. (YI, 12-3-1925, p91)

I am not aware of having done a single thing in my life as a matter of expedience. I have ever held that the highest morality is also the highest expedience. (H, 8-12-1933, p8)

Compromise

I have often been charged with having an unyielding nature. I have been told that I would not bow to the decisions of the majority. I have been accused of being autocratic. ... I have never been able to subscribe to the charge of obstinacy or autocracy. On the contrary, I pride myself on my yielding nature in non-vital matters. I detest autocracy. Valuing my freedom and independence, I equally cherish them for others. I have no desire to carry a single soul with me if I cannot appeal to his or her reason.

My unconventionality I carry to the point of rejecting the divinity of the oldest Shastras if they cannot convince my reason. But I have found by experience that, if I wish to live in society and retain my independence, I must limit the points of utter independence to matters of first-rate importance. In all others which do not involve a departure from one's personal religion or moral code, one must yield to the majority. (YI, 14-7-1920, p4)

All my life through, the very insistence on truth has taught me to appreciate the beauty of compromise. I saw in later life that this spirit was an essential part of Satyagraha. It has often meant endangering my life and incurring the displeasure of friends. But truth is hard as adamant and tender as a blossom. (A, p107)

Human life is a series of compromises, and it is not always easy to achieve in practice what one has found to be true in theory. (H, 5-9-1936, p237)

There are eternal principles, which admit of no compromise, and one must be prepared to lay down one's life in the practice of them. (ibid, p238)

MY WRITINGS

My hesitancy in speech, which was once an annoyance, is now a pleasure. Its greatest benefit has been that it has taught me the economy of words. I have naturally formed the habit of restraining my thoughts. And I can now give myself the certificate that a thoughtless word hardly ever escapes my tongue or pen. I do not recollect ever having had to regret anything in my speech or writing. I have thus been spared many a mishap and waste of time. (A, p45)

In the very first month of Indian Opinion, I realized that the sole aim of journalism should be service. The newspaper press is a great power, but just as an unchained torrent of water submerges whole country sides and devastates crops, even so an uncontrolled pen serves but to destroy. If the control is from without, it proves more poisonous than want of control. It can be profitable only when exercised from within. If this line of reasoning is correct, how many of the journals in the world would stand the test? But who would stop those that are useless? The useful and the useless must, like good and evil generally, go on together, and man must make his choice. (ibid, p211)

There can be no room for untruth in my writings, because it is my unshakable belief that there is no religion other than truth and because I am capable of rejecting aught obtained at the cost of truth.

My writings cannot but be free from hatred towards any individual because it is my firm belief that it is love that sustains the earth. (SL, No. 5, 17-9-1919)

My Journalism

I have taken up journalism not for its sake but merely as an aid to what I have conceived to be my mission in life. My mission is to teach by example and precept under severe restraint the use of the matchless weapon of Satyagraha which is a direct corollary of nonviolence and truth. ... To be true to my faith, therefore, I may not write in anger or malice. I may not write idly. I may not write merely to excite passion.

The reader can have no idea of the restraint I have to exercise from week to week in the choice of topics and my vocabulary.

It is a training for me. It enables me to peep into myself and to make discoveries of my weaknesses. Often my vanity dictates a smart expression or my anger a harsh adjective. It is a terrible ordeal but a fine exercise to remove these weeds. (YI, 2-7-1925, p232)

I write just as the Spirit moves me at the time of writing. I do not claim to know definitely that all conscious thought and action on my part is directed by the Spirit. But on an examination of the greatest steps that I have taken in my life, as also of those that may be regarded as the least, I think it will not be improper to say that all of them were directed by the Spirit. (A, p206)

As for giving ideas, I have some originality. But writing is a by-product; I write to propagate my ideas. Journalism is not my profession. (H, 18-8-1946, p270)

What I have done will endure, not what I have said or written. (H, 1-5-1947, p93)

TRUTH

The Gospel of Truth

What...is Truth? A difficult question; but I have solved it for myself by saying that it is what the voice within tells you. How then, you ask, [do] different people think of different and contrary truths? Well, seeing that the human mind works through innumerable media and that the evolution of the human mind is not the same for all, it follows that what may be truth for one may be untruth for another, and hence those who have made these experiments have come to the conclusion that there are certain conditions to be observed in making those experiments...

It is because we have at the present moment everybody claiming the right of conscience without going through any discipline whatsoever, and there is so much untruth being delivered to a bewildered world. All that I can in true humility present to you is that Truth is not to be found by anybody who has not got an abundant sense of humility. If you would swim on the bosom of the ocean of Truth, you must reduce yourself to a zero. YI, 31-12-1931, p428)

Truth and Love-ahimsa-is the only thing that counts. Where this is present, everything rights itself in the end. This is a law to which there is no exception. (YI, 18-8-1927, p265)

Sovereign Principle

For me truth is the sovereign principle, which includes numerous other principles. This truth is not only truthfulness in word, but truthfulness in thought also, and not only the relative truth of our conception, but the Absolute Truth, the Eternal Principle, that is God. There are innumerable definitions of God, because His manifestations are innumerable. They overwhelm me with wonder and awe and for a moment stun me.

But I worship God as Truth only. I have not yet found Him, but I am seeking after Him. I am prepared to sacrifice the things dearest to me in pursuit of this quest. Even if the sacrifice demanded be my very life, I hope I may be prepared to give it. But as long as I have not realized this Absolute Truth, so long must I hold by the relative truth as I have conceived it. That relative truth must, meanwhile, be my beacon, my shield and buckler. Though this path is strait and narrow and sharp as the razor's edge, for me it has been the quickest and easiest. Even my Himalayan blunders have seemed trifling to me because I have kept strictly to this path. For the path has saved me from coming to grief, and I have gone forward according to my light. Often in my progress I have had faint glimpses of the Absolute Truth, God, and daily the conviction is growing upon me that He alone is real and all else is unreal.

Quest for Truth

.....The further conviction has been growing upon me that whatever is possible for me is possible even for a child, and I have found sound reasons for saying so. The instruments for the quest of Truth are as simple as they are difficult. They may appear quite impossible to an arrogant person, and quite possible to an innocent child.

The seeker after Truth should be humbler than the dust. The world crushes the dust under its feet, but the seeker after Truth should so humble himself that even the dust could crush him. Only then, and not till then, will he have a glimpse of Truth. (A, p xv)

Truth is like a vast tree, which yields more and more fruit the more you nurture it. The deeper the search in the mine of truth the richer the discovery of the gems buried there, in the shape of openings for an even greater variety of service. (ibid, p159)

I think it is wrong to expect certainties in this world, where all else but God that is Truth is an uncertainty. All that appears and happens about and around is uncertain, transient. But there is a Supreme Being hidden therein as a Certainty, and one would be blessed if one could catch a glimpse of that certainty and hitch one's wagon to it. The quest for that Truth is the summum bonum of life. (ibid, p184)

In the march towards Truth, anger, selfishness, hatred, etc., naturally give way, for otherwise Truth would be impossible to attain. A man who is swayed by passions may have good enough intentions, may be truthful in word, but he will never find the Truth. A successful search for Truth means complete deliverance from the dual throng such as of love and hate, happiness and misery. (ibid, pp254-5)

Vision of Truth

To see the universal and all-pervading spirit of Truth face to face one must be able to love the meanest of creation as oneself. And a man who aspires after that cannot afford to keep out of any field of life. That is why my devotion to Truth has drawn me into the field of politics; and I can say without the slightest hesitation, and yet in all humility, that those who say that religion has nothing to do with politics do not know what religion means. (ibid, pp370-1)

My uniform experience has convinced me that there is no other God than Truth... The little fleeting glimpses... that I have been able to have of Truth can hardly convey an idea of the indescribable luster of Truth, a million times more intense than that of the sun we daily see with our eyes. (YI, 7-2-1929, p42)

In fact, what I have caught is only the faintest gleam of that mighty effulgence. But this much I can say with assurance, as a result of all my experiments, that a perfect vision of Truth can only follow a complete realization of ahimsa. (ibid)

Truth resides in every human heart, and one has to search for it there, and to be guided by truth as one sees it. But no one has a right to coerce others to act according to his own view of truth. (H, 24-11-1933, p6)

Absolute Truth

It is not given to man to know the whole Truth. His duty lies in living up to the truth as he sees it, and in doing so, to resort to the purest means, i.e., to nonviolence. (ibid)

God alone knows absolute truth. Therefore, I have often said, Truth is God. It follows that man, a finite being, cannot know absolute truth. (H, 7-4-1946, p70)

Nobody in this world possesses absolute truth. This is God's attribute alone. Relative truth is all we know. Therefore, we can only follow the truth as we see it. Such pursuit of truth cannot lead anyone astray. (H, 2-6-1946, p167)

Truth and I

I have in my life never been guilty of saying things I did not mean-my nature is to go straight to the heart and, if often I fail in doing so for the time being, I know that Truth will ultimately make itself heard and felt, as it has often done in my experience. (YI, 20-8-1925, pp285-6)

Let hundreds like me perish, but let Truth prevail. Let us not reduce the standards of Truth even by a hair's breadth for judging erring mortals like myself. (A, p xv)

In judging myself I shall try to be as harsh as truth, as I want others also to be. Measuring myself by that standard I must exclaim with Surdas.

Where is there a wretch?

So wicked and loathsome as I?

I have forsaken by Maker,

So faithless have I been. (ibid, p xvi)

My Errors

I may be a despicable person, but when Truth speaks through me, I am invincible. (EF, p71)

I am devoted to none but Truth and I owe no discipline to anybody but Truth. (H, 25-5-1935, p115)

I have no God to serve but Truth. (H, 15-4-1939, p87)

I have no strength except what comes from insistence on truth. Nonviolence, too, springs from the same insistence. (H, 7-4-1946, p70)

I am a humble but very earnest seeker after Truth. And in my search, I take all fellow-seekers in uttermost confidence so that I may know my mistakes and correct them. I confess that I have often erred in my estimates and judgments... And inasmuch as in every case I retraced my steps, no permanent harm was done. On the contrary, the fundamental truth of nonviolence has been made infinitely more manifest than it ever has been, and the country has in no way been permanently injured. (YI, 21-4-1927, p126) I am a learner myself, I have no axe to grind, and wherever I see a truth, I take it up and try to act up to it. (YI, 11-8-1927, p250)

I believe that, if in spite of the best of intentions, one is led into committing mistakes, they do not really result in harm to the world or, for the matter of that, any individual. God always saves the world from the consequences of unintended errors or men who live in fear of Him.

Those who are likely to be misled by my example would have gone that way all the same even if they had not known of my action. For, in the final analysis, a man is guided in his conduct by his own inner promptings, though the example of others might sometimes seem to guide him. But be it as it may, I know that the world has never had to suffer on account of my errors because they were all due to my ignorance. It is my firm belief that not one of my known errors was willful. (YI, 3-1-1929, p6)

Indeed, what may appear to be an obvious error to one may appear to another as pure wisdom. He cannot help himself even if he is under a hallucination. Truly as Tulsidas said: 'Even though there never is silver in mother o' pearl nor water in the sunbeams, while the illusion of silver in the shinning shell or that of water in the beam lasts, no power on earth can shake the deluded man free from the spell.' Even so must it be with men like me who, it may be, are labouring under a great hallucination. Surely God will pardon them and the world should bear with them. Truth will assert itself in the end. (ibid)

Truth never damages a cause that is just. (H, 10-11-1946, p389)

Life is an aspiration. Its mission is to strive after perfection, which is self-realization. The ideal must not be lowered because of our weaknesses or imperfections. I am painfully conscious of both in me. The silent cry daily goes out to Truth to help me to remove these weakness and imperfections of mine. (H, 22-6-1935, p145)

No Abandonment of Truth

Believe me when I tell you, after 60 years of personal experience, that the only real misfortune is to abandon the path of truth. If you but realize this, your one prayer to God will always be to enable you to put up, without flinching, with any number of trials and hardships that may fall to your lot in the pursuit of truth. (H, 28-7-1946, p243)

Truth alone will endure, all the rest will be swept away before the tide of time. I must, therefore, continue to bear testimony to Truth even if I am forsaken by all. Mine may today be a voice in the wilderness, but it will be heard when all other voices are silenced, if it is the voice of Truth. (H, 15-8-1946, p284)

A man of faith will remain steadfast to truth, even-though the whole world might appear to be enveloped in falsehood. (H, 22-9-1946, p322)

When it is relevant, truth has to be uttered, however unpleasant it may be. Irrelevance is always untruth and should never be uttered. (H, 21-12-1947, p473)

TRUTH IS GOD

God Is

There is an indefinable mysterious Power that pervades everything. I feel it, though I do not see it. It is this unseen Power which makes itself felt and yet defies all proof, because it is so unlike all that I perceive through my senses. It transcends the senses. But it is possible to reason out the existence of God to a limited extent.

I do dimly perceive that whilst everything around me is ever changing, ever-dying, there is underlying all that change a Living Power that is changeless, that holds all together, that creates, dissolves, and recreates. That informing Power or Spirit is God. And since nothing else I see merely through the senses can or will persist, He alone is.

And is this Power benevolent or malevolent? I see it as purely benevolent. For I can see, that in the midst of death life persists, in the midst of untruth truth persists, in the midst of darkness light persists. Hence I gather that God is Life, Truth, Light. He is Love. He is the Supreme Good.

I confess... that I have no argument to convince... through reason. Faith transcends reason. All I can advise... is not to attempt the impossible. I cannot account for the existence of evil by any rational method. To want to do so is to be co-equal with God. I am, therefore, humble enough to recognize evil as such; and I call God long-suffering and patient precisely because He permits evil in the world. I know that He has no evil in Him and yet if there is evil, He is the author of it and yet untouched by it.

I know, too, that I shall never know God if I do not wrestle with and against evil even at the cost of life itself. I am fortified in the belief by my own humble and limited experience. The purer I try to become the nearer to God I feel myself to be. How much more should I be near to Him when my faith is not a mere apology, as it is today, but has become as immovable as the Himalayas and as white and bright as the snows on their peaks? (YI, 11-10-1928, pp340-1)

My Faith

I can easily put up with the denial of the world, but any denial by me of my God is unthinkable. (YI, 23-2-1922, p112)

I know that I can do nothing. God can do everything. O God, make me Thy fit instrument and use me as thou wilt! (YI, 9-10-1924, p329)

I have not seen Him, neither have I known Him. I have made the world's faith in God my own and as my faith is ineffaceable, I regard that faith as amounting to experience. However, as it may be said that to describe faith as experience is to tamper with truth, it may perhaps be more correct to say that I have no word for characterizing my belief in God. (A, p206)

I am surer of His existence than of the fact that you and I are sitting in this room. Then I can also testify that I may live without air and water but not without Him. You may pluck out my eyes, but that cannot kill me. You may chop off my nose, but that will not kill me. But blast my belief in God, and I am dead.

You may call this a superstition, but I confess it is a superstition that I hug, even as I used to hug the name of Rama in my childhood when there was any cause of danger or alarm.

That was what an old nurse had taught me. (H, 14-5-1938, p109)

I believe that we can all become messengers of God, if we cease to fear man and seek only God's Truth. I do believe I am seeking only God's Truth and have lost all fear of man.

...I have no special revelation of God's will. My firm belief is that He reveals Himself daily to every human being, but we shut our ears to the 'still small voice'. We shut our eyes to the Pillar of Fire in front of us. I realize His omnipresence. (YI, 25-5-1921, pp161-2)

Some of my correspondents seem to think that I can work wonders. Let me say as a devotee of truth that I have no such gift. All the power I may have comes from God. But He does not work directly. He works through His numberless agencies. (H, 8-10-1938, p285)

Nature of God

To me God is Truth and Love; God is ethics and morality; God is fearlessness. God is the source of Light and Life and yet He is above and beyond all these. God is conscience. He is even the atheism of the atheist. For in His boundless love God permits the atheist to live. He is the searcher of hearts. He transcends speech and reason. He knows us and our hearts better than we do ourselves. He does not take us at our word, for He knows that we often do not mean it, some knowingly and others unknowingly.

He is a personal God to those who need His personal presence. He is embodied to those who need His touch. He is the purest essence. He simply is to those who have faith. He is all things to all men. He is in us and yet above and beyond us... He cannot cease to be because hideous immoralities or inhuman brutalities are committed in His name. He is long-suffering. He is patient but He is also terrible. He is the most exacting personage in the world and the world to come. He metes out the same measure to us that we mete out to our neighbors-men and brutes.

With Him ignorance is no excuse. And withal He is ever forgiving, for He always gives us the chance to repent.

He is the greatest democrat the world knows, for He leaves us 'unfettered' to make our own choice between evil and good. He is the greatest tyrant ever known, for He often dashes the cup from our lips and under cove of free will leaves us a margin so wholly inadequate as to provide only mirth for Himself at our expense.

Therefore it is that Hinduism calls it all His sport-lila, or calls it all an illusion-maya. We are not, He alone Is. And if we will be, we must eternally sing His praise and do His will. Let us dance to the tune of His bansi-lute, and all would be well. (YI, 5-3-1925, p81)

God is the hardest taskmaster I have known on this earth, and He tries you through and through. And when you find that your faith is failing or your body is failing you and you are sinking, He comes to your assistance somehow or other and proves to you that you must not lose your faith and that He is always at your beck and call, but on His terms, not on your terms. So I have found. I cannot really recall a single instance when, at the eleventh hour, He has forsaken me. (SW, p1069)

In my early youth I was taught to repeat what in Hindu scriptures are known as one thousand names of God. But these one thousand names of God were by no means exhaustive. We believe-and I think it is the truth-that God has as many names as there are creatures and, therefore, we also say that God is nameless and, since God has many forms, we also consider Him formless, and since He speaks to us through many tongues, we consider Him to be speechless and so on. And so when I came to study Islam, I found that Islam too had many names for God.

I would say with those who say God is Love, God is Love. But deep down in me I used to say that though God may be Love, God is Truth, above all. If it is possible for the human tongue to give the fullest description of God, I have come to the conclusion that, for myself, God is Truth.

But two years ago I went a step further and said that Truth is God. You will see the fine distinction between the two statements, viz., that God is Truth and Truth is God. And I came to the conclusion after a continuous and relentless search after Truth which began nearly fifty years ago.

I then found that the nearest approach to Truth was through love. But I also found that love has many meanings in the English language at least and that human love in the sense of passion could become a degrading thing also. I found too that love in the sense of ahimsa had only a limited number of votaries in the world. But I never found a double meaning in connection with truth and not even atheists had demurred to the necessity or power of truth.

But, in their passion for discovering truth, the atheists have not hesitated to deny the very existence of God-from their own point of view, rightly. And it was because of this reasoning that I saw that, rather than say that God is Truth, I should say that Truth is God. (YI, 31-12-1931, p427-8)

God is Truth, but God is many other things also. That is why I say Truth is God.... Only remember that Truth is not one of the many qualities that we name. It is the living embodiment of God, it is the only Life, and I identify Truth with the fullest life, and that is how it becomes a concrete thing, for God is His whole creation, the whole Existence, and service of all that exists-Truth-is service of God. (H, 25-5-1935, p115)

Perfection is the attribute of the Almighty, and yet what a great democrat He is! What an amount of wrong and humbug He suffers on our part! He even suffers us insignificant creatures of His to question His very existence, though He is in every atom about us, around us and within us. But He has reserved to Himself the right of becoming manifest to whomsoever He chooses. He is a Being without hands and feet and other organs, yet he can see Him to whom He chooses to reveal Himself. (H, 14-11-1936, p314)

God Through Service

If I did not fee the presence of God within me, I see so much of misery and disappointment every day that I would be a raving maniac and my destination would be the Hooghli. (YI, 6-8-1925, p275)

If I am to identify myself with the grief of the least in India, aye, if I have the power, the least in the world, let me identify myself with the sins of the little ones who are under my care.

And so doing in all humility, I hope some day to see God-Truth-face to face. (YI, 3-12-1925, p422)

I am endeavoring to see God through service of humanity, for I know that God is neither in heaven, nor down below, but in every one. (YI, 4-8-1927, p247-8)

I am a part and parcel of the whole, and I cannot find Him apart from the rest of humanity. My countrymen are my nearest neighbors. They have become so helpless, so resourceless, so inert that I must concentrate on serving them. If I could persuade myself that I should find Him in a Himalayan cave, I would proceed there immediately. But I know that I cannot find Him apart from humanity. (H, 29-8-1936, p226)

I claim to know my millions. All the 24 hours of the day I am with them. They are my first care and last because I recognize no God except the God that is to be found in the hearts of the dumb millions. They do not recognize His presence; I do. And I worship the God that is Truth or Truth which is God through the service of these millions. (H, 11-3-1939, p44)

Guide and Protector

I must go... with God as my only guide. He is a jealous Lord. He will allow no one to share His authority. One has, therefore, to appear before Him in all one's weakness, empty-handed and in a spirit of full surrender, and then He enables you to stand before a whole world and protects you from all harm. (YI, 3-9-1931, p247)

I have learned this one lesson-that what is impossible with man is child's play with God and if we have faith in that Divinity which presides on the destiny of the meanest of His creation, I have no doubt that all things are possible; and in that final hope, I live and pass my time and endeavor to obey His will. (YI, 19-11-1931, p361)

Even in darkest despair, where there seems to be no helper and no comfort in the wide, wide world, His Name inspires us with strength and puts all doubts and despairs to flight. The sky may be overcast today with clouds, but a fervent prayer to Him is enough to dispel them. It is because of prayer that I have known no disappointment.

...I have known no despair. Why then should you give way to it? Let us pray that He may cleanse our hearts of pettiness, meanness and deceit and He will surely answer our prayers. Many I know have always turned to that unfailing source of strength. (H, 1-6-1935, p123)

I have seen and believe that God never appears to you in person, but in action which can only account for your deliverance in your darkest hour. (H, 10-12-1938, p373)

Individual worship cannot be described in words. It goes on continuously and even unconsciously. There is not a moment when I do not feel the presence of a Witness whose eye misses nothing and with whom I strive to keep in tune.

I have never found Him lacking in response. I have found Him nearest at hand when the horizon seemed darkest in my ordeals in jails when it was not all-smooth sailing for me. I cannot recall a moment in my life when I had a sense of desertion by God. (H, 24-12-1938, p395)

Self-realization

I believe it to be possible for every human being to attain to that blessed and indescribable, sinless state in which he feels within himself the presence of God to the exclusion of everything else. (YI, 17-11-1921, p368)

What I want to achieve, what I have been striving and pining to achieve..., is self-realization, to see God face to face, to attain moksha. I live and move and have my being in pursuit of this goal. All that I do by way of speaking and writing and all my ventures in the political field are directed to this same end. (A, p xiv)

For it is an unbroken torture to me that I am still so far from Him, who, as I fully know, governs every breath of my life, and whose offspring I am. I know that it is the evil passions within that keep me so far from Him, and yet I cannot get away from them. (ibid, p xvi)

This belief in God has to be based on faith, which transcends reason. Indeed, even the so-called realization has at bottom an element of faith without which it cannot be sustained. In the very nature of things it must be so. Who can transgress the limitations of his being? I hold that complete realization is impossible in this embodied life. Nor is it necessary. A living immovable faith is all that is required for reaching the full spiritual height attainable by human beings. God is not outside this earthly case of ours. Therefore, exterior proof is not of much avail, if any at all.

We must ever fail to perceive Him through the senses, because He is beyond them. We can feel Him if we will but withdraw ourselves from the senses. The divine music is incessantly going on within ourselves, but the loud senses drown the delicate music, which is unlike and infinitely superior to anything we can perceive or hear with our senses. (H, 13-6-1936, pp140-1)

TRUTH AND BEAUTY

Inwardness of Art

There are two aspects of things - the outward and the inward....The outward has no meaning except in so far as it helps the inward. All true Art is thus an expression of the soul. The outward forms have value only in so far as they are the expression of the inner spirit of man. (YI, 13-11-1924, p.377)

I know that many call themselves artists, and are recognized as such, and yet in their works there is absolutely no trace of the soul's upward urge and unrest. (ibid)

All true Art must help the soul to realize its inner self. In my own case, I find that I can do entirely without external forms in my soul's realization. I can claim, therefore, that there is truly efficient Art in my life, though you might not see what you call works of Art about me.

My room may have blank walls; and I may even dispense with the roof, so that I may gaze out at the starry heavens overhead that stretch in an unending expanse. What conscious Art of man can give me the panoramic scenes that open out before me, when I look up to the sky above with all its shining stars?

This, however, does not mean that I refuse to accept the value of productions of Art, generally accepted as such, but only that I personally feel how inadequate these are compared with the eternal symbols of beauty in Nature. These productions of man's Art have their value only in so far as they help the soul onward towards self-realization. (ibid)

Truth First

Truth is the first thing to be sought for, and Beauty and Goodness will then be added unto you. Jesus was, to my mind, a supreme artist because he saw and expressed Truth; and so was Muhammad, the Koran being, the most perfect composition in all Arabic literature - at any rate, that is what scholars say. It is because both of them strove first for Truth that the grace of expression naturally came in and yet neither Jesus not Muhammad wrote on Art. That is the Truth and Beauty I crave for, live for, and would die for. (YI, 20-11-1924, p.386)

Art for the Millions

Here too, just as elsewhere, I must think in terms of the millions. And to the millions we cannot give that training to acquire a perception of Beauty in such a way as to see Truth in it. Show them Truth first and they will see Beauty afterwards... Whatever can be useful to those starving millions is beautiful to my mind. Let us give today first the vital things of life and all the graces and ornaments of life will follow. (ibid)

I want art and literature that can speak to the millions. (H, 14-11-1936, p.135)

Art to be art must soothe. (YI, 27-5-1926, p.196)

After all, Art can only be expressed not through inanimate power-driven machinery designed for mass-production, but only through the delicate living touch of the hands of men and women. (YI, 14-3-1929, p.86)

Inner Purity

True art takes note not merely of form but also of what lies behind. There is an art that kills and an art that gives life... True art must be evidence of happiness, contentment and purity of its authors. (YI, 11-8-1921, p. 253)

True beauty after all consists in purity of heart. (A, p. 228)

I love music and all the other arts, but I do not attach such value to them as is generally done. I cannot, for example, recognize the value of those activities which require technical knowledge for their understanding.

Life is greater than all art. I would go even further and declare that the man whose life comes nearest to perfection is the greatest artist; for what is art without the sure foundation and framework of a noble life? (AG, pp. 65-66)

We have somehow accustomed ourselves to the belief that art is independent of the purity of private life. I can say with all the experience at my command that nothing could be more untrue. As I am nearing the end of my earthly life, I can say that purity of life, is the highest and truest art. The art of producing good music from a cultivated voice can be achieved by many, but the art of producing that music from the harmony of a pure life is achieved very rarely. (H, 19-2-1938, p. 10)

Beauty in Truth

I see and find Beauty in Truth or through Truth. All Truths, not merely true ideas, but truthful faces, truthful pictures, or songs, are highly beautiful. People generally fail to see Beauty in Truth, the ordinary man runs away from it and becomes blind to the beauty in it. Whenever men begin to see Beauty in Truth, then true Art will arise. (YI, 13-11-1924, p. 377)

To a true artist only that face is beautiful which, quite apart from its exterior, shines with the Truth within the soul. There is... no Beauty apart from Truth. On the other hand, Truth may manifest itself in forms, which may not be outwardly beautiful at all. Socrates, we are told, was the most truthful man of his time, and yet his features are said to have been the ugliest in Greece. To my mind he was beautiful, because all his life was a striving after Truth, and you may remember that his outward form did not prevent Phidias from appreciating the beauty of Truth in him, though as an artist he was accustomed to see Beauty in outward forms also. (ibid)

Truth and Untruth often coexist; good and evil are often found together. In an artist also not seldom [do] the right perception of things and the wrong coexist. Truly beautiful creations come when right perception is at work. If these monuments are rare in life, they are also rare in Art. (ibid)

These beauties ['a sunset or a crescent moon that shines amid the stars at night'] are truthful, inasmuch as they make me think of the Creator at the back of them. How else could these be beautiful, but for the Truth that is in the centre of creation? When I admire the wonder of a sunset or the beauty of the moon, my soul expands in worship of the Creator. I try to see Him and His mercies in all these creations. But even the sunsets and sunrises would be mere hindrances if they did not help me to think of Him. Anything which is a hindrance to the flight of the soul is a delusion and a snare; even like the body, which often does hinder you in the path of salvation. (H, 13-11-1924, p. 379)

Why can't you see the beauty of colour in vegetables? And then, there is beauty in the speckles sky. But no, you want the colours of the rainbow, which is a mere optical illusion. We have been taught to believe that what is beautiful need not be useful and what is useful cannot be beautiful. I want to show that what is useful can also be beautiful. (H, 7-4-1946, p. 67)

FEARLESSNESS

The Gospel of Fearlessness

Fearlessness is the first requisite of spirituality. Cowards can never be moral. (YI, 13-10-1921, p. 323)

Where there is fear there is no religion. (YI, 2-9-1926, p. 308)

Every reader of the Gita is aware that fearlessness heads the list of the Divine Attributes enumerated in the 16th Chapter. Whether this is merely due to the exigencies of metre, or whether the pride of place has been deliberately yielded to fearlessness is more than I can say. In my opinion, however, fearlessness richly deserves the first rank assigned to it there, perhaps, by accident.

Fearlessness is a sine qua non for the growth of the other noble qualities. How can one seek truth or cherish Love without fearlessness? As Pritam has it, 'The Path of Hari (the Lord) is the path of the brave, not of cowards.' Hari here means Truth, and the brave are those armed with fearlessness, not with the sword, the rifle or other carnal weapons, which are affected only by cowards. (YI, 11-9-1930, pp. 1-2)

Fearlessness connotes freedom from all external fear - fear of disease, bodily injury or death, of dispossession, of losing one's nearest and dearest, of losing reputation or giving offence, and so on. (ibid)

Attainment of Fearlessness

Perfect fearlessness can be attained only by him who has realized the Supreme, as it implies the height of freedom from delusions. But one can always progress towards this goal by determined and constant endeavour and by increasing confidence in oneself....

As for the internal foes, we must ever walk in their fear. We are rightly afraid of Animal Passion, Anger and the like. External fears cease of their own accord when once we have conquered these traitors within the camp. All fears revolve round the body as the centre, and would, therefore, disappear as soon as one got rid of the attachment for the body.

We thus find that all fear is the baseless fabric of our own vision. Fear has no place in our hearts when we have shaken off the attachment for wealth, for family and for the body. 'Tena tyaktena bhunjithah' (enjoy the things of the earth by renouncing them) is a noble commandment. The wealth, the family and the body will be there, just the same; we have only to change our attitude to them. All these are not ours but God's. Nothing whatever in this world is ours. Even we ourselves are His. Why then should we entertain any fears?

The Upanishad, therefore, directs us 'to give up attachment for things while we enjoy them'. That is to say, we must be interested in them not as proprietors but only as trustees. He on whose behalf we hold them will give us the strength and the weapons requisite for defending them against all comers.

When we thus cease to be masters and reduce ourselves to the rank of servants humbler than the very dust under our feet, all fears will roll away like mists; we shall attain ineffable peace and see Satya- Narayan (the God of Truth) face to face. (ibid)

Fear of God

Let us fear God and we shall cease to fear man. (SW, p. 130)

There is so much superstition and hypocrisy around that one is afraid even to do the right thing. But if one gives way to fear, even truth will have to be suppressed. The golden rule is to act fearlessly upon what one believes to be right. (H, 2-6-1946, p. 160)

Fearlessness does not mean arrogance or aggressiveness. That in itself is a sign of fear. Fearlessness presupposes calmness and peace of mind. For that it is necessary to have a living faith in God. (H, 3-11-1946, p. 388)

Fear is a thing which I dislike. Why should one man be afraid of another man? Man should stand in fear of God alone, and then he can shed all other fears. (H, 5-1-1947, p. 477)

Bravery of the Soul

Each individual must be taught the art of self-defense. It is more a mental state that has to be inculcated than that our bodies should be trained for retaliation. Our mental training has been one of feeling helpless. Bravery is not a quality of the body, it is the soul. I have seen cowards encased in tough muscle and rare courage in the frailest body... The weakest of us physically must be taught the art of facing dangers and giving a good account of ourselves. (YI, 20-10-1921, p. 335)

We stand on the threshold of twilight-whether morning or evening twilight we know not. One is followed by the night, the other heralds the dawn. If we want to see the dawning day after the twilight and not the mournful night, it behoves everyone of us...to realize the truth at this juncture, to stand for it against any odds and to preach and practice it, at any cost, unflinchingly. (SW, p. 303)

We have chosen for our march towards freedom the ancient path of truth and nonviolence, and we must let God's covenant, that those who tread on the straight and narrow path shall never come to grief, inspire us with faith and hope. (YI, 2-4-1931, p. 54)

In-this country of self-suppression and timidity, almost bordering on cowardice, we cannot have too much bravery, too much self-sacrifice... I want... the greater bravery of the meek, the gentle and the nonviolent, the bravery that will mount the gallows without injuring, or harbouring any thought of injury to a single soul. (ibid, p. 58)

There is no bravery greater than a resolute refusal to bend the knee to an earthly power, no matter how great, and that, without bitterness of spirit and in the fullness of faith that the spirit alone lives, nothing else does. (H, 15-10-1938, p. 291)

We have two choices before us. We can become a great military power or, if we follow my way, we can become a great nonviolent and invincible power. In either case the first condition is the shedding of all fear. (H, 26-10-1947, p. 382)

FAITH

The Gospel Of Faith

It is faith that steers us through stormy seas, faith that moves mountains and faith that jumps across the ocean. That faith is nothing but a living, wide-awake consciousness of God within. He who has achieved that faith wants nothing. Bodily diseased, he is spiritually healthy; physically poor, he rolls in spiritual riches. (YI, 24-9-1925, p. 331)

Without faith this world would come to naught in a moment. True faith is appropriation of the reasoned experience of people whom we believe to have lived a life purified by prayer and penance. Belief, therefore, in prophets or incarnations who have lived in remote ages is not an idle superstition but a satisfaction of an inmost spiritual want. (YI, 14-4-1927, p. 120)

Faith is not a delicate flower, which would wither under the slightest stormy weather. Faith is like the Himalaya mountains which cannot possibly change. No storm can possibly remove the Himalaya mountains from their foundations. ... And I want every one of you to cultivate that faith in God and religion. (H, 26-1-1934, p. 8)

Limitations of Reason

Experience has humbled me enough to let me realize the specific limitations of reason. Just as matter misplaced becomes dirt, reason misused becomes lunacy.

Rationalists are admirable beings, rationalism is a hideous monster when it claims for itself omnipotence. Attribution of omnipotence to reason is as bad a piece of idolatry as is worship of stock and stone believing it to be God. (YI, 14-10-1924, p. 359)

I plead not for the suppression of reason, but for a due recognition of that in us which sanctifies reason itself. (ibid) To me it is as plain as a pikestaff that, where there is an appeal to reason pure and undefiled, there should be no appeal to authority however great it may be. (YI, 26-9-1929, p. 316)

There are subjects where Reason cannot take us far and we have to accept things on faith. Faith then does not contradict Reason but transcends it. Faith is a kind of sixth sense which works in cases which are without the purview of Reason. (H, 6-3-1937, p.26)

Meaning of Religion

Let me explain what I mean by religion. It is not the Hindu religion which I certainly prize above all other religions, but the religion which transcends Hinduism, which changes one's very nature, which binds one indissolubly to the truth within and which ever purifies. It is the permanent element in human nature which counts no cost too great in order to find full expression and which leaves the soul utterly restless until it has found itself, known its Maker and appreciated the true correspondence between the Maker and itself. (YI, 12-5-1920, p. 2) By religion, I do not mean formal religion, or customary religion, but that religion which underlies all religions, which brings us face to face with our Maker. (MKG, p.7)

My Religion

My religion has no geographical limits. If I have a living faith in it, it will transcend my love for India herself. (YI, 11-8-1920, p. 4)

Mine is not a religion of the prison-house. It has room for the least among God's creation. But it is proof against insolence, pride of race, religion or colour. (YI, 1-6-1921, p. 171)

There is undoubtedly a sense in which the statement is true when I say that I hold my religion dearer than my country and that, therefore, I am a Hindu first and nationalist after. I do not become on that score a less nationalist than the best of them. I simply thereby imply that the interests of my country are identical with those of my religion.

Similarly when I say that I prize my own salvation above everything else, above the salvation of India, it does not mean that my personal salvation requires a sacrifice of India's political or any other salvation. But it implies necessarily that the two go together. (YI, 23-2-1922, p. 123) This is the maxim of life which I have accepted, namely, that no work done by any man, no matter how great he is, will really prosper unless he has religious backing. (SW, pp. 377-8)

I have abundant faith in my cause and humanity. Indian humanity is no worse than any other; possibly it is better. Indeed, the cause presumes faith in human nature. Dark though the path appears, God will light it and guide my steps, if I have faith in His guidance and humility enough to acknowledge my helplessness without that infallible guidance. (YI, 27-11-1924, p. 391)

This may be considered to be quixotic, but it is my firm faith that he who undertakes to do something in the name of God, and in full faith in Him, even at the end of his days, does not work in vain; and I am sure that the work I have undertaken is not mine, but is God's. (H, 1-3-1935, p. 24)

That is dharma which is enjoined by the holy books, followed by the sages, interpreted by the learned and which appealed to the heart. The first three conditions must be fulfilled before the fourth comes into operation. Thus one has no right to follow the precepts of an ignorant man or a rascal even though they commend themselves to one. Rigorous observance of harmlessness, non-enmity and renunciation are the first requisites for a person to entitle him to lay down the law, i.e., dharma. (H, 17-11-1946, p. 397)

Futility of Force

I have a deep conviction that no religion can be sustained by brute force. On the contrary, those who take the sword always perish by the sword. (H, 9-3-1934, p. 29)

Religions, like nations, are being weighed in the balance. That religion and that nation will be blotted out of the face of earth, which pins its faith to injustice, untruth or violence. (H, 12-9-1936, p. 247)

Morality

With me moral includes spiritual. ...In my career as a reformer, I have regarded everything from the moral standpoint. Whether I am engaged in tackling a political question or a social or an economic one, the moral side of it always obtrudes itself and it pervades my whole attitude. (H, 29-3-1935, p. 51)

There is no such thing as absolute morality for all times. But there is a relative morality, which is absolute enough for imperfect mortals that we are. Thus, it is absolutely immoral to drink spirituous liquors except as medicine, in medicinal doses and under medical advice.

Similarly, it is absolutely wrong to see lustfully any woman other than one's wife. Both these positions have been proved by cold reason. Counter-arguments have always been advanced. They have been advanced against the very existence of God-the Sum of all that Is. Faith that transcends reason is our only Rock of Ages. ...My faith has saved me and is still saving me from pitfalls. It has never betrayed me. It has never been known to betray anyone. (H, 23-12-1939, p. 387)

Diversity of Religion

In reality there are as many religions as there are individuals. (HS, p. 49)

Religions are different roads converging upon the same point. What does it matter that we take different roads, so long as we reach the same goal? (ibid, p. 50)

I do not share the belief that there can or will be on earth one religion. I am striving, therefore, to find a common factor and to induce mutual tolerance. (YI, 31-7-1924, p. 254)

Basic Unity

The soul of religions is one, but it is encased in a multitude of forms. The latter will persist to the end of time. Wise men will ignore the outward crust and see the same soul living under a variety of crusts. (YI, 25-9-1924, p. 318)

I believe that all the great religions of the world are true more or less. I say 'more or less' because I believe that everything that the human hand touches, by reason of the very fact that human beings are imperfect, becomes imperfect. Perfection is the exclusive attribute of God and it is indescribable, untranslatable. I do believe that it is possible for every human being to become perfect even as God is perfect. It is necessary for us all to aspire after perfection, but when that blessed state is attained, it becomes indescribable, indefinable. And I therefore admit, in all humility, that even the Vedas, the Koran and the Bible are imperfect word of God and, imperfect beings that we are, swayed to and fro by a multitude of passions, it is impossible for us even to understand this word of God in its fullness. (YI, 22-9-1927, p. 319)

I should love all the men-not only in India but in the world-belonging to the different faiths, to become better people by contact with one another, and if that happens, the world will be a much better place to live in than it is today. I plead for the broadest toleration, and I am working to that end. I ask people to examine every religion from the point of the religionists themselves. I do not expect the India of my dream to develop one religion, i.e., to be wholly Hindu, or wholly Christian, or wholly Mussalman, but I want it to be wholly tolerant, with its religions working side by side with one another. (YI, 22-12-1927, p. 425)

I came to the conclusion long ago, after prayerful search and study and discussion with as many people as I could meet, that all religions were true and also that all had some error in them, and that, whilst I hold by my own, I should hold others as dear as Hinduism, from which it logically follows that we should hold all as dear as our nearest kith and kin and that we should make no distinction between them. (YI, 19-1-1928, p.22)

Belief in one God is the corner stone of all religions. But I do not foresee a time when there would be only one religion on earth in practice. In theory, since there is one God, there can be only one religion. But in practice, no two persons I have known have had the same identical conception of God. Therefore, there will, perhaps, always be different religions answering to different temperaments and climatic conditions. (H, 2-2-1934, p. 8)

I believe in the fundamental truth of all great religions of the world. I believe that they are all God-given, and I believe that they were necessary for the people to whom these religions were revealed. And I believe that, if only we could all of us read the scriptures of the different faiths from the standpoint of the followers of those faiths, we should find that they were at the bottom all one and were all helpful to one another. (H, 16-12-1934, p. 5-6)

Religions are not for separating men from one another. They are meant to bind them. (H, 8-6-1940, p. 157)

The Scriptures

For me the Vedas are divine and unwritten. 'The letter killeth.' It is the spirit that giveth the light. And the spirit of the Vedas is purity, truth, innocence, chastity, humility, simplicity, forgiveness, godliness, and all that makes a man or woman noble and brave. (YI, 19-1-1921, p. 22)

I do not believe in the exclusive divinity of the Vedas. I believe the Bible, the Koran and Zend Avesta to be as much divinely inspired as the Vedas. My belief in the Hindu scriptures does not require me to accept every word and every verse as divinely inspired.....I decline to be bound by an interpretation, however learned it may be, if it is repugnant to reason or moral sense. (YI, 6-10-1921, p. 317)

I am not a literalist. Therefore, I try to understand the spirit of the various scriptures of the world. I apply the test of Truth and ahimsa laid down by these very scriptures for interpretation. I reject what is inconsistent with that test, and appropriate all that is consistent with it. (YI, 27-8-1925, p. 293)

I have not been able to see any difference between the Sermon on the Mount and the Bhagavad Gita. What the Sermon describes in a graphic manner, the Bhagavad Gita reduces to a scientific formula. It may not be a scientific book in the accepted sense of the term, but it has argued out the law of love-the law of abandon, as I would call it-in a scientific manner. The Sermon on the Mount gives the same law in wonderful language. The New Testament gave me comfort and boundless joy, as it came after the repulsion that parts of the Cld had given me. Today, supposing I was deprived of the Gita and forgot all its contents but had a copy of the Sermon, I should derive the same joy from it as I do from the Gita. (YI, 22-12-1927, p. 426)

There is one thing in me and that is that I love to see the bright side of things and not the seamy side, and so I can derive comfort and inspiration from any great book of any great religion. I may not be able to reproduce a single verse from the Gita or the New Testament; a Hindu child or Christian child may be able to repeat the verses better; but those clever children cannot deprive me of the assimilation that is in me today of the spirit of the two books. (ibid)

Onc's experience, therefore, must be the final guide. The written word undoubtedly helps, but even that has to be interpreted, and when there are conflicting interpretations, the seeker is the final arbiter. (H, 22-12-1933, p. 3)

I believe I have no superstition in me. Truth is not truth merely because it is ancient. Nor is it necessarily to be regarded with suspicion because it is ancient. There are some fundamentals of life, which may not be lightly given up because they are difficult of enforcement in one's life. (H, 14-3-1936, p. 36)

Religious Instruction

If India is not to declare spiritual bankruptcy, religious instruction of its youth must be held to be at least as necessary as secular instruction. It is true that knowledge of religious books is no equivalent of that of religion. But if we cannot have religion, we must be satisfied with providing our boys and girls with what is next best. And whether there is such instruction given in the schools or not, grown-up students must cultivate the art of self-help about matters religious as about others. They may start their own class just as they have their debating, and now, spinners' clubs. (YI, 25-8-1927, p. 272)

I do not believe that the State can concern itself or cope with religious education. I believe that religious education must be the sole concern of religious associations. Do not mix up religion and ethics. I believe that fundamental ethics is common to all religions. Teaching of fundamental ethics is undoubtedly a function of the State. By religion I have not in mind fundamental ethics but what goes by the name of denominationalism. We have suffered enough from State-aided religion and a State Church. A society or a group, which depends partly or wholly on State aid for the existence of its religion, does not deserve, or, better still, does not have any religion worth the name. (H, 23-3-1947, p. 76)

A curriculum of religious instruction should include a study of the tenets of faiths other than one's own. For this purpose the students should be trained to cultivate the habit of understanding and appreciating the doctrines of various great religions of the world in a spirit of reverence and broad-minded tolerance. (YI, 6-12-1928, p406)

THE MEANING OF GOD

Law-giver and Law

God may be called by any other name so long as it connotes the living Law of Life-in other words, the Law and the Law-giver rolled into one. (H, 14-4-1946, p80)

God Himself is both the Law and the Law-giver. The question of anyone creating Him, therefore, does not arise, least of all by an insignificant creature such as man. Man can build a dam, but he cannot create a river. He can manufacture a chair, but it is beyond him to make the wood. He can, however, picture God in his mind in many ways. But how can man who is unable to create even a river or wood create God? That God has created man is, therefore, the pure truth. The contrary is an illusion. However, anyone may, if he likes, say that God is neither the doer nor the cause. Either is predicable of him. (ibid)

No Personal God

I do not regard God as a person. Truth for me is God, and God's Law and God are not different things or facts, in the sense that an earthly king and his law are different. Because God is an Idea, Law Himself. Therefore, it is impossible to conceive God as breaking the Law. He, therefore, does not rule our actions and withdraw Himself. When we say He rules our actions, we are simply using human language and we try to limit Him. Otherwise He and His Law abide everywhere and govern everything.

Therefore, I do not think that He answers in every detail every request of ours, but there is no doubt that He rules our action. ...The free will we enjoy is less than that of a passenger on a crowded deck.

...Although I know that my freedom is less than that of a passenger, I appreciate that freedom, as I have imbibed through and through the central teaching of the Gita that man is the maker of his own destiny in the sense that he has freedom of choice as to the manner in which he uses that freedom. But he is no controller of results. The moment he thinks he is, he comes to grief. (H, 23-2-1940, p55)

Let this however be quite clear. The Almighty is not a person like us. He or It is the greatest living Force or Law in the world. Accordingly, He does not act by caprice, nor does that Law admit of any amendment or improvement. His will is fixed and changeless, everything else changes every second. (H, 28-7-1946, p233)

His Personality

I have not seen God face to face. If I had, I would have no need to be speaking to you. My thought would be potent enough to render speech and action on my part unnecessary. But I have an undying faith in the existence of God. Millions all over the world share this faith with me. The most learned cannot shake the faith of the illiterate millions. (H, 3-8-1947, p262)

God is wholly good. There is no evil in Him. God made man in His own image. Unfortunately for us, man has fashioned Him in his own. This arrogation has landed mankind in a sea of troubles. God is the Supreme Alchemist. In His presence all iron and dross turn into pure gold. Similarly does all evil turn into good.

Again, God lives, but not as we. His creatures live but to die. But God is life. Therefore, goodness and all it connotes is not an attribute.

Goodness is God. Goodness conceived as apart from Him is a lifeless thing and exists only whilst it is a paying policy. So are all morals. If they are to live in us, they must be considered and cultivated in their relation to God. We try to become good because we want to reach and realize God. All the dry ethics of the world turn to dust because apart from God they are lifeless. Coming from God, they come with life in them. They become part of us and ennoble us. Conversely, God conceived without goodness is without life. We give Him life in our vain imagining. (H, 24-8-1947, p285)

There is a big gulf between 'seeing God face to face' and 'seeing Him in the embodiment of Truth from a far distance'. In my opinion, the two statements are not only not incompatible but each explains the other. We see the Himalayas from a very great distance and when we are on the top, we have seen the Himalayas face to face. Millions can see them from hundreds of miles if they are within the range of that seeing distance, but few having arrived at the top, after years of travel, see them face to face. (H, 23-11-1947, p432)

I have never had [the slightest doubt] about the reality that God Is and that His most graphic name is Truth. (H, 25-1-1948, p535)

Power of God

Everything that has a beginning must end. The sun, the moon and the earth must all perish one day, even though it might be after an incalculable number of years. God alone is immortal, imperishable. How can anyone find words to describe Him? (H, 16-6-1946, p183)

God cannot be realized through the intellect. Intellect can lead one to a certain extent and no further. It is a matter of faith and experience derived from faith. One might rely on the experience of one's betters or else be satisfied with nothing less than personal experience. Full faith does not feel the want of experience. (H, 4-8-1946, p249)

God alone knows Absolute Truth. Therefore, I have often said, Truth is God. It follows that man, a finite being, cannot know Absolute Truth. (H, 7-4-1946, p70)

I call that great Power not by the name of Allah, not by the name of Khuda or God, but by the name of Truth. For me Truth is God and Truth overrides all our plans. The whole truth is only embodied within the heart of that Great Power—Truth. I was taught from my early days to regard Truth as unapproachable—something that you cannot reach. A great Englishman taught me to believe that God is unknowable. He is knowable, but knowable only to the extent that our limited intellect allows. (H, 20-4-1947, p109)

God is all-powerful. He can change the hearts of man and bring real peace among them. (H, 3-8-1947, p262)

His Rule

Today, in the West, people talk of Christ, but it is really the Anti-Christ that rules their lives. Similarly, there are people who talk of Islam, but really follow the way of Satan. It is a deplorable state of affairs. ...If people follow the way of God, there will not be all this corruption and profiteering that we see in the world. The rich are becoming richer and the poor poorer. Hunger, nakedness and death stare one in the face. These are not the marks of the Kingdom of God, but that of Satan, Ravana or Anti-Christ. We cannot expect to bring the reign of God on earth by merely repeating His name with the lips. Our conduct must conform to His ways instead of Satan's. (H, 23-6-1946, pp186-7)

Only when God reigns in men's hearts will they be able to shed their anger. (H, 20-4-1947, p118)

All universal rules of conduct known as God's commandments are simple and easy to understand and carry out if the will is there. They only appear to be difficult because of the inertia, which governs mankind. Man is a progressive being. There is nothing at a standstill in nature. Only God is motionless for, He was, is and will be the same yesterday, today and tomorrow, and yet is ever moving. We need not, however, worry ourselves over the attributes of God. We have to realize that we are ever progressing. Hence, I hold that if mankind is to live, it has to come growingly under the sway of truth and nonviolence. It is in view of these two fundamental rules of conduct that I and you have to work and live. (H, 9-11-1947, p406)

A mind not set on God is given to wandering and lacks the quality of a temple of worship. (ibid)

Genesis of Evil

Why is there evil in the world is a difficult question to answer. I can only give what I may call a villager's answer. If there is good, there must also be evil, just as where there is light there is also darkness, but it is true only so far as we human mortals are concerned. Before God there is nothing good, nothing evil. We poor villagers may talk of His dispensation in human terms, but our language is not God's.

The Vedanta says the world is maya. Even that explanation is a babbling of imperfect humanity. I, therefore, say that I am not going to bother my head about it. Even if I was allowed to peep into the innermost recesses of God's chamber I should not care to do it. For I should not know what to do there. It is enough for our spiritual growth to know that God is always with the doer of good. That again is a villager's explanation. (H, 7-9-1935, p233)

I cannot account for the existence of evil by any rational method. To want to do so is to be coequal with God. I am therefore humble enough to recognize evil as such. And I call God long-suffering and patient precisely because He permits evil in the world. I know that He has no evil. He is the author of it and yet untouched by it.

I know too that I shall never know God if I do not wrestle with and against evil even at the cost of life itself. I am fortified in the belief by my own humble and limited experience. The purer I try to become, the nearer I feel to be to God. How much more should I be, when my faith is not a mere apology as it is today but has become as immovable as the Himalayas and as white and bright as the snows on their peaks? (YI, 11-10-1928, p341)

In a strictly scientific sense God is at the bottom of both good and evil. He directs the assassin's dagger no less than the surgeon's knife. But for all that good and evil are, for human purposes, from each other distinct and incompatible, being symbolical of light and darkness, God and Satan... (H, 20-2-1937, p9)

To say that God permits evil in this world may not be pleasing to the ear. But if He is held responsible for the good, it follows that He has to be responsible for the evil too. Did not God permit Ravana to exhibit unparalleled strength? Perhaps, the root cause of the perplexity arises from a lack of the real understanding of what God is. God is not a person. He transcends description. He is the Law-maker, the Law and the Executor. No human being can well arrogate these powers to himself. If he did, he would be looked upon as an unadulterated dictator. They become only Him whom we worship as God. This is the reality, a clear understanding of which will answer the question ['Does God permit evil?'] (H, 24-2-1946, p24)

There is a saying to the effect that the outer is only the reflection of the inner. If you are good, the whole world will be good to you. On the contrary, if you feel tempted to regard anybody as evil, the odds are that the evil is within you....

We must neither think evil about others nor suspect others of thinking evil about us. Proneness to lend ear to evil reports is a sign of lack of faith. (H, 28-4-1946, p111)

Miracles

I do [believe in miracles] and I do not. God does not work through miracles. But the divine mind is revealed in a flash and it appears like a miracle to man. We do not know God, we know Him only through the working of His law. He and His law are one. There is nothing outside His law. Even earthquakes and tempests do not occur without His will-not a blade of grass grows but He will it. Satan is here only on His sufferance, not independently of Him. (H, 7-4-1946, pp75-76)

Man cannot be transformed from bad to good overnight. God does not exercise magic. He too is within His own law. His law, however, is different from the law of the State. There may be mistakes in the latter, but God cannot err. If he were to go beyond the limits of His law, the world will be lost. (H, 19-5-1946, p136)

History provides us with a whole series of miracles of masses of people being converted to a particular view-point in the twinkling of an eye. Take the Boer War. It has given to the English language the word 'Maffeking'. People went mad on the Maffeking Day. Yet, inside of two years, the whole British nation underwent a transformation. Henry Campbell Bannerman became the Premier and practically all the gains of war were given up.

The recent Labour victory at the polls is another instance in point. To me it is a sufficient miracle that, in spite of his oratory and brilliance, Churchill should cease to be the idol of the British people who till yesterday hung on his lips and listened to him in awe. All these instances are enough to sustain the faith of a believer like me that, when all other powers are gone one will remain, call it God, Nature or whatever you like. (H, 10-11-1946, p389)

Incarnation

All embodied life is in reality an incarnation of God, but it is not usual to consider every living being an incarnation. Future generations pay this homage to one who, in his own generation, has been extraordinarily religious in his conduct. I can see nothing wrong in this procedure; it takes nothing from God's greatness, and there is no violence done to Truth.....

This belief in incarnation is a testimony of man's lofty spiritual ambition. Man is not at peace with himself till he has become like unto God. The endeavour to reach this state is the supreme, the only ambition worth having. And this is self-realization. And this self-realization is the subject of the Gita, as it is of all scriptures. (YI, 6-8-1931, p206) Belief, therefore, in prophets or incarnations who have lived in remote ages is not an idle superstition, but a satisfaction of an inmost spiritual want. (YI, 14-4-1927, p120)

God's Laws

Human language can but imperfectly describe God's ways. I am sensible of the fact that they are indescribable and inscrutable. But if mortal man will dare to describe them, he has no better medium than his own inarticulate speech. (A, p317). We do not know all the laws of God nor their working. Knowledge of the tallest scientist or the greatest spiritualist is like a particle of dust. If God is not a personal being for me like my earthly father, He is infinitely more. He rules me in the tiniest detail of my life. I believe literally that not a leaf moves but by His will. Every breath I take depends upon His sufferance.

He and His law are one. The Law is God. Anything attributed to Him is not a mere attribute. He is the attribute. He is Truth, Love, Law and a million other things that human ingenuity can name. (H, 16-2-1934, p4)

The laws of Nature are changeless, unchangeable, and there are no miracles in the sense of infringement or interruption of Nature's laws. But we, limited beings, fancy all kinds of things and impute our limitations to God. We may copy God, but not He us. We may not divide Time for Him. Time for Him is eternity. For us there is past, present and future. And what is human life of a hundred years but less than a mere speck in the eternity of Time? (H, 17-4-1947, p87)

Nature's Visitations

I share the belief with the whole world-civilized and uncivilized-that calamities such as the Bihar one [earth-quake] come to mankind as chastisement for their sins. When that conviction comes from the heart, people pray, repent and purify themselves....

I have but a limited knowledge of His purpose. Such calamities are not a mere caprice of the deity or Nature. They obey fixed laws as surely as the planets move in obedience to laws governing their movements. Only we do not know the laws governing these events and, therefore, call them calamities or disturbances. (H, 2-2-1934, p1)

This earthly existence of ours is more brittle than the glass bangles that ladies wear. You can keep glass bangles for thousands of years if you treasure them in a chest and let them remain untouched. But this earthly existence is so fickle that it may be wiped out in the twinkling of an eye. Therefore, while we have yet breathing time, let us get rid of the distinctions of high and low, purify our hearts and be ready to face our Maker when an earthquake or some natural calamity or death in the ordinary course overtakes us. (ibid, p5)

There is a divine purpose behind every physical calamity. That perfected science will one day be able to tell us beforehand when earthquakes will occur, as it tells us today of eclipses, is quite possible. It will be another triumph of the human mind. But such triumph even indefinitely multiplied can bring about no purification of self without which nothing is of any value.

I ask those who appreciate the necessity of inward purification to join the prayer that we may read the purpose of God behind such visitations, that they may humble us and prepare us to face our Maker whenever the call comes, and that we may be ever ready to share the sufferings of our fellows whosoever they may be. (H, 8-6-1935, p132)

God's Names

God has a thousand names, or rather, He is Nameless. We may worship or pray to Him by whichever name that pleases us. Some call Him Rama, some Krishna, others call Him Rahim, and yet others call Him God. All worship the same spirit, but as all foods do not agree with all, all names do not appeal to all. Each chooses the name according to his associations, and He, being the In-Dweller, All-Powerful and Omniscient knows our innermost feelings and responds to us according to our deserts.

Worship or prayer, therefore, is not to be performed with the lips, but with the heart. And that is why it can be performed equally by the dumb and the stammerer, by the ignorant and the stupid. And the prayers of those whose tongues are nectared but whose hearts are full of poison are never heard. He, therefore, who would pray to God, must cleanse his heart.

Rama was not only on the lips of Hanuman, He was enthroned in his heart. He gave Hanuman exhaustless strength. In His strength he lifted the mountain and crossed the ocean. (YI, 24-9-1925, p331)

I talk of God exactly as I believe Him to be... I believe God to be creative as well as non-creative. This too is the result of my acceptance of the doctrine of the manyness of reality. From the platform of the Jains I prove the non-creative aspect of God, and from that of Ramanuja the creative aspect. As a matter of fact, we are all thinking of the Unthinkable, describing the Indescribable, seeking to know the Unknown, and that is why our speech falters, is inadequate and even often contradictory. That is why the Vedas describe Brahman as 'not this', 'not this'. (H, 21-1-1926, p30)

In my opinion, Rama, Rahaman, Ahuramazda, God or Krishna are all attempts on the part of man to name that invisible force which is the greatest of all forces. It is inherent in man, imperfect though he be, ceaselessly to strive after perfection. In the attempt he falls into reverie. And, just as a child tries to stand, falls down again and again and ultimately learns how

to walk, even so man, with all his intelligence, is a mere infant as compared to the infinite and ageless God. This may appear to be an exaggeration but is not. Man can only describe God in his own poor language. (H, 18-8-1946, p267)

RAMANAMA

My Saviour

Though my reason and heart long ago realized the highest attribute and name of God as Truth, I recognize Truth by the name of Rama. In the darkest hour of my trial, that one name has saved me and is still saving me. It may be the association of childhood, it may be the fascination that Tulsidas has wrought on me.

But the potent fact is there, and as I write these lines, my memory revives the scenes of my childhood, when I used daily to visit the Ramji Mandir adjacent to my ancestral home. My Rama then resided there. He saved me from many fears and sins. It was no superstition for me. The custodian of the idol may have been a bad man. I know nothing against him. Misdeeds might have gone on in the temple. Again I know nothing of them. Therefore, they would not affect me. What was and is true of me is true of millions of Hindus. (H, 18-3-1933, p6)

When a child, my nurse taught me to repeat Ramanama whenever I felt afraid or miserable, and it has been second nature with me with growing knowledge and advancing years. I may even say that the Word is in my heart, if not actually on my lips, all the twenty-four hours. It has been by saviour and I am ever stayed on it. In the spiritual literature of the world, the Ramayana of Tulsidas takes a foremost place. It has charms that I miss in the Mahabharata and even in Valmiki's Ramayana. (H, 17-8-1934, p213)

Best Worship

I myself have been a devotee of Tulasidas from my childhood and have, therefore, always worshipped God as Rama. But I know that if, beginning with Omkar, one goes through the entire gamut of God's names current in all climes, all countries and languages, the result is the same. He and His law are one. To observe His law is, therefore, the best form of worship. (H, 24-3-1946, p56)

One God

I laugh within myself when someone objects that Rama or the chanting of Ramanama is for the Hindus only, how can Mussalmans therefore take part in it? Is there one God for the Mussalmans and another for the Hindus, Paris or Christians? No, there is only one omnipotent and omnipresent God. He is named variously and we remember Him by the name which is most familiar to us.

My Rama, the Rama of our prayers is not the historical Rama, the son Dasharatha, the King of Ayodhya. He is the eternal, the unborn, the one without a second. Him alone I worship. His aid alone I see, and so should you. He belongs equally to all. I, therefore, see no reason why a Mussalman or anybody should object to taking His name. But he is in no way bound to recognize God as Ramanama. He may utter to himself Allah or Khuda so as not to mar the harmony of the sound. (H, 28-4-1946, p111)

To me...Rama, described as the Lord of Sita, son of Dasharatha, is the all-powerful essence whose name, inscribed in the heart, removes all suffering-mental, moral and physical. (H, 2-6-1946, p158)

Curative Power

An apt question is as to why a man who recites Ramanama regularly and leads a pure life should ever fall ill. Man is by nature imperfect. A thoughtful man strives after perfection, but never attains it. He stumbles on the way, however unwittingly. The whole of God's law is embodied in a pure life.

The first thing is to realize one's limitations. It should be obvious that, the moment one transgresses those limits, one falls ill. Thus a balanced diet eaten in accordance with needs gives one freedom from disease. How is one to know what is the proper diet for one? Many such enigmas can be imagined. The purport of it all is that everyone should be his own doctor and find out his limitations. The man who does so will surely live up to 125. (H, 19-5-1946, p148)

Ramanama cannot perform the miracle of restoring to you a lost limb. But it can perform the still greater miracle of helping you to enjoy an ineffable peace in spite of the loss while you live and rob death of its sting and the grave its victory at the journey's end. Since death must come soon or late to everyone, why should one worry over the time? (H, 7-4-1946, p69)

The practice of nature cure does not require high academic qualifications or much erudition. Simplicity is the essence of universality. Nothing that is meant for the benefit of the millions requires much erudition. The latter can be acquired only by the few and, therefore, can benefit the rich only. But India lives in her seven lakhs of villages-obscure, tiny, out-of-the-way villages, where the population in some cases hardly exceeds a few hundred, very often not even a few score.

I would like to go and settle down in some such village. That is real India, my India. You cannot take to these humble people the paraphernalia of highly qualified doctors and hospital equipment. In simple, natural remedies and Ramanama lies their only hope. (ibid)

Purity of Thought

Mere lip recitation of Ramanama has nothing to do with cure. Faith cure, if I know it correctly, is blind cure, such as the friend describes and thereby ridicules the living name of the living God. The latter is not a figment of one's imagination. It has to come from the heart.

It is conscious belief in God and a knowledge of His law that make perfect cure possible without any further aid. That law is that a perfect mind is responsible for perfect health of he body. A perfect mind comes from a perfect heart, not the heart known by a doctor's stethoscope but the heart which is the seat of God. It is claimed that realization of God in the heart makes it impossible for an impure or an idle thought to cross the mind.

Disease is impossible where there is purity of thought. Such a state may be difficult to attain. But the first step in the ascent to health is taken with its recognition. The next is taken when the corresponding attempt is made. This radical alteration in one's life is naturally accompanied by the observance of all other nature's laws hitherto discovered by man. One cannot play with them and claim to have a pure heart.

It can be said with justice that possession of a pure heart should do equally well without Ramanama. Only, I know no other way of attaining purity. And it is the way trodden by the sages of old all over the world. They were men of God, not supersitious men or charlatans. (H, 9-6-1946, p171)

Spiritual force is like any other force at the service of man. Apart from the fact that it has been used for physical ailments for ages, with more or less success, it would be intrinsically wrong not to use it, if it can be successfully used for the cure of physical ailments. For, man is both matter and spirit, each acting on and affecting the other.

If you get rid of malaria by taking quinine, without thinking of the millions who do not get it, why should you refuse to use the remedy which is within you, because millions will not use it through their ignorance?

May you not be clean and well because millions of others will not be so, ignorantly or, may be even cussedly? If you will not be clean out of false notions of philanthropy, you will deny yourself the duty of serving the very millions by remaining dirty and ill. Surely refusal to be spiritually well or clean is worse than the refusal to be physically clean and well. (H, 1-9-1946, p286)

To repeat Ramanama and to follow the way of Ravana in actual practice is worse than useless. It is sheer hypocrisy. One may deceive oneself or the world, but one cannot deceive the Almighty. (H, 23-6-1946, p186)

PRAYER THE FOOD OF MY SOUL

I claim to be a man of faith and prayer, and even if I were cut to pieces, I trust God would give me the strength not to deny Him and to assert that He is. (YI, 8-12-1927, p413)

No act of mine is done without prayer. Man is a fallible being. He can never be sure of his steps. What he may regard as answer to prayer may be an echo of his pride. For infallible guidance man has to have a perfectly innocent heart incapable of evil. I can lay no such claim. Mine is a struggling, striving, erring, imperfect soul. (YI, 25-9-1924, p313)

Even if I am killed, I will not give up repeating the names of Rama and Rahim, which mean to me the same God. With these names on my lips, I will die cheerfully. (H, 20-4-1947, p118)

Safeguard in Trial

On all occasions of trial He has saved me. I know that the phrase 'God saved me' has a deeper meaning for me today, and still I feel that I have not yet grasped its entire meaning. Only richer experience can help me to a fuller understanding.

But in all my trials-of a spiritual nature, as a lawyer, in conducting institutions, and in politics-I can say that God saved me. When every hope is gone, 'when helpers fail and comforts flee', I experience that help arrives somehow, from I know not where.

Prayer has been the saving of my life. Without it I should have been a lunatic long ago. My autobiography will tell you that I have had my fair share of the bitterest public and private experiences. They threw me into temporary despair, but if I was able to get rid of it, it was because of prayer.

Now I may tell you that prayer has not been part of my life in the sense that truth has been. It came out of sheer necessity, as I found myself in a plight when I could not possibly be happy without it. And the more my faith in God increased, the more irresistible became the yearning for prayer. Life seemed to be dull and vacant without it.

I had attended the Christian service in South Africa, but it had failed to grip me. I could not join them in prayer. They supplicated God, but I could not do so, I failed egregiously. I started with disbelief in God and prayer, and, until at a late stage in life, I did not feel anything like a void in life. But at that stage I felt that, as food was indispensable for the body, so was prayer indispensable for the soul. In fact, food for the body is not so necessary as prayer for the soul. For starvation is often necessary in order to keep the body in health, but there is no such thing as prayer-starvation....

In spite of despair staring me in the face on the political horizon, I have never lost my peace. In fact, I have found people who envy my peace. That peace, I tell you, comes from prayer; I am not a man of learning, but I humbly claim to be a man of prayer. I am indifferent as to the form. Every one is a law unto himself in that respect. But there are some well-marked roads, and it is safe to walk along the beaten tracks, trod by the ancient teachers.

...I have given my personal testimony. Let every one try and find that, as a result of daily prayer, he adds something new to his life, something with which nothing can be compared. (YI, 24-4-1931, p274)

God's Response

Never own defeat in a sacred cause and make up your minds henceforth that you will be pure and that you will find a response from God. But God never answers the prayers of the arrogant, nor the prayers of those who bargain with Him....

If you would ask Him to help you, you would go to Him in all your nakedness, approach Him without reservations, also without fear or doubts as to how He can help a fallen being like you. He who has helped millions who have approached Him, is He going to desert you? He makes no exceptions whatsoever and you will find that every one of your prayers will be answered. I am telling this out of my personal experience. I have gone through the purgatory. Seek first the Kingdom of Heaven and everything will be added unto you. (YI, 4-4-1929, p111)

I have never found Him lacking in response. I have found Him nearest at hand when the horizon seemed darkest-in my ordeals in jails when it was not at all smooth sailing for me. I cannot recall a moment in my life when I had a sense of desertion by God. (H, 24-12-1938, p395)

Character of Prayer

Supplication, worship, prayer are no superstition; they are acts more real than the acts of eating, drinking, sitting or walking. It is no exaggeration to say that they alone are real, all else is unreal.

Such worship or prayer is no flight of eloquence; it is no lip-homage. It springs from the heart. If, therefore, we achieve that purity of the heart when it is 'emptied of all but love', if we keep all the chords in proper tune, they 'trembling pass in music out of sight'.

Prayer needs no speech. It is in itself independent of any sensuous effort. I have not the slightest doubt that prayer is an unfailing means of cleansing the heart of passions. But it must be combined with the utmost humility. (A, pp51-52)

It is better in prayer to have a heart without words than words without a heart. (YI, 23-1-1930, p25)

We go to the temple to worship not the stone or the metal image, but God who resides in it. The image becomes what man makes of it. It has no power independently of the sanctity with which it is invested by the worshipper. Therefore everyone, including children, should observe perfect silence at the time of prayer. (H, 28-4-1946, p112)

Prayer is an impossibility without a living faith in the presence of God within. (YI, 20-12-1928, p420)

Prayer is the first and the last lesson in learning the noble and brave art of sacrificing self in the various walks of life, culminating in the defense of one's nation's liberty and honour. Undoubtedly, prayer requires a living faith in God. (H, 14-4-1946, p80)

Man often repeats the name of God parrot-wise and expects fruit from so doing. The true seeker must have that living faith which will not only dispel the untruth of parrot-wise repetition from within him, but also from the hearts of others. (H, 5-5-1956, p113)

Need for Prayer

As food is necessary for the body, prayer is necessary for the soul. A man may be able to do without food for a number of days-as Mac Swiney did for over 70 days—but, believing in God, man cannot, should not live a moment without prayer. (YI, 15-12-1927, p424)

There are many who, whether from mental laziness or from having fallen into a bad habit, believe that God is and will help us unasked. Why, then, is it necessary to recite His name? It is true that if God is, He is irrespective of our belief. But realization of God is infinitely more than mere belief. That can come only by constant practice. This is true of all science. How much more true of the science of all sciences? (H, 28-4-1946, p109)

Prayer is the key of the morning and the bolt of the evening. (YI, 23-1-1930, p25)

I am giving you a bit of my experience and that of my companions when I say that he who had experienced the magic of prayer may do without food for days together, but not a single moment without prayer. For without prayer there is no inward peace. (ibid)

I agree that, if a man could practice the presence of God all the twenty-four hours, there would be no need for a separate time for prayer. But most people find this impossible. The sordid everyday world is too much with them. For them the practice of complete withdrawal of the mind from all outward things, even though it might be only for a few minutes everyday, will be found to be of infinite use. Silent communion will help them to experience an undisturbed peace in the midst of turmoil, to curb anger and cultivate patience. (H, 28-4-1946, p109)

It should be the general rule that prayers must not be delayed for anybody on earth. God's time never stops. From the very beginning the wheel of His time has gone ceaselessly on. As a matter of fact, there is no beginning for Him or His time....How can anyone afford to miss the time of offering prayers to Him whose watch never stops? (H, 5-5-1946, p113)

In the first shloka of Ishopanishad that is repeated everyday at the beginning of the prayer, one is asked to dedicate everything to God and then use it to the required extent. The principle condition laid down is that one must not covet what belongs to another. These two maxims contain the quintessence of the Hindu religion.

Essence of Prayer

In another shloka which is recited during the morning prayer it is said, 'I do not ask for temporal power, not do I ask to go to heaven, nor even to attain Nirwana, What I ask for is that I may be able to relieve the pain of those who are in pain.' The pain might be physical, mental or spiritual. Spiritual pain due to slavery to one's passions is sometimes greater even than the physical.

But God does not come down in person to relieve suffering. He works through human agency. Therefore, prayer to God to enable one to relieve the suffering of others must mean a longing and a readiness on one's part to labour for it.

The prayer... is not exclusive. It is not restricted to one's own caste or community. It is all inclusive. It comprehends the whole of humanity. Its realization would thus mean the establishment of the Kingdom of Heaven on earth. (H, 28-4-1946, p111)

True meditation consists in closing the eyes and ears of the mind to all else except the object of one's devotion. Hence the closing of eyes during prayers is a n aid to such concentration. Man's conception of God is naturally limited. Each one has, therefore, to think of Him as best appeals to him, provided that the conception is pure and uplifting. (H, 18-4-1946, p265)

He can truly pray who has the conviction that God is within him. He who has not, need not pray. God will not be offended, but I can say from experience that he who does not pray is certainly a loser.

What matters, then, whether one man worships God as Person and another as Force? Both do right according to their lights. None knows and, perhaps, never will know what is the absolutely proper way to pray. The ideal must always remain the ideal. One need only remember that God is the Force among all the forces. All other forces are material. But God is the vital force or spirit which is all-pervading, all-embracing and, therefore, beyond human ken. (ibid, p267)

Efficacy of Silence

It has often occurred to me that a seeker after truth has to be silent. I know the wonderful efficacy of silence. I visited a Trappist monastery in South Africa. A beautiful place it was. Most of the inmates of that place were under a vow of silence. I inquired of the Father the motive of it and he said the motive is apparent: 'We are frail human beings. We do not know very often what we say. If we want to listen to the still small voice that is always speaking within us, it will not be heard if we continually speak.' I understood that precious lesson. I know the secret of silence. (YI, 6-8-1925, pp274-5)

Experience has taught me that silence is a part of the spiritual discipline of a votary of truth. Proneness to exaggerate, to suppress or modify the truth, wittingly or unwittingly, is a natural weakness of man, and silence is necessary in order to surmount it. A man of few words will rarely be thoughtless in his speech; he will measure every word. (A, p45). Silence of the sewn-up lips is no silence. One may achieve the same result by chopping off one's tongue, but that too would not be silence. He is silent who, having the capacity to speak, utters no idle word. (H, 24-6-1933, p5)

It [silence] has now become both a physical and spiritual necessity for me. Originally it was taken to relieve the sense of pressure. Then I wanted time for writing. After, however, I had practiced it for some time, I saw the spiritual value of it. It suddenly flashed across my mind that was the time when I could best hold communion with God. And now I feel as though I was naturally built for silence. (H, 10-12-1938, p323-4)

Prayer is for remembering God, and for purifying the heart, and can be offered even when observing silence. (H, 20-4-1947, p118)

As I believe that silent prayer is often a mightier [force] than any overt act, in my helplessness I continuously pray in the faith that the prayer of a pure heart never goes unanswered. (YI, 22-9-1927, p321)

Power of Prayer

I can give my own testimony and say that a heartfelt prayer is undoubtedly the most potent instrument that man possesses for overcoming cowardice and all other bad old habits. (YI, 20-12-1928, p420)

Not until we have reduced ourselves to nothingness can we conquer the evil in us. God demands nothing less than complete self-surrender as the price for the only real freedom that is worth having. And when a man thus loses himself, he immediately finds himself in the service of all that lives. It becomes his delight and his recreation. He is a new man, never weary of spending himself in the service of God's creation. (ibid)

There is an eternal struggle raging in man's breast between the powers of darkness and of light, and he who has not the sheet-anchor of prayer to rely upon will be a victim to the powers of darkness. The man of prayer will be at peace with himself and with the whole world; the man who goes about the affairs of the world without a prayerful heart will be miserable and will make the world also miserable....

Prayer is the only means of bringing about orderliness and peace and repose in our daily acts....Take care of the vital thing and other things will take care of themselves. Rectify one angle of a square, and the other angles will be automatically right. (YI, 23-1-1930, p26)

Prayer is not an old woman's idle amusement. Properly understood and applied, it is the most potent instrument of action. (H, 14-4-1946, p80)

When the mind is completely filled with His spirit, one cannot harbour ill-will or hatred towards anyone and, reciprocally, the enemy will shed his enmity and become a friend. It is not my claim that I have succeeded in converting enemies into friends, but in numerous cases it has been my experience that, when the mind is filled with His peace, all hatred ceases. An unbroken succession of world teachers since the beginning of time have borne testimony to the same. I claim to merit for it. I know it is entirely due to God's grace. (H, 28-4-1946, p109)

One with a wicked heart can never be conscious of the all-purifying presence of God. (H, 29-6-1946, p209)

God answers prayer in His own way, not ours. His ways are different from the ways of mortals. Hence they are inscrutable. Prayer presupposes faith. No prayer goes in vain. Prayer is like any other action. It bears fruit whether we see it or not, and the fruit of heart prayer is far more potent than action so-called. (ibid, p215)

MY HINDUISM IS NOT EXCLUSIVE

All-embracing

For me Hinduism is all-sufficing. Every variety of belief finds protection under its ample folk. (SW, p329)

I can no more describe my feelings for Hinduism than for my own wife. She moves me as no other woman in the world can. Not that she has no faults; I dare say she has many more than I see myself. But the feeling of an indescribable bond is there. Even so I feel for and about Hinduism with all its faults and limitations. (YI, 6-10-1921, p318)

...Hinduism is not an exclusive religion. In it there is room for the worship of all the prophets in the world. It is not a missionary religion in the ordinary sense of the term. It has no doubt absorbed many tribes in its fold, but this absorption has been of an evolutionary, imperceptible character. Hinduism tells every one to worship God according to his own faith or Dharma and so it lives at peace with all the religions. (ibid)

There is nothing in the world that would keep me from professing Christianity or any other faith, the moment I felt the truth of and the need for it. Where there is fear, there is no religion...If I could call myself, say, a Christian, or a Mussalman, with my own interpretation of the Bible or the Koran, I should not hesitate to call myself either. For then Hindu, Christian and Mussalman would be synonymous terms. I do believe that in the other world there are neither Hindus, nor Christians nor Mussalmans. They all are judged not according to their labels, or professions, but according to their actions, irrespective of their professions. During our earthly existence there will always be these labels. I, therefore, prefer to retain the label of my forefathers so long as it does not cramp my growth and does not debar me from assimilating all that is good anywhere else. (YI, 2-7-1926, p308)

I know that friends get confused when I say I am a Sanatanist Hindu and they fail to find in me things they associate with a man usually labeled as such. But that is because, in spite of my being a staunch Hindu, I find room in my faith for Christian and Islamic and Zoroastrian teaching, and, therefore, my Hinduism seems to some to be a conglomeration and some have even dubbed me an eclectic. Well, to call a man eclectic is to say that he has no faith, but mine is a broad faith which does not oppose Christians-not even a Plymouth Brother-not even the most fanatical Mussalman. It is a faith based on the broadest possible toleration. I refuse to abuse a man for his fanatical deeds because I try to see them from his point of view. It is that broad faith that sustains me. It is a somewhat embarrassing position,

I know-but to others, not to me! (YI, 22-12-1927, p426). The chief value of Hinduism lies in holding the actual belief that all life (not only human beings, but all sentient beings) is one, i.e., all life coming from the One universal source, call it Allah, God or Parameshwara. (H, 26-12-1936, p365)

My Hinduism is not sectarian. It includes all that I know to be best in Islam, Christianity, Buddhism and Zoroastrianism....Truth is my religion and ahimsa is the only way of its realization. I have rejected once and for all the doctrine of the sword. (H, 30-4-1938, p99)

Hinduism and Ahimsa

Hinduism with its message of ahimsa is to me the most glorious religion in the world-as my wife to me is the most beautiful woman in the world—but others may feel the same about their own religion. (YI, 19-1-1928, p22)

The most distinctive and the largest contribution of Hinduism to India's culture is the doctrine of ahimsa. It has given a definite bias to the history of the country for the last three thousand years and over and it has not ceased to be a living force in the lives of India's millions even today. It is a growing doctrine, its message is still being delivered. Its teaching has so far permeated our people that an armed revolution has almost become an impossibility in India not because, as some would have it, we as a race are physically weak, for it does not require much physical strength so much as a devilish will to press a trigger to shoot a person, but because the tradition of ahimsa has struck deep root among the people. (H, 24-3-1929, p95)

Mother Gita

I do not believe that the Gita teaches violence for doing good. It is pre-eminently a description of the duel that goes on in our own hearts. The divine author has used a historical incident for inculcating the lesson of doing one's duty even at the peril of one's life. It inculcates performance of duty irrespective of the consequences, for we mortals, limited by our physical frames, are incapable of controlling actions, save our own. The Gita distinguished between the powers of light and darkness and demonstrates their incompatibility. (YI, 25-8-1920, p2)

Though I admire much in Christianity, I am unable to identify myself with orthodox Christianity...Hinduism as I know it entirely satisfies my soul, fills my whole being, and I find a solace in the Bhagavad Gita and Upanishads that I miss even in the Sermon on the Mount. Not that I do not prize the ideal presented therein; not that some of the precious teaching in the Sermon on the Mount have not left a deep impression upon me, but I must confess.... that, when doubt haunts me, when disappointments stare me in the face, and when I see not one ray of light on the horizon, I turn to the Bhagavad Gita, and find a verse to comfort me; and I immediately begin to smile in the midst of overwhelming sorrow. My life has been full of external tragedies, and if they have not left any visible and indelible effect on me, I owe it to the teachings of the Bhagavad Gita. (YI, 6-8-1925, p274)

As for myself, I run to my Mother Gita whenever I find myself in difficulties, and up to now she has never failed to comfort me. It is possible that those who are getting comfort from the Gita may get greater help, and see something altogether new, if they come to know the way in which I understand it from day to day. (YI, 13-11-1930, p1)

Today the Gita is not only my bible or my Koran; it is more than that—it is my mother. I lost my earthly mother who gave me birth long ago; but this eternal mother has completely filled her place by my side ever since. She has never changed, she has never failed me. When I am in difficulty or distress, I seek refuge in her bosom. (H, 24-8-1934, p222)

The Way of the Buddha

It is my deliberate opinion that the essential part of the teachings of the Buddha now forms an integral part of Hinduism. It is impossible for Hindu India today to retrace her steps and go behind the great reformation that Gautama effected in Hinduism. By his immense sacrifice, by his great renunciation, and by the immaculate purity of his life he left an indelible impress upon Hinduism, and Hinduism owes an eternal debt of gratitude to that great teacher... What Hinduism did not assimilate of what passes as Buddhism today was not an essential part of the Buddha's life and his teachings.

It is my fixed opinion that Buddhism or, rather, the teaching of the Buddha found its full fruition in India and it could not be otherwise, for Gautama was himself a Hindu of Hindus. He was saturated with the best that was in Hinduism, and he gave life to some of the teachings that were buried in the Vedas and which were overgrown with weeds. His great Hindu spirit cut its way through the forest of words, meaningless words, which had overlaid the golden truth that was in the Vedas. He made some of the words in the Vedas yield a meaning to which the men of his generation were utter strangers, and he found in India the most congenial soil.

And wherever the Buddha went, he was followed by and surrounded not by non-Hindus but Hindus, those who were themselves saturated with vedic law. But the Buddha's teaching, like his heart, was all-expanding and all-embracing and so it has survived his own body and swept across the face of the earth. And at the risk of being called a follower of the Buddha, I claim this achievement as a triumph of Hinduism. The Buddha never rejected Hinduism, but he broadened its base. He gave it a new life and a new interpretation. But...I want to submit to you that the teaching of the Buddha was not assimilated in its fullness whether it was in Ceylon, or in Burma, or in China, or in Tibet... (YI, 24-11-1927, pp392-3)

Moral Government of World

I have heard it contended times without number and I have read in books also claiming to express the spirit of Buddhism that the Buddha did not believe in God. In my humble opinion such a belief contradicts the very central fact of the Buddha's teaching...The confusion has arisen over his rejection, and just rejection, of all the base things that passed in his generation under the name of God. He undoubtedly rejected the notion that a being called God was actuated by malice, could repent of his actions and, like the Kings of the earth, could possibly be open to temptations and bribes and could possibly have favourites. His whole soul rose in mighty indignation against the belief that a being called God required for his satisfaction the living blood of animals in order that he might be pleased-animals who were his own creation. He, therefore, reinstated God in the right place and dethroned the usurper who for the time being seemed to occupy that White Throne. He emphasized and re-declared the eternal and unalterable existence of the moral government of this universe. He unhesitatingly said that the law was God Himself.

God's laws are eternal and unalterable and not separable from God Himself. It is an indispensable condition of His very perfection. And hence the great confusion that the Buddha disbelieved in God and simply believed in the moral law, and because of this confusion about God Himself, arose the confusion about the proper understanding of the great word Nirvana. Nirvana is undoubtedly not utter extinction. So far as I have been able to understand the central fact of the Buddha's life, Nirvana is utter extinction of all that is base in us, all that is vicious in us, all that is corrupt and corruptible in us. Nirvana is not like the black, dead peace of the grave, but the living peace, the living happiness of a soul which is conscious of itself, and conscious of having found its own abode in the heart of the Eternal....

Great as the Buddha's contribution to humanity was in restoring God to His eternal place, in my humble opinion, greater still was his contribution to humanity in his exacting regard of all life, be it ever so low. (ibid, p393)

Christianity in the West

It is my firm opinion that Europe today represents not the spirit of God or Christianity, but the spirit of Satan. And Satan's successes are the greatest when he appears with the name of God on his lips. Europe is today only nominally Christian. In reality it is worshipping Mammon. 'It is easier for a camel to pass through the eye of a needle than for a rich man to enter the Kingdom.' Thus really spoke Jesus Christ. His so-called followers measure their moral progress by their material possessions (YI, 8-9-1920, pp2-3)

It is a very curious commentary on the West that although it professes Christianity, there is no Christianity or Christ in the West, or there should haye been no war. That is how I understand the message of Jesus. (H, 17-11-1946, p405)

Christianity became disfigured when it went to the West. I am sorry to have to say that. (H, 20-4-1947, p116)

I ask my Christian brethren...not to take their Christianity as it is interpreted in the West. There, we know, they fight with one another as never before. After all, Jesus was an Asiatic depicted as wearing the Arabian flowing robe. He was the essence of meekness. I hope that the Christians of India will express in their lives Jesus the crucified, of the Bible, and not as interpreted in the West with her blood-stained fingers. I have no desire to criticize the West. I know and value the many virtues of the West. But I am bound to point out that Jesus of Asia is misrepresented in the West except in individuals. (H, 7-9-1947, p315)

The indirect influence of Christianity has been to quicken Hinduism into life... But the effect of Christianity upon India in general must be judged by the life lived in our midst by the average Christian and its effect upon us. I am sorry to have to record my opinion that it has been disastrous. (YI, 31-7-1924, p254)

Personality of Christ

I may say that I have never been interested in a historical Jesus. I should not care if it was proved by someone that the man called Jesus never lived, and that [what] was narrated in the Gospels was a figment of the writer's imagination. For the Sermon on the Mount would still be true for me. (YI, 31-12-1931, p429)

I cannot ascribe exclusive divinity to Jesus. He is as divine as Krishna or Rama or Mohamed or Zoroaster. Similarly, I do not regard every word of the Bible as the inspired word of God, even as I do not regard every word of the Vedas or the Koran as inspired. The sum total of each of these books is certainly inspired, but I miss that inspiration in many of the things taken individually. The Bible is as much a book of religion with me as the Gita and the Koran. (H, 6-3-1937, p25). Though, I cannot claim to be a Christian in the sectarian sense, the example of Jesus' suffering is a factor in the composition of my undying faith in nonviolence which rules all my actions, worldly and temporal. (H, 7-1-1939, p417)

What Christ Means to Me

What...does Jesus mean to me? To me, He was one of the greatest teachers humanity has ever had. To His believers, He was God's only begotten Son. Could the fact that I do or do not accept this belief make Jesus have any more or less influence in my life? Is all the grandeur of His teaching and of His doctrine to be forbidden to me? I cannot believe so. (MR, Oct. 1941, pp406-7)

To me it [the word 'begotten'] implies a spiritual birth. My interpretation, in other words, is that in Jesus' own life is the key of His nearness to God; that He expressed, as no other could, the spirit and will of God. It is in this sense that I see Him and recognize Him as the Son of God. (ibid)

I believe that it is impossible to estimate the merits of the various religions of the world, and, moreover, I believe that it is unnecessary and harmful even to attempt it. But each one of them, in my judgment, embodies a common motivating force: the desire to uplift man's life and give it purpose. And because the life of Jesus has the significance and the transcendency to which I have alluded, I believe that He belongs not solely to Christianity, but to the entire world, to all races and people- it matters little under what flag, name or doctrine they may work, profess a faith, or worship a God inherited from their ancestors. (ibid)

There is much ignorance and superstition in India. But deep down in us is that faith in God-the instinct for religion. (H, 17-11-1946, p405)

If Mohamed came to India today, he would disown many of his so-called followers and own me as a true Muslim, as Jesus would own me as a true Christian. (ibid)

"How can we bring man back to God or the teaching of Jesus, or that of Mohamed?" I might give the answer that Jesus gave to one of his followers: "Do the will of my Father who is in Heaven, not merely say Lord, Lord." That holds true of you, me and everybody. If we have faith in the living God, all will be well with us. I hope not to lose that faith even to my dying day. In spite of my numerous failings and shortcomings of which I am but too well aware, my faith in God is burning brighter every day. (ibid)

If it did not, I would take the same prescription that I gave a women threatened with dishonour and with no prospect of help or escape, viz., commit suicide. (ibid)

Islam a Religion of Peace

I do regard Islam to be a religion of peace in the same sense as Christianity, Buddhism and Hinduism are. No doubt there are differences in degree, but the object of these religions is peace. (YI, 20-1-1927, p21)

Islam's distinctive contribution to India's national culture is its unadulterated belief in the oneness of God and a practical application of the truth of the brotherhood of man for those who are nominally within its fold. I call these two distinctive contributions. For in Hinduism the spirit of brotherhood has become too much philosophized. Similarly, though philosophical Hinduism has no other god but God, it cannot be denied that practical Hinduism is not so emphatically uncompromising as Islam. (YI, 21-3-1929, p95)

Use of Force

There is nothing in the Koran to warrant the use of force for conversion. The Holy Book says in the clearest language possible, 'There is no compulsion in religion'. The Prophet's whole life is a repudiation of compulsion in religion. No Mussalman, to my knowledge, has ever approved of compulsion. Islam would cease to be a world religion of it were to rely upon force for its propagation. (YI, 29-9-1921, p307)

I have given my opinion that the followers of Islam are too free with the sword. But that is not due to the teaching of the Koran. This is due, in my opinion, to the environment in which Islam was born. Christianity has a bloody record against it not because Jesus was found wanting, but because the environment in which it spread was not responsive to his lofty teaching. (YI, 20-1-1927, p21)

The Koran

I have more than once read the Koran. My religion enables me, obliges me, to imbibe all that it good in all the great religions of the earth. (H, 28-10-1939, p317)

I certainly regard Islam as one of the inspired religions and, therefore, the Holy Koran as an inspired book and Muhammad as one of the prophets. (H, 13-7-1940, p207)

I have come to the conclusion that the teaching of the Koran is essentially in favour of nonviolence. Nonviolence is better than violence, it is said in the Koran. Nonviolence is enjoined as a duty; violence is permitted as a necessity. (ibid, p193)

RELIGION AND POLITICS

Life an Integral Whole

I Claim that human mind or human society is not divided into watertight compartments called social, political and religious. All act and react upon one another. (YI, 2-3-1922, p. 131)

Human life being an undivided whole, no line can ever be drawn between its different compartments, not between ethics and politics. A trader who earns his wealth by deception only succeeds in deceiving himself when he thinks that his sins can be washed away by spending some amount of his ill-gotten gains on the so-called religious purposes. One's everyday life is never capable of being separated from one's spiritual being. Both act and react upon one another. (H, 30-3-1947, p. 85)

The politician in me has never dominated a single decision of mine, and if I seem to take part in politics, it is only because politics encircle us today like the coil of a snake from which one cannot get out, no matter how much one tries. I wish, therefore, to wrestle with the snake as I have been doing with more or less success consciously since 1894, unconsciously, as I have now discovered, ever since reaching years of discretion. Quite selfishly, as I wish to live in peace in the midst of a bellowing storm howling round me, I have been experimenting with myself and my friends by introducing religion into politics. (YI, 12-5-1920, p. 2)

To see the universal and all-pervading Spirit of Truth face to face, one must be able to love the meanest of creation as oneself. And a man who aspires after that cannot afford to keep out of any field of life. That is why my devotion to Truth has drawn me into the field of politics; and I can say without the slightest hesitation, and yet in all humility, that those who say that religion has nothing to do with politics do not know what religion means. (A, pp. 370-1)

I could not be leading a religious life unless I identified myself with the whole of mankind, and that I could not do unless I took part in politics. The whole gamut of man's activities today constitutes an indivisible whole. You cannot divide social, economic, political and purely religious work into watertight compartments. I do not know any religion apart from human activity. It provides a moral basis to all other activities which they would otherwise lack, reducing life to a maze of 'sound and fury signifying nothing'. (H, 24-12-1938, p. 393)

I felt compelled to come into the political field because I found I could not do even social work without touching politics. I feel that political work must be looked upon in terns of social and moral progress. In democracy no fact of life is untouched by politics. (H, 6-10-1946, p. 341)

For me, politics bereft of religion are absolute dirt, ever to be shunned. Politics concern nations and that which concerns the welfare of nations must be one of the concerns of a man who is religiously inclined, in other words, a seeker after God and Truth. For me, God and Truth are convertible terms, and if anyone told me that God was a god of untruth or a god of torture, I would decline to worship Him. Therefore, in politics also we have to establish the kingdom of Heaven. (YI, 18-6-1925, p. 214)

I cannot isolate politics from the deepest things of my life, for the simple reason that my politics are not corrupt, they are inextricably bound up with nonviolence and truth. (YI, 1-10-1931, p. 281)

I could not live for a single second without religion. Many of my political friends despair of me because they say that even my politics are derived from religion. And they are right. My politics and all other activities of mine are derived from my religion. I go further and say that every activity of a man of religion must be bound to God, that is to say, God rules your every breath. (H, 2-3-1934, p. 23)

Indeed, religion should pervade every one of our actions. Here religion does not mean sectarianism. It means a belief in ordered moral government of the universe. It is not less real because it is unseen. This religion transcends Hinduism, Islam, Christianity, etc. It does not supersede them. It harmonizes them and gives them reality. (H, 10-2-1940, p. 445)

The life of the millions is my politics, from which I dare not free myself without denying my life-work and God. That my politics may take a different turn [after the 15th August 1947, when India will be free] is quite possible. But that will be determined by circumstances. (H, 17-8-1947, p. 281)

There is undoubtedly a sense in which the statement is true when I say that I hold my religion dearer than my country and that, therefore, I am a Hindu first and nationalist after. I do not become on that score less a nationalist than the best of them. I simply thereby imply that the interests of my country are identical with those of my religion. Similarly, when I say that I prize my own salvation above everything else, above the salvation of India, it does not mean that my personal salvation requires a sacrifice of necessarily that the two go together. (YI, 23-2-1922, p. 123)

Religion is no test of nationality, but a personal matter between man and his God. In the sense of nationality they are Indians first and Indians last, no matter what religion they profess. (H, 29-6-1947, p. 215)

TEMPLES AND IDOLATRY

Character of Idolatry

I do not disbelieve in idol worship. An idol does not excite any feeling of veneration in me. But I think that idol worship is part of human nature. We hanker after symbolism. Why should one be more composed in a church than elsewhere? Images are an aid to worship. No Hindu considers an image to be God. I do not consider idol worship a sin. (YI, 6-10-1921, p318)

I am both an idolater and an iconoclast in what I conceive to be the true sense of the terms. I value the spirit behind idol worship. It plays a most important part in the uplift of the human race... I am an iconoclast in the sense that I break down the subtle form of idolatry in the shape of fanaticism that refuses to see any virtue in any other form of worshipping the Deity save one's own. This form of idolatry is more deadly for being more fine and evasive than the tangible and gross form of worship that identifies the Deity with a little bit of a stone or a golden image. (YI, 28-8-1924, p284)

I am both a supporter and opponent of image worship. When image worship degenerates into idolatry and becomes encrusted with false beliefs and doctrines, it becomes a necessity to combat it as a gross social evil. On the other hand, image worship in the sense of investing one's ideal with a concrete shape is inherent in man's nature, and even valuable as an aid to devotion. Thus we worship an image when we offer homage to a book which we regard as holy or sacred. We worship an image when we visit a temple or a mosque with a feeling of sanctity or reverence. Nor do I see any harm in all this. On the contrary, endowed as man is with a finite, limited understanding, he can hardly do otherwise. Even so, far from seeing anything inherently evil or harmful in tree worship, I find in it a thing instinct with a deep pathos and poetic beauty. It symbolizes true reverence for the entire vegetable kingdom which, with its endless panorama of beautiful shapes and forms, declares to us, as it were with a million tongues, the greatness and glory of God.... (YI, 26-9-1929, p320)

Far different, however, is the case of vows and prayers which votaries offer before trees. The offering of vows and prayers for selfish ends, whether offered in churches, mosques, temples or before trees and shrines, is a thing not to be encouraged. Making of selfish requests or offering of vows is not related to image worship as effect and cause. A personal selfish prayer is bad whether made before an image or an unseen God. Let no one, however, from this understand me to mean that I advocate tree worship in general. I do not defend tree worship because I consider it to be a necessary aid to devotion, but only because I recognize that God manifests Himself in innumerable forms, in this universe, and every such manifestation commands my spontaneous reverence. (ibid)

As for idol worship, you cannot do without it in some form or other. Why does a Mussalman give his life for defending a mosque which he calls a house of God? And why does a Christian go to a church, and when he is required to take an oath, he swears by the Bible? Not that I see any objection to it. And what is it if not idolatry to give untold riches for building mosques and tombs? And what do the Roman Catholics do when they kneel before Virgin Mary and before saints, quite imaginary figures in stone or painted on canvas or glass? Even so, it is not the stone we worship, but it is God we worship in images of stone or metal, however rude they may be. (H, 13-3-1937, p39)

Place of Worship

I do not regard the existence of temples as a sin or superstition. Some form of common worship and a common place of worship appear to be a human necessity. Whether the temples should contain images or not is a matter of temperament and taste. I do not regard a Hindu or a Roman Catholic place of worship containing images as necessarily bad or superstitious and a mosque or a Protestant place of worship being good or free of superstition merely because of their exclusion of images. A symbol such as a Cross or a book may easily become idolatrous, and therefore, superstitious. And the worship of the image of Child Krishna or Virgin Mary may become ennobling and free of all superstition. It depends upon the attitude of the heart of the worshipper. (YI, 5-11-1925, p378)

Places of worship to me are not merely brick and mortar. They are but a shadow of the reality. Against every church and every mosque and every temple destroyed, hundreds have risen in their places. (YI, 4-11-1926, p386)

I know of no religion or sect that has done or is doing without its house of God, variously described as a temple, mosque, church, synagogue or agissari. Nor is it certain that any of the great reformers including Jesus destroyed or discarded temples altogether. All of them sought to banish corruption from temples as well as from society...I have ceased to visit temples for years, but I do not regard myself on that account as a better person than before. My mother never missed going to the temple when she was in fit state to go there. Probably her faith was far greater than mine, though I do not visit temples. (H, 11-3-1933, p5)

Temples or mosques or churches... I make no distinction between these different abodes of God. They are what faith has made them. They are an answer to man's craving somehow to reach the Unseen. (H, 18-3-1933, p6). Acquisition of consciousness [of the living presence of God within one] does not require or mean temple-going. (H, 29-6-1947, p209)

Our bodies are the real temples rather than buildings of stone. The best place for congregational worship is in the open with the sky above as the canopy and mother earth below for the floor. (H, 4-1-1948, p498)

THE CURSE OF UNTOUCHABILITY

I do not want to be reborn. But if I have to be reborn, I should be born an untouchable, so that I may share their sorrows, sufferings, and the affronts levelled at them, in order that I may endeavour to free myself and them from that miserable condition. I, therefore, prayed that, if I should be born again, I should do so not as a Brahmin, Kshatriya, Vaishya or Shudra, but as an Atishudra. (YI, 4-5-1921, p144)

I was wedded to the work for the extinction of 'untouchability' long before I was wedded to my wife. There were two occasions in our joint life when there was choice between working for the untouchables and remaining with my wife and I would have preferred the first. But thanks to my good wife, the crisis was averted. In my Ashram, which is my family, I have several untouchables and a sweet but naughty girl living as my own daughter. (YI, 5-11-1931, p341)

Love of the people brought the problem of untouchability early into my life. My mother said. 'You must not touch this boy, he is an untouchable.' 'Why not?' I questioned back, and from that day my revolt began. (H, 24-12-1938, p393)

Swaraj is a meaningless term, if we desire to keep a fifth of India under perpetual subjection, and deliberately deny to them the fruits of national culture. We are seeking the aid of God in this great purifying movement, but we deny to the most deserving among his creatures the rights of humanity. Inhuman ourselves we may not plead before the Throne for deliverance from the inhumanity of others. (YI, 25-5-1921, p165)

It is simple fanatical obstinacy to persist in persecuting man in the sacred name of religion. (YI, 11-3-1926, p95)

For reforms of Hinduism and for its real protection, removal of untouchability is the greatest thing...Removal of untouchability is....a spiritual process. (YI, 6-1-1927,p2). If untouchability lives, Hinduism must die. (H, 28-9-1947, p349)

I would far rather that Hinduism died than that untouchability lived. In battling against untouchability and in dedicating myself to that battle, I have no less an ambition than to see a complete regeneration of humanity. It may be a mere dream, as unreal as the silver in the sea-shell. It is not so to me while the dream lasts, and in the words of Romain Rolland, 'Victory lies not in realization of the goal, but in a relentless pursuit after it. (YI, 26-11-1931, p372)

Untouchability and Caste

It is a wrong to destroy caste because of the outcaste, as it would be to destroy a body because of an ugly growth in it or of a crop because of the weeds. The outcasteness, in the sense we understand it, has therefore to be destroyed altogether. It is an excess to be removed, if the whole system is not to perish. Untouchability is the product, therefore, not of the caste system, but of the distinction of high and low that has crept into Hinduism and is corroding it. The attack on untouchability is thus an attack upon this 'high-and-low'-ness. The moment untouchability goes, the caste system itself will be purified, that is to say, according to my dream, it will resolve itself into the true Varnadharma, the four division of society, each complementary of the other and none inferior or superior to any other, each as necessary for the whole body of Hinduism as any other. (H, 11-2-1933, p3)

Varnashrama Dharma

Varnashrama Dharma defines man's mission on this earth. He is not born day after day to explore avenues for amassing riches and to explore different means of livelihood; on the contrary, man is born in order that he may utilize every atom of his energy for the purpose of knowing his Maker. It restricts him, therefore, for the purpose of holding body and soul together, to the occupation of his forefathers. That and nothing more or nothing less is Varnashrama Dharma. (YI, 27-10-1927, p357)

I do, however, believe in varna which is based on hereditary occupations. Varnas are four to mark four universal occupations,-imparting knowledge, defending the defenseless, carrying on agriculture and commerce, and performing service through physical labour. These occupations are common to all mankind, but Hinduism, having recognized them as the law of our being, has made use of it in regulating social relations and conduct. Gravitation affects us all, whether one knows its existence or not. But scientists who knew the law have made it yield results that have startled the world. Even so has Hinduism startled the world by its discovery and application of the law of varna. When Hindus were seized with inertia, abuse of varna resulted in innumerable castes, with unnecessary and harmful restrictions as to intermarriage and inter-dine. These restrictions may be necessary in the interest of chastity and hygiene. But a Brahmana who marries a Shudra girl, or vice versa, commits no offence against the law of varnas. (YI, 4-6-1931, p129)

Today Brahmins and Kshatriyas, Vaishyas and Shudras are mere labels. There is utter confusion of varna as I understand it and I wish that all the Hindus will voluntarily call themselves Shudras. That is the only way to demonstrate the truth of Brahminism and to revive Varnadharma in its true state. (H, 25-3-1933, p3)

I believe that every man is born in the world with certain natural tendencies. Every person is born with certain definit limitations which he cannot overcome. From a careful observation of those limitations the law of varna was deduced. It established certain spheres of actions for certain people with certain tendencies. This avoided all unworthy competition. Whilst recognizing limitations, the law of varna admitted of no distinctions of high and low; on the one hand, it guaranteed to each the fruits of his labours, and one the other, it prevented him from pressing upon his neighbours. This great law has been degraded and fallen into disrepute. But my conviction is that an ideal social order will only be evolved when the implications of this law are fully understood and given effect to. (MR, Oct. 1935, p413)

Intermarriage and Inter-dining

Though there is in Varnashrama no prohibition against intermarriage and inter-dining, there can be no compulsion. It must be left to the unfettered choice of the individual as to where he or she will marry or dine. (H, 16-11-1935, p316)

Caste

......I consider the four divisions alone to be fundamental, natural and essential. The innumerable sub castes are sometimes a convenience, often a hindrance. The sooner there is fusion the better. (YI, 8-12-1920, p3)

From the economic point of view, its value was once very great. It ensured hereditary skill; it limited competition. It was the best remedy against pauperism. And it had all the advantages of trade guilds. Although it did not foster adventure or invention there, it is not known to have come in the way either...

Historically speaking, caste may regarded as man's experiment or social adjustment in the laboratory of Indian society. If we can prove it to be a success, it can be offered to the world as a leaven and as the best remedy against heartless competition and social disintegration born of avarice and greed. (YI, 5-1-1921, p2)

Caste and Varna

...I have frequently said that I do not believe in caste in the modern sense. It is an excrescence and a -handicap on progress. Nor do I believe in inequalities between human beings. We are all absolutely equal. But equality is of souls and not bodies. Hence, it is a mental state. We need to thing of, and to assert, equality because we see great inequalities in the physical world. We have to realize equality in the midst of this apparent external inequality. Assumption of superiority by any person over any other is a sin against God and man. Thus caste, in so far as it connotes distinctions in status, is an evil. (YI, 4-6-1931, p129)

Caste distinctions have taken such deep root amongst us that they have also infected the Muslims, Christians and followers of other religions in India. It is true that class barriers are also to be found in more or less degree in other parts of the world. This means that it is a distemper common to the human race. It can be eliminated only by the inculcation of religion in its true sense. I have not found sanction for such barriers and distinctions in the scriptures of any religion.

In the eye of religion all men are equal. Learning, intellect or riches do not entitle one to claim superiority over those who are lacking in these. If any person is suffused and sanctified with the purifying essence and discipline of true religion, he regards himself under the obligation to share his advantages with those who have fewer. That being so, in our present fallen state, true religion requires us all to become Atishudras by choice.

We must regard ourselves not as owners, but as trustees of our wealth, and use it for the service of society, taking for ourselves no more than a fair return for service rendered. Under this system there would be none poor, none rich. All religions would be held equal. All quarrels arising out of religion, caste or economic grievance would cease to disturb peace on earth. (Hu, 19-9-1945)

4

VIEWS OF GANDHI

NONVIOLENCE

The Gospel of Nonviolence

The Law of Our Species

I am not a visionary. I claim to be a practical idealist. The religion of nonviolence is not meant merely for the rishis and saints. It is meant for the common people as well. Nonviolence is the law of our species as violence is the law of the brute. The spirit lies dormant in the brute and he knows no law but that of physical might. The dignity of man requires obedience to a higher law-to the strength of the spirit....

The rishis who discovered the law of nonviolence in the midst of violence were greater geniuses than Newton. They were themselves known the use of arms, they realized their uselessness, and taught a weary world that its salvation lay not through violence but through nonviolence. (YI, 11-8-1920, p3)

My Ahimsa

I know only one way-the way of ahimsa. The way of himsa goes against my grain. I do not want to cultivate the power to inculcate himsa...The faith sustains me that He is the help of the helpless, that He comes to one's succour only when one throws himself on His mercy. It is because of that faith that I cherish the hope that God will one day show me a path which I may confidently commend to the people. (YI, 10-10-1928, p342)

I have been a 'gambler' all my life. In my passion for finding truth and in relentlessly following out my faith in nonviolence, I have counted no stake too great. In doing so I have erred, if at all, in the company of the most distinguished scientist of any age and any clime. (YI, 20-2-1930, p61)

I learnt the lesson of nonviolence from my wife, when I tried to bend her to my will. Her determined resistance to my will, on the one hand, and her quiet submission to the suffering my stupidity involved, on the other, ultimately made me ashamed of myself and cured me of my stupidity in thinking that I was born to rule over her and, in the end, she became my teacher in nonviolence. (H, 24-12-1938, p394)

The doctrine that has guided my life is not one of inaction but of the highest action. (H, 28-6-1942, p201)

I must not...flatter myself with the belief—nor allow friends...to entertain the belief that I have exhibited any heroic and demonstrable nonviolence in myself. All I can claim is that I am sailing in that direction without a moment's stop. (H, 11-1-1948, p504)

Character of Nonviolence

Non-violence is the law of the human race and is infinitely greater than and superior to brute force. In the last resort it does not avail to those who do not possess a living faith in the God of Love.

Nonviolence affords the fullest protection to one's self-respect and sense of honour, but not always to possession of land or movable property, though its habitual practice does prove a better bulwark than the possession of armed men to defend them. Nonviolence, in the very nature of things, is of no assistance in the defence of ill-gotten gains and immoral acts. Individuals or nations who would practice nonviolence must be prepared to sacrifice (nations to last man) their all except honour. It is, therefore, inconsistent with the possession of other people's countries, i.e., modern imperialism, which is frankly based on force for its defence.

Nonviolence is a power which can be wielded equally by all-children, young men and women or grown-up people, provided they have a living faith in the God of Love and have therefore equal love for all mankind. When nonviolence is accepted as the law of life, it must pervade the whole being and not be applied to isolated acts.

It is a profound error to suppose that, whilst the law is good enough for individuals, it is not for masses of mankind. (H, 5-9-1936, p236)

For the way of nonviolence and truth is sharp as the razor's edge. Its practice is more than our daily food. Rightly taken, food sustains the body; rightly practiced nonviolence sustains the soul. The body food we can only take in measured quantities and at stated intervals; nonviolence, which is the spiritual food, we have to take in continually. There is no such thing as satiation. I have to be conscious every moment that I am pursuing the goal and have to examine myself in terms of that goal.

Changeless Creed

The very first step in nonviolence is that we cultivate in our daily life, as between ourselves, truthfulness, humility, tolerance, loving kindness. Honesty, they say in English, is the best policy. But, in terms of nonviolence, it is not mere policy. Policies may and do change. Nonviolence is an unchangeable creed. It has to be pursued in face of violence raging around you. Nonviolence with a nonviolent man is no merit. In fact it becomes difficult to say whether it is nonviolence at all. But when it is pitted against violence, then one realizes the difference between the two. This we cannot do unless we are ever wakeful, ever vigilant, ever striving. (H, 2-4-1938, p64)

The only thing lawful is nonviolence. Violence can never be lawful in the sense meant here, i.e., not according to man-made law but according to the law made by Nature for man. (H, 27-10-1946, p369)

Faith in God

[A living faith in nonviolence] is impossible without a living faith in God. A nonviolent man can do nothing save by the power and grace of God. Without it he won't have the courage to die without anger, without fear and without retaliation. Such courage comes from the belief that God sits in the hearts of all and that there should be no fear in the presence of God. The knowledge of the omnipresence of God also means respect for the lives even of those who may be called opponents.... (H, 18-6-1938, p64)

Nonviolence is an active force of the highest order. It is soul force or the power of Godhead within us. Imperfect man cannot grasp the whole of that Essence-he would not be able to bear its full blaze, but even an infinitesimal fraction of it, when it becomes active within us, can work wonders.

The sun in the heavens fills the whole universe with its life-giving warmth. But if one went too near it, it would consume him to ashes. Even so it is with God-head. We become Godlike to the extent we realize nonviolence; but we can never become wholly God. (H, 12-11-1938, p326)

The fact is that nonviolence does not work in the same way as violence. It works in the opposite way. An armed man naturally relies upon his arms. A man who is intentionally unarmed relies upon the Unseen Force called God by poets, but called the Unknown by scientists. But that which is unknown is not necessarily non-existent. God is the Force among all forces known and unknown. Nonviolence without reliance upon that Force is poor stuff to be thrown in the dust. (H, 28-6-1942, p201)

Consciousness of the living presence of God within one is undoubtedly the first requisite. (H, 29-6-1947, p209)

Religious Basis

My claim to Hinduism has been rejected by some, because I believe and advocate nonviolence in its extreme form. They say that I am a Christian in disguise. I have been even seriously told that I am distorting the meaning of the Gita, when I ascribe to that great poem the teaching of unadulterated nonviolence. Some of my Hindu friends tell me that killing is a duty enjoined by the Gita under certain circumstances. A very learned shastri only the other day scornfully rejected my interpretation of the Gita and said that there was no warrant for the opinion held by some commentators that the Gita represented the eternal duel between forces of evil and good, and inculcated the duty of eradicating evil within us without hesitation, without tenderness.

I state these opinions against nonviolence in detail, because it is necessary to understand them, if we would understand the solution I have to offer....

I must be dismissed out of considerations. My religion is a matter solely between my Maker and myself. If I am a Hindu, I cannot cease to be one even though I may be disowned by the whole of the Hindu population. I do however suggest that nonviolence is the end of all religions. (YI, 29-5-1924, p175)

The lesson of nonviolence is present in every religion, but I fondly believe that, perhaps, it is here in India that its practice has been reduced to a science. Innumerable saints have laid down their lives in tapashcharya until poets had felt that the Himalayas became purified in their snowy whiteness by means of their sacrifice. But all this practice of nonviolence is nearly dead today. It is necessary to revive the eternal law of answering anger by love and of violence by nonviolence; and where can this be more readily done than in this land of Kind Janaka and Ramachandra? (H, 30-3-1947, p86)

Hinduism's Unique Contribution

Nonviolence is common to all religions, but it has found the highest expression and application in Hinduism. (I do not regard Jainism or Buddhism as separate from Hinduism).

Hinduism believes in the oneness not of merely all human life but in the oneness of all that lives. Its worship of the cow is, in my opinion, its unique contribution to the evolution of humanitarianism. It is a practical application of the belief in the oneness and, therefore, sacredness of all life. The great belief in transmigration is a direct consequence of that belief. Finally, the discovery of the law of Varnashrama is a magnificent result of the ceaseless search for truth. (YI, 20-10-1927, p352)

I have also been asked wherefrom in Hinduism I have unearthed ahimsa. Ahimsa is in Hinduism, it is in Christianity as well as in Islam. Whether you agree with me or not, it is my bounden duty to preach what I believe to be the truth as I see it. I am also sure that ahimsa has never made anyone a coward. (H, 27-4-1947, p126)

The Koran and Nonviolence

[Barisaheb] assured me that there was warrant enough for Satyagraha in the Holy Koran. He agreed with the interpretation of the Koran to the effect that, whilst violence under certain well-defined circumstances is permissible, self-restraint is dearer to God than violence, and that is the law of love. That is Satyagraha. Violence is concession to human weakness, Satyagraha is an obligation. Even from the practical standpoint it is easy enough to see that violence can do no good and only do infinite harm. (YI, 14-5-1919, quoted in Communal Unity, p985)

Some Muslim friends tell me that Muslims will never subscribe to unadulterated nonviolence. With them, they say, violence is as lawful and necessary as nonviolence. The use of either depends upon circumstances. It does not need Koranic authority to justify the lawfulness of both. That is the well-known path the world has traversed through the ages. There is no such thing as unadulterated violence in the world. But I have heard it from many Muslim friends that the Koran teaches the use of nonviolence. It regards forbearance as superior to vengeance. The very word Islam means peace, which is nonviolence. Badshahkhan, a staunch Muslim who never misses his namaz and Ramzan, has accepted out and out nonviolence as his creed. It would be no answer to say that he does not live up to his creed, even as I know to my shame that I do not one of kind, it is of degree. But, argument about nonviolence in the Holy Koran is an interpolation, not necessary for my thesis. (H, 7-10-1939, p296)

No Matter of Diet

Ahimsa is not a mere matter of dietetics, it transcends it. What a man eats or drinks matters little; it is the self-denial, the self-restraint behind it that matters. By all means practice as much restraint in the choice of the articles of your diet as you like. The restraint is commendable, even necessary, but it touches only the fringe of ahimsa. A man may allow himself a wide latitude in the matter of diet and yet may be a personification of ahimsa and compel our homage, if is heart overflows with love and melts at another's woe, and has been purged of all passions. On the other hand a man always over-scrupulous in diet is an utter stranger to ahimsa and pitiful wretch, if he is a slave to selfishness and passions and is hard of heart. (YI, 6-9-1928, pp300-1)

Road to Truth

My love for nonviolence is superior to every other thing mundane or supramundane. It is equaled only by my love for Truth, which is to me synonymous with nonviolence through which and which alone I can see and reach Truth. (YI, 20-2-1930, p61)

....Without ahimsa it is not possible to seek and find Truth. Ahimsa and Truth are so intertwined that it is practically impossible to disentangle and separate them. They are like the two sides of a coin, or rather of a smooth, unstamped, metallic disc. Who can say which is the obverse, and which is the reverse? Nevertheless ahimsa is the means; Truth is the end. Means to be means must always be within our reach, and so ahimsa is our supreme duty. If we take care of the means, we are bound to reach the end sooner of latter. When once we have grasped this point, final victory is beyond question. (FYM, pp12-3)

Ahimsa is not the goal. Truth is the goal. But we have no means of realizing truth in human relationships except through the practice of ahimsa. A steadfast pursuit of ahimsa is inevitably bound to truth—not so violence. That is why I swear by ahimsa. Truth came naturally to me. Ahimsa I acquired after a struggle. But ahimsa being the means, we are naturally more concerned with it in our everyday life. It is ahimsa, therefore, that our masses have to be educated in. Education in truth follows from it as a natural end. (H, 23-6-1946, p199)

No Cover for Cowardice

My nonviolence does not admit of running away from danger and leaving dear ones unprotected. Between violence and cowardly flight, I can only prefer violence to cowardice. I can no more preach nonviolence to a coward than I can tempt a blind man to enjoy healthy scenes. Nonviolence is the summit of bravery. And in my own experience, I have had no difficulty in demonstrating to men trained in the school of violence the superiority of nonviolence. As a coward, which I was for years, I harboured violence. I began to prize nonviolence only when I began to shed cowardice. Those Hindus who ran away from the post of duty when it was attended with danger did so not because they were nonviolent, or because they were afraid to strike, but because they were unwilling to die or even suffer an injury. A rabbit that runs away from the bull terrier is not particularly nonviolent. The poor thing trembles at the sight of the terrier and runs for very life. (YI, 28-5-1924, p178)

Nonviolence is not a cover for cowardice, but it is the supreme virtue of the brave. Exercise of nonviolence requires far greater bravery than that of swordsmanship. Cowardice is wholly inconsistent with nonviolence. Translation from swordsmanship to nonviolence is possible and, at times, even an easy stage. Nonviolence, therefore, presupposes ability to strike. It is a conscious deliberate restraint put upon one's desire for vengeance. But vengeance is any day superior to passive, effeminate and helpless submission. Forgiveness is higher still. Vengeance too is weakness.

The desire for vengeance comes out of fear of harm, imaginary or real. A dog barks and bites when he fears. A man who fears no one on earth would consider it too troublesome even to summon up anger against one who is vainly trying to injure him. The sun does not wreak vengeance upon little children who throw dust at him. They only harm themselves in the act. (YI, 12-8-1926, p285)

The path of true nonviolence requires much more courage than violence. (H, 4-8-1946, pp248-9)

The minimum that is required of a person wishing to cultivate the ahimsa of the brave is first to clear one's thought of cowardice and, in the light of the clearance, regulate his conduct in every activity, great or small. Thus the votary must refuse to be cowed down by his superior, without being angry.

He must, however, be ready to sacrifice his post, however remunerative it may be. Whilst sacrificing his all, if the votary has no sense of irritation against his employer, he has ahimsa of the brave in him.

Assume that a fellow-passenger threatens my son with assault and I reason with the would-be-assailant who then turns upon me. If then I take his blow with grace and dignity, without harbouring any ill-will against him, I exhibit the ahimsa of the brave. Such instances are of every day occurrence and can be easily multiplied. If I succeed in curbing my temper every time and, though able to give blow for blow, I refrain, I shall develop the ahimsa of the brave which will never fail me and which will compel recognition from the most confirmed adversaries. (H, 17-11-1946, p404)

Inculcation of cowardice is against my nature. Ever since my return from South Africa, where a few thousand had stood up not unsuccessfully against heavy odds, I have made it my mission to preach true bravery which ahimsa means. (H, 1-6-1947, p175)

Humility Essential

If one has...pride and egoism, there is no nonviolence. Nonviolence is impossible without humility. My own experience is that, whenever I have acted non-violently, I have been led to it and sustained in it by the higher promptings of an unseen power. Through my own will I should have miserably failed. When I first went to jail, I quailed at the prospect. I had heard terrible things about jail life. But I had faith in God's protection. Our experience was that those who went to jail in a prayerful spirit came out victorious, those who had gone in their own strength failed. There is no room for self-pitying in it either when you say God is giving you the strength. Self-pity comes when you do a thing for which you expect recognition from others. But there is no question of recognition. (H, 28-1-1939, p442)

It was only when I had learnt to reduce myself to zero that I was able to evolve the power of Satyagraha in South Africa. (H, 6-5-1939, p113)

THE POWER NONVIOLENCE

Nonviolence in its dynamic condition means conscious suffering. It does not mean meek submission-to the will of the evildoer, but it means the pitting of one's whole soul against the will of the tyrant. Working under this law of our being, it is possible for a single individual to defy the whole might of an unjust empire to save his honour, his religion, his soul and lay the foundation for that empire's fall or its regeneration. (YI, 1-8-1920, p3)

Active Force

The nonviolence of my conception is a more active and more real fighting against wickedness than retaliation whose very nature is to increase wickedness. I contemplate a mental and, therefore, a moral opposition to immoralities. I seek entirely to blunt the edge of the tyrant's sword, not by putting up against it a sharper-edged weapon, but by disappointing his expectation that I would be offering physical resistance. The resistance of the should that I should offer instead would elude him. It would at first dazzle him, and at last compel recognition from him, which recognition would not humiliate him but would uplift him. It may be urged that this again is an ideal state. And so it is. The propositions from which I have drawn my arguments are as true as Euclid's definitions, which are none the less true because in practice we are unable to even draw Euclid's line on a blackboard. But even a geometrician finds it impossible to get on without bearing in mind Euclid's definitions. Nor may we...dispense with the fundamental propositions on which the doctrine of Satyagraha is based. (YI, 8-10-1925, p346)

I admit that the strong will rob the weak and that it is sin to be weak. But this is said of the soul in man, not of the body. If it be said of the body, we could never be free from the sin of weakness. But the strength of soul can defy a whole world in arms against it. This strength is open to the weakest in body. (YI, 6-5-1926, p164)

Nonviolence is the greatest force at the disposal of mankind. It is mightier than the mightiest weapon of destruction devised by the ingenuity of man. Destruction is not the law of the humans. Man lives freely by his readiness to die, if need be, at the hands of his brother, never by killing him. Every murder or other injury, no matter for what cause, committed or inflicted on another is a crime against humanity. (H, 20-7-1935, pp180-1)

Nonviolence is like radium in its action. An infinitesimal quantity of it embedded in a malignant growth acts continuously, silently and ceaselessly till it has transformed the whole mass of the diseased tissue into a healthy one. Similarly, even a little of true nonviolence acts in a silent, subtle, unseen way and leavens the whole society. (H, 12-11-1938, p327)

Matchless Bravery

An armed soldier relies on his weapons for his strength. Take away from him his weapons-his gun or his sword, and he generally becomes helpless. But a person who has truly realized the principle of nonviolence has the God-given strength for his weapon and the world has not known anything that can match it. (H, 19-11-1938, pp341-2)

A small body of determined spirits fired by an unquenchable faith in their mission can alter the course of history. (ibid, p343)

Nonviolence of the strong is any day stronger than that of the bravest soldier fully armed or a whole host. (H, 12-5-1946, p128)

Exercise in Faith

The hardest metal yields to sufficient heat. Even so the hardest heart must melt before sufficiency of the heat of nonviolence. And there is no limit to the capacity of nonviolence to generate heat.

Every action is a resultant of a multitude of forces even of a contrary nature. There is no waste of energy. So we learn in the books on mechanics. This is equally true of human actions. The difference is that in the one case we generally know the forces at work, and when we do, we can mathematically foretell the resultant. In the case of human actions, they result from a concurrence of forces of most of which we have no knowledge. But our ignorance must not be made to serve the cause of disbelief in the power of these forces. Rather is our ignorance a cause for greater faith. And nonviolence being the mightiest force in the world and also the most elusive in its working, it demands the greatest exercise of faith. Even as we believe in God in faith, so have we to believe in nonviolence in faith. (H, 7-1-1939, p417)

Violence like water, when it has an outlet, rushes forward furiously with an overwhelming force. Nonviolence cannot act madly. It is the essence of discipline. But, when it is set going, no amount of violence can crush it. For full play, it requires unsullied purity and an unquenchable faith... (H, 21-3-1939, p433)

A Science

Ahimsa is a science. The word 'failure' has no place in the vocabulary of science. Failure to obtain the expected result is often the precursor to further discoveries. (H, 6-5-1939, p113)

If the function of himsa is to devour all it comes across, the function of ahimsa is to rush into the mouth of himsa. In an atmosphere of ahimsa one has no scope to put his ahimsa to the test. It can be tested only in the face of himsa. (H, 13-5-1939, p121)

Violence can only be effectively met by nonviolence. This is an old, established truth...that the weapon of violence, even if it was the atom bomb, became useless when matched against nonviolence. That very few understand how to wield this mighty weapon is true. It requires a lot of understanding and strength of mind. It is unlike what is needed in military schools and colleges. The difficulty one experiences in meeting himsa with ahimsa arises from weakness of mind. (H, 1-6-1947, p172)

The Deed, not Doer

'Hate the sin and not the sinner' is a precept which, though easy enough to understand, is rarely practised, and that is why the poison of hatred spreads in the world. This ahimsa is the basis of the search for truth. I am realizing every day that the search is vain unless it is founded on ahimsa as the basis. It is quite proper to resist and attack a system, but to resist and attack its author is tantamount to resisting and attacking oneself. For we are all tarred with the same brush, and are children of one and the same creator, and as such, the divine powers within us are infinite. To slight a single human being is to slight those divine powers, and thus to harm not only that Being but with Him the whole world. (A, p203)

Man and his deed are two distinct things. Whereas a good deed should call forth approbation and a wicked deed disapprobation, the doer of the deed, whether good or wicked, always deserves respect or pity as the case may be. (ibid)

Those who seek to destroy men rather than manners adopt the latter and become worse than those whom they destroy under the mistaken belief that the manners will die with the men. They do not know the root of the evil. (YI, 17-3-1927, p85)

It is the acid test of nonviolence that, in a nonviolent conflict, there is no rancour left behind, and in the end the enemies are converted into friends. That was my experience in South Africa, with General Smuts. He started with being my bitterest opponent and critic. Today he is my warmest friend. (H, 12-11-1938, p327)

The principal implication of ahimsa is that the ahimsa in us ought to soften and not to stiffen our opponents' attitude to us; it ought to melt him; it ought to strike a responsive chord in his heart.

As ahimsa-ites, can you say that you practice genuine ahimsa? Can you say that you receive the arrows of the opponent on your bare breasts without returning them? Can you say that you are not angry, that you are not perturbed by his criticism? (H, 13-5-1939, p121)

By reason of life-long practice of ahimsa, I claim to be an expert in it, though very imperfect. Speaking in absolute terms, the more I practice it the clearer I see how far I am from the full expression of ahimsa in my life. It is his ignorance of this, the greatest duty of man in the world, which makes him say that in this age nonviolence has little scope in the face of violence, whereas I make bold to say that in this age of the Atom Bomb unadulterated nonviolence is the only force that can confound all the tricks put together of violence. (H, 16-11-1947, p412)

TRAINING FOR NONVIOLENCE

"How are we to train individuals or communities in this difficult art?"

There is no royal road, except through living the creed in your life which must be a living sermon. Of course, the expression in one's own life presupposes great study, tremendous perseverance, and thorough cleansing of one's self of all the impurities.

If for mastering of the physical sciences you have to devote a whole life-time, how many lifetimes may be needed for mastering the greatest spiritual force that mankind has known? But why worry even if it means several lifetimes? For, if this is the only permanent thing in life, if this is the only thing that counts, then whatever effort you bestow on mastering it is well spent. Seek ye first the Kingdom of Heaven and everything else shall be added unto you. The Kingdom of Heaven is ahimsa. (H, 14-3-1936, p39)

Arms are surely unnecessary for a training in ahimsa. In fact the arms, if any, have to be thrown away, as the Khansaheb did in the Frontier Province. Those who hold that it is essential to learn violence before we can learn nonviolence, would hold that only sinners can be saints.

Fearlessness the Prerequisite

Just as one must learn the art of killing in the training for violence, so one must learn the art of dying in the training for nonviolence. Violence does not mean emancipation from fear, but discovering the means of combating the cause of fear. Nonviolence, on the other hand, has no cause for fear. The votary of nonviolence has to cultivate the capacity for sacrifice of the highest type in order to be free from fear. He racks not if he should lose his land, his wealth, his life. He who has not overcome all fear cannot practice ahimsa to perfection.

The votary of ahimsa has only one fear, that is of God. He who seeks refuge in God ought to have a glimpse of the Atman that transcends the body; and the moment one has a glimpse of the Imperishable Atman, one sheds the love of the perishable body. Training in nonviolence is thus diametrically opposed to training in violence. Violence is needed for the protection of things external, nonviolence is needed for the protection of the Atman, for the protection of one's honour.

This nonviolence cannot be learnt by staying at home. It needs enterprise. In order to test ourselves we should learn to dare danger and death, mortify the flesh, and acquire the capacity to endure all manner of hardships. He who trembles or take to his heels the moment he sees two people fighting is not nonviolent, but a coward. A nonviolent person will lay down his life in preventing such quarrels. The bravery of the nonviolent is vastly superior to that of the violent. The badge of the violent is his weapon-spear, or sword, or rifle. God is the shield of the nonviolent. This is not course of training for one intending to learn nonviolence. But it is easy to evolve one from the principles I have laid down. (H, 1-9-1940, p268)

Nonviolence of the Brave

Nonviolence does not require any outside or outward training. It simply requires the will not to kill even in retaliation and the courage to face death without revenge. This is no sermon on ahimsa but cold reason and the statement of a universal law. Given the unquenchable faith in the law, no provocation should prove too great for the exercise of forbearance. This I have described as the nonviolence of the brave. (H, 8-9-1946, p296)

That nonviolence which only an individual can use is not of much use in terms of society. Man is a social being. His accomplishments to be of use must be such as any person with sufficient diligence can attain. That which can be exercised only among friends is of value only as a spark of nonviolence. It cannot merit the appellation of ahimsa. 'Enmity vanishes before ahimsa' is a great aphorism. It means that the greatest enmity requires an equal measure of ahimsa for its abatement.

Cultivation of this virtue may need long practice, ever extending to several births. It does not become useless on that account. Travelling along the route, the pilgrim will meet richer experiences from day to day, so that he may have a glimpse of the beauty he is destined to see at the top. This will add to his zest. No one is entitled to infer from this that the path will be a continuous carpet of roses without thorns. A poet has sung that the way to reach God accrues only to the very brave, never to the fainthearted. The atmosphere today is so much saturated with poison that one refuses to recollect the wisdom of the ancients and to perceive the varied little experience of ahimsa in action. 'A bad turn is neutralized by a good' ,is a wise saying of daily experience in practice. Why can we not see that if the sum total of the world's activities was destructive, it would have come to an end long ago? Love, otherwise, ahimsa, sustains this planet of ours. This much must be admitted. The precious grace of life has to be strenuously cultivated, naturally so because it is uplifting. Descent is easy, not so ascent. A large majority of us being undisciplined, our daily experience is that of fighting or swearing at one another on the slightest pretext.

This, the richest grace of ahimsa, will descend easily upon the owner of hard discipline. (H, 14-12-1947, p468)

APPLICATION OF NONVIOLENCE

If one does not practice nonviolence in one's personal relations with others, and hopes to use it in bigger affairs, one is vastly mistaken. Nonviolence like charity must begin at home.

But if it is necessary for the individual to be trained in nonviolence, it is even more necessary for the nation to be trained likewise. One cannot be nonviolent in one's own circle and violent outside it. Or else, one is not truly nonviolent even in one's own circle; often the nonviolence is only in appearance. It is only when you meet with resistance, as for instance, when a thief or a murderer appears, that your nonviolence is put on its trail. You either try or should try to oppose the thief with his own weapons, or you try to disarm him by love. Living among decent people, your conduct may not be described as a nonviolent. Mutual forbearance is nonviolence. Immediately, therefore, you get the conviction that nonviolence is the law of life, you have to practice it towards those who act violently towards you, and the law must apply to nations as individuals. Training no doubt is necessary. And beginnings are always small. But if the conviction is there, the rest will follow. (H, 28-1-1939, pp441-2)

Universality of Nonviolence

Nonviolence to be a creed has to be all-pervasive. I cannot be nonviolent about one activity of mine and violent about others. (H, 12-10-1935, p376)

It is a blasphemy to say that nonviolence can only be practiced by individuals and never by nations which are composed of individuals. (H, 12-11-1938, p328)

In my opinion, nonviolence is not passivity in any shape or form. Nonviolence, as I understand it, is the most active force in the world...Non-violence is the supreme law. During my half a century of experience, I have not yet come across a situation when I had to say that I was helpless, that I had no remedy in terms of nonviolence. (H, 24-12-1938, p393)

Cultivation of Nonviolence

I am an irrepressible optimist. My optimism rests on my belief in the infinite possibilities of the individual to develop nonviolence. The more you develop it in your own being, the more infectious it becomes till it over-whelms your surroundings and by and by might over sweep the world. (H, 28-1-1939, p443)

I have known from early youth that nonviolence is not a cloistered virtue to be practiced by the individual for his peace and final salvation, but it is a rule of conduct for society if it is to live consistently with human dignity and make progress towards the attainment of peace for which it has been yearning for ages past. (GCG, pp42-44, pp170-1)

To practice nonviolence in mundane matters is to know its true value. It is to bring heaven upon earth. There is no such thing as the other world. All works are one. There is no 'here' and no 'there'. As Jeans has demonstrated, the whole universe including the most distant stars, invisible even through the most powerful telescope in the world, is compressed in an atom.

I hold it, therefore, to be wrong to limit the use of nonviolence to cave-dwellers and for acquiring merit for a favoured position in the other world. All virtue ceases to have use if it serves no purpose in every walk of life. (H, 26-7-1942, p248)

Use on Mass Scale

Unfortunately for us, we are strangers to the nonviolence of the brave on a mass scale. Some even doubt the possibility of the exercise of nonviolence by groups, much less by masses of people. They restrict its exercise to exceptional individuals. Only, mankind can have no use of it if it is always reserved only for individuals. (H, 8-9-1946, p296)

Efficacy

I have been practicing with scientific precision nonviolence and its possibilities for an unbroken period of over fifty years. I have applied it in every walk of life, domestic, institutional, economic and political. I know of no single case in which it has failed. Where it has seemed sometimes to have failed, I have ascribed it to my imperfections. I claim no perfection for myself. But I do claim to be a passionate seeker after Truth, which is but another name for God. In the course of that search, the discovery of nonviolence came to me. Its spread is my life mission. I have no interest in living except for the prosecution of that mission. (H, 6-7-1940, pp185-6)

There is no hope for the aching world except through the narrow and straight path of nonviolence. Millions like me may fail to prove the truth in their own lives, that would be their failure, never of the eternal law. (H, 29-6-1947, p209)

THE NONVIOLENT SOCIETY

I hold that nonviolence is not merely a personal virtue. It is also a social virtue to be cultivated like the other virtues. Surely society is largely regulated by the expression of nonviolence in its mutual dealings. What I ask for is an extension of it on a larger, national and international scale. (H, 7-1-1939, p417)

All society is held together by nonviolence, even as the earth is held in her position by gravitation. But when the law of gravitation was discovered, the discovery yielded results of which our ancestors had no knowledge.

Even so, when society is deliberately constructed in accordance with the law of nonviolence, its structure will be different in material particulars from what it is today. But I cannot say in advance what the government based on nonviolence will be like.

What is happening today is disregard of the law of nonviolence and enthronement of violence as if it were an eternal law. (H, 11-12-1939, p8)

Society based on nonviolence can only consist of groups settled in villages in which voluntary cooperation is the condition of dignified and peaceful existence. (H, 13-1-1940, pp410-11)

The Government

The Government cannot succeed in becoming entirely nonviolent, because it represents all the people. I do not today conceive of such a golden age. But I do believe in the possibility of a predominantly nonviolent society. And I am working for it. (H, 9-3-1940, p31)

There remains the question as to whether in an ideal society, there should be any or no government. I do not think we need worry ourselves about this at the moment. If we continue to work for such a society, it will slowly come into being to an extent, such that the people can benefit by it. Euclid's line is one without breadth, but no one has so far been able to draw it and never will. All the same, it is only by keeping the ideal line in mind that we have made progress in geometry. What is true here is true of every ideal.

Anarchy

It must be remembered that nowhere in the world does a State without government exist. If at all it could ever come into being, it would be in India; for, ours is the only country where the attempt has, at any rate, been made. We have not yet been able to show that bravery to the degree which is necessary and for the attainment of which there is only one way. Those who have faith in the latter have to demonstrate it. In order to do so, the fear of death has to be completely shed, just as we have shed the fear of prisons. (H, 15-9-1946, p309)

Democracy and Nonviolence

Science of war leads one to dictatorship pure and simple. Science of nonviolence can alone lead one to pure democracy. (H, 15-10-1938, p290)

Democracy and violence can ill go together. The State that are today nominally democratic have either to become frankly totalitarian, or if they are to become truly democratic, they must become courageously nonviolent. (H, 12-11-1938, p328)

Holding the view that, without the recognition of nonviolence on a national scale, there is no such thing as a constitutional or democratic government, I devote my energy to the propagation of nonviolence as the law of our life, individual, social, political, national and international.

I fancy that I have seen the light, though dimly. I write cautiously for I do not profess to know the whole of the Law. If I know the success of my experiments, I know also my failures. But the successes are enough to fill me with undying hope.

I have often said that if one takes care of the means, the end will take care of itself. Nonviolence is the means, the end for everyone is complete independence. There will be an international League only when all the nations, big or small, composing it are fully independent. The nature of that independence will correspond to the extent of nonviolence assimilated by the nations concerned. One thing is certain. In a society based on nonviolence, the smallest nation will feel as tall as the tallest. The idea of superiority and inferiority will be wholly obliterated.

...The conclusion is irresistible that for one like me, wedded to nonviolence, constitutional or democratic government is a distant dream so long as nonviolence is not recognized as a living force, an inviolable creed, not a mere policy. While I prate about universal nonviolence, my experiment is confined to

India. If it succeeds, the world will accept it without effort. There is however a bit BUT. The pause does not worry me. My faith is brightest in the midst of impenetrable darkness. (H, 11-12-1939, p8)

Use of Power

By its very nature, nonviolence cannot 'seize' power, nor can that be its goal. But nonviolence can do more; it can effectively control and guide power without capturing the machinery of government. That is its beauty.

There is an exception, of course. If the nonviolent noncooperation of the people is so complete that the administration ceases to function or if the administration crumbles under the impact of a foreign invasion and a vacuum results, the people's representatives will then step in and fill it. Theoretically that is possible.

But the use of power need not necessarily be violent. A father wields power over his children; he may even punish but not by inflicting violence. The most effective exercise of power is that which irks least. Power rightly exercised must sit light as a flower; no one should feel the weight of it.

The people accepted the authority of the Congress willingly. I was on more than one occasion invested with the absolute power of dictatorship. But everybody knew that my power rested on their willing acceptance. They could set me aside at any time and I would have stepped aside without a murmur.

Prophets and supermen are born only once in an age. But if even a single individual realizes the ideal of ahimsa in its fullness, he covers and redeems the whole society. Once Jesus had blazed the trail, his twelve disciples could carry on his mission without his presence.

It needed the perseverance and genius of so many generations of scientists to discover the laws of electricity, but today everybody, even children use electric power in their daily life. Similarly, it will not always need a perfect being to administer an ideal State once it has come into being. What is needed is a thorough social awakening to begin with. The rest will follow.

To take an instance nearer home, I have presented to the working class the truth that true capital is not silver or gold, but the labour of their hands and feet and their intelligence. Once labour develops that awareness, it would not need my presence to enable it to make use of the power that it will release. (TNH, pp91-93)

THE NONVIOLENT STATE

Many have shaken their heads as they have said, "But you can't teach nonviolence to the masses. It is only possible for individuals and that too in rare cases." That is, in my opinion, a gross self-deception. If mankind was not habitually nonviolent, it would have been self-destroyed ages ago. But in the duel between forces of violence and nonviolence, the latter have always come out victorious in the end.

The truth is that we have not had patience enough to wait and apply ourselves whole-heartedly to the spread of nonviolence among the people as a means for political ends. (YI, 2-1-1930, p4)

Political Power

To me political power is not an end but one of the means of enabling people to better their condition in every department of life. Political power means capacity to regulate national life through national representatives. If national life becomes so perfect as to become self-regulated, no representation become necessary. There is then a state of enlightened anarchy. In such a state everyone is his own ruler. He rules himself in such a manner that he is never a hindrance to his neighbour.

In the ideal State, therefore, there is no political power because there is no State. But the ideal is never fully realized in life. Hence the classical statement of Thoreau that Government is best which governs the least. (YI, 2-7-1931, p162)

Capitalism a Trusteeship

It is my firm conviction that if the State suppressed capitalism by violence, it will be caught in the coils of violence itself, and fail to develop nonviolence at any time. The State represents violence in a concentrated and organized form. The individual has a soul, but as the State is a soulless machine, it can never be weaned from violence to which it owes its very existence. Hence I prefer the doctrine of trusteeship.

The fear is always there that the State may use too much violence against those who differ from it. I would be very happy, indeed, if the people concerned behaved as trustees; but if they fail, I believe we shall have to deprive them of their possessions through the State with the minimum exercise of violence.

That is why I said at the Round Table Conference that every vested interest must be subjected to scrutiny, and confiscation ordered where necessary with or without compensation as the case demanded.

What I would personally prefer would be not centralization of power in the hands of the State, but an extension of the sense of trusteeship, as, in my opinion, the violence of private ownership is less injurious than the violence of the State. However, if it is unavoidable, I would support a minimum of State-ownership.

While admitting that man actually lives by habit, I hold that it is better for him to live by the exercise of will. I also believe that men are capable of developing their will to an extent that will reduce exploitation to a minimum.

I look upon an increase in the power of the State with the greatest fear because, although while apparently doing good by minimizing exploitation, it does the greatest harm to mankind by destroying individuality, which lies at the root of the progress.

We know of so many cases where men have adopted trusteeship, but non where the State has really lived for the poor. (MR, October, 1935, p412)

Nonviolent Swaraj

In Swaraj based on ahimsa, people need not know their rights, but it is necessary for them to know their duties. There is no duty but creates a corresponding right, and those only are true rights which flow from a due performance of one's duties. Hence rights of true citizenship accrue only to those who serve the State to which they belong. And they alone can do justice to the rights that accrue to them.

Everyone possesses the right to tell lies or resort to goondaism. But the exercise of such right is harmful both to the exerciser and society. But to him who observes truth and nonviolence comes prestige, and prestige brings rights. And people who obtain rights as a result of performance of duty, exercise them only for the service of society, never for themselves.

Swaraj of a people means the sum total of the Swaraj (self-rule) of individuals. And such Swaraj comes only from performance by individuals of their duty as citizens. In it no one thinks of his rights. They come, when they are needed, for better performance of duty. (YI, 25-3-1939, p64)

Under Swaraj based on nonviolence nobody is anybody's enemy, everybody contributes his or her due quota to the common goal, all can read and write, and their knowledge keeps growing from day to day. Sickness and disease are reduced to the minimum. No one is a pauper and labour can always find employment. There is no place under such a government for gambling, drinking and immorality or for class hatred.

The rich will use their riches wisely and usefully, and not squander them in increasing their pomp and worldly pleasures. It should not happen that a handful of rich people should live in jeweled palaces and the millions in miserable hovels devoid of sunlight or ventilation.....

In nonviolent Swaraj there can be no encroachment upon just rights; contrariwise no one can possess unjust rights. In a well-organized State, usurpation should be an impossibility and it should be unnecessary to resort to force for dispossessing a usurper. (ibid, p65)

Decentralization

I suggest that, if India is to evolve along nonviolent lines, it will have to decentralize many things. Centralization cannot be sustained and defended without adequate force. Simple homes from which there is nothing to take away require no policing; the palaces of the rich must have strong guards to protect them against decoity. So must huge factories. Rurally organized India will run less risk of foreign invasion than urbanized India well equipped with military, naval and air forces.

Centralization as a system is inconsistent with nonviolent structure of society. (YI, 18-1-1942, p5)

Modern State

It is not possible for a modern State based on force nonviolently to resist forces of disorder, whether external or internal. A man cannot serve God and Mammon, nor be 'temperate and furious' at the same time. It is claimed that a State can be based on nonviolence, i.e., it can offer nonviolent resistance against a world combination based on armed force. Such a State was Ashoka's. The example can be repeated. But the case does not become weak even if it be shown that Ashoka's State was not based on nonviolence. It has to be examined on its merits.....

There can be no nonviolence offered by the militarily strong. Thus, Russia in order to express nonviolence has to discard all her power of doing violence. What is true is that if those, who were at one time strong in armed might, change their mind, they will be better able to demonstrate their nonviolence to the world and, therefore, also to their opponents. (YI, 12-5-1946, p128)

VIOLENCE AND TERRORISM

My experience teaches me that truth can never be propagated by doing violence. Those who believe in the justice of their cause have need to possess boundless patience and those alone are fit to offer civil disobedience who are above committing criminal disobedience or doing violence. (YI, 28-4-1920, p. 8)

Popular Violence

If I can have nothing to do with the organized violence of the Government, I can have less to do with the unorganized violence of the people. I would prefer to be crushed between the two. (YI, 24-11-1921, p. 382)

For me popular violence is as much an obstruction in our path as the Government violence. Indeed, I can combat the Government violence more successfully than the popular. For one thing, in combating the latter, I should not have the same support as in the former. (YI, 24-4-1930, p. 140)

I make bold to say that violence is the creed of no religion and that, whereas nonviolence in most cases is obligatory in all, violence is merely permissible in some cases. But I have not put before India the final form of nonviolence. (YI, 2-3-1922, p. 130)

I object to violence because, when it appears to do good, the good is only temporary; the evil it does is permanent. (YI, 21-5-1925, p. 178)

No Faith in Violence

It is an unshakable faith with me that a cause suffers exactly to the extent that it is supported by violence. I say this in spite of appearances to the contrary. If I kill a man who abstracts me, I may experience a sense of false security. But the security will be short-lived. For I shall not have dealt with the root cause. In due course, other men will surely rise to obstruct me. My business, therefore, is not to kill the man or men who obstruct me, but to discover the cause that impels them to obstruct me and deal with it. (YI, 26-2-1931, p. 1)

I do not believe in armed risings. They are a remedy worse than the disease sought to be cured. They are a token of the spirit of revenge and impatience and anger. The method of violence cannot do good in the long run. (YI, 9-6-1920, p. 3)

The Revolutionary

I do not deny the revolutionary's heroism and sacrifice. But heroism and sacrifice in a bad cause are so much waste of splendid energy and hurt the good cause by drawing away attention from it by the glamour of the misused heroism and sacrifice in a bad cause.

I am not ashamed to stand erect before the heroic and self-sacrificing revolutionary because I am able to pit an equal measure of nonviolent men's heroism and sacrifice untarnished by the blood of the innocent. Self-sacrifice of one innocent man is a million times more potent than the sacrifice of a million men who die in the act of killing others. The willing sacrifice of the innocent is the most powerful retort to insolent tyranny that has yet been conceived by God or man.

I invite the attention of the revolutionaries to the three great hindrances to Swaraj-the incomplete spread of the spinning wheel, the discord between Hindus and Mussalmans and the inhuman ban on the suppressed classes. I ask them patiently to take their due share in this work of patient construction. It may not be spectacular enough. But on that very account it requires all the heroic patience, silent and sustained effort and self-effacement of which the tallest among the revolutionaries is capable. Impatience will blur the revolutionary's vision and lead him astray.

Slow and inglorious self-imposed starvation among the starved masses is every time more heroic than the death on the scaffold under false exaltation. (YI, 12-2-1925, p. 60)

Prevention of Brutalization

I am more concerned in preventing the brutalization (human nature than in the preventing of the sufferings of my own people....I know that people who voluntarily undergo a course of suffering raise themselves and the whole of humanity. but I also know that people, who become brutalized in their desperate efforts to get victory over their opponents or to exploit weaker nations or weaker men, not only drag down themselves but making also. (YI, 29-10-1931, p. 325)

There is no necessary charm about death on the gallows; often such death is easier than a life of drudgery and toil in malarious tracts....I suggest to my friend the revolutionary that death on the gallows serves the country only when the victim is a 'spotless lamb'. (YI, 9-4-1925, p. 124)

....I do not condemn everything European. But I condemn for all climes and for all times secret murders and unfair methods even for a fair cause....Armed conspiracies against something satanic is like matching Satans against Satan. But since one Satan is one too many for me, I would not multiply him..... (ibid, p. 125)

Cowardice, whether philosophical or otherwise, I abhor. And if I could be persuaded that revolutionary activity has dispelled cowardice, it will go a long way to soften my abhorrence of the method, however much I may still oppose it on principle....

I do not regard killing or assassination or terrorism as good in any circumstances whatsoever. I do believe that ideas ripen quickly when nourished by the blood of martyrs. But a man who dies slowly of jungle fever in service bleeds as certainly as the one on the gallows. And if the one who dies on the gallows is not innocent of another's blood, he never had ideas that deserved to ripen.

Heroes of History

....To compare their (revolutionaries') activities with those of Guru Govind Singh or Washington or Garibaldi or Lenin would be most misleading and dangerous. But, by test of the theory of nonviolence, I do not hesitate to say that it is highly likely that, had I lived as their contemporary and in the respective countries, I would have called every one of them a misguided patriot, even though a successful and brave warrior....

I disbelieve history so far as details of acts of heroes are concerned. I accept broad facts of history and draw my own lessons for my conduct. I do not want to repeat it in so far as the broad facts contradict the highest laws of life. But I positively refuse to judge men from the scanty material furnished to us by history. De mortuis nil nisi bonum.

Kemal Pasha and De Valera, too, I cannot judge. But, for me as a believer in nonviolence out and out, they cannot be my guides in life in so far as their faith in war is concerned. I believe in Krishna. But my Krishna is the Lord of the Universe, the creator, preserver and destroyer of us all. He may destroy because He creates....

Revolution Suicidal....

I have not the qualifications for teaching my philosophy of life. I have barely qualifications for practicing the philosophy

I believe....The revolutionaries are at liberty to reject the whole of my philosophy....But India is not like Turkey or Ireland or Russia and that revolutionary activity is suicidal at this stage of the country's life at any rate, if not for all time in a country so vast, so hopelessly divided and with the masses so deeply sunk in pauperism and so fearfully terror-struck. (YI, 9-4-1925, p. 126). The revolutionary destroys the body for the supposed benefit of the adversary's soul....I do not know a single revolutionary who has even thought of the adversary's soul. His single aim has been to benefit the country, even though the adversary may perish body and soul. (YI, 30-4-1925, p. 153)

I honour the anarchist for his love of the country. I honour him for his bravery in being willing to die for his country; but I ask him: Is killing honourable death? I deny it. (SW, p. 323)

I repeat my deliberate opinion that, whatever may be true of other countries, in India at least political murder can only harm the country. (YI, 16-4-1931, p. 75)

The page of history is soiled red with the blood of those who have fought for freedom. I do not know an instance in which nations have attained their own without having to go through an incredible measure of travail. The dagger of he assassin, the poison bowl, the bullet of the rifle-man, the spear—and all these weapons and methods of destruction have been used up to now by what I consider blind lovers of liberty and freedom...I hold no brief for the terrorist. (YI, 24-12-1931, p. 408)

Let the revolutionary pray with and for me that I may soon become that [free from passions, wholly incapable of sin]. But, meanwhile, let him take with me the one step to it which I see as clearly as day-light, viz. to win India's freedom with strictly nonviolent means. (H, 25-1-1942, p. 15)

BETWEEN COWARDICE AND VIOLENCE

I would risk violence a thousand times rather than risk the emasculation of a whole race. (YI, 4-8-1920, p5)

Violence the Choice

I do believe that, where there is only a choice between cowardice and violence, I would advise violence....I would rather have India resort to arms in order to defend her honour than that she should, in a cowardly manner, become or remain a helpless witness to her own dishonour.

But I believe that nonviolence is infinitely superior to violence, forgiveness is more manly than punishment. Forgiveness adorns a soldier...But abstinence is forgiveness only when there is the power to punish; it is meaningless when it pretends to proceed from a helpless creature....

But I do not believe India to be helpless....I do not believe myself to be a helpless creature....Strength does not come from physical capacity. It comes from an indomitable will. (YI, 11-8-1920, p3)

We do want to drive out the best in the man, but we do not want on that account to emasculate him. And in the process of finding his own status, the beast in him is bound now and again to put up his ugly appearance. (YI, 15-12-1921, p419)

The world is not entirely governed by logic. Life itself involves some kind of violence and we have to choose the path of least violence. (H, 28-9-1934, p259)

No Cowardice

I want both the Hindus and Mussalmans to cultivate the cool courage to die without killing. But if one has not that courage, I want him to cultivate the art of killing and being killed rather than, in a cowardly manner, flee from danger. For the latter, in spite of his flight, does commit mental himsa. He flees because he has not the courage to be killed in the act of killing. (YI, 20-10-1921, p335)

My method of nonviolence can never lead to loss of strength, but it alone will make it possible, if the nation wills it, to offer disciplined and concerted violence in time of danger. (YI, 29-5-1924, p176)

My creed of nonviolence is an extremely active force. It has no room for cowardice or even weakness. There is hope for a violent man to be some day nonviolent, but there is none for a coward. I have, therefore, said more than once....that, if we do not know how to defend ourselves, our women and our places of worship by the force of suffering, i.e., nonviolence, we must, if we are men, be at least able to defend all these by fighting. (YI, 16-6-1927, p196)

No matter how weak a person is in body, if it is a shame to flee, he will stand his ground and die at his post. This would be nonviolence and bravery. No matter how weak he is, he will use what strength he has in inflicting injury on his opponent, and die in the attempt. This is bravery, but not nonviolence. If, wnen his duty is to face danger, he flees, it is cowardice. In the first case, the man will have love or charity in him. In the second and third cases, there would be a dislike or distrust and fear. (H, 17-8-1935, p211)

My nonviolence does admit of people, who cannot or will not be nonviolent, holding and making effective use of arms. Let me repeat for the thousandth time that nonviolence is of the strongest, not of the weak. (YI, 8-5-1941)

To run away from danger, instead of facing it, is to deny one's faith in man and God, even one's own self. It were better for one to drown oneself than live to declare such bankruptcy of faith. (H, 24-11-1946, p410)

Self-defence by Violence

I have been repeating over and over again that he who cannot protect himself or his nearest and dearest or their honour by nonviolently facing death may and ought to do so by violently dealing with the oppressor. He who can do neither of the two is a burden. He has no business to be the head of a family. He must either hide himself, or must rest content to live for ever in helplessness and be prepared to crawl like a worm at the bidding of a bully. (YI, 11-10-1928, p342)

The strength to kill is not essential for self-defence; one ought to have the strength to die. When a man is fully ready to die, he will not even desire to offer violence. Indeed, I may put it down as a self-evident proposition that the desire to kill is in inverse proportion to the desire to die. And history is replete with instances of men who, by dying with courage and compassion on their lips, converted the hearts of their violent opponents. (YI, 21-1-1930, p27)

Nonviolence cannot be taught to a person who fears to die and has no power of resistance. A helpless mouse is not nonviolent because he is always eaten by pussy. He would gladly eat the murderess if he could, but he ever tries to flee from her. We do not call him a coward, because he is made by nature to behave no better than he does.

But a man who, when faced by danger, behaves like a mouse, is rightly called a coward. He harbours violence and hatred in his heart and would kill his enemy if he could without hurting himself. He is a stranger to nonviolence. All sermonizing on it will be lost on him. Bravery is foreign to his nature. Before he can understand nonviolence, he has to be taught to stand his ground and even suffer death, in the attempt to defend himself against the aggressor who bids fair to overwhelm him. To do otherwise would be to confirm his cowardice and take him further away from nonviolence.

Whilst I may not actually help anyone to retaliate, I must not let a coward seek shelter behind nonviolence so-called. Not knowing the stuff of which nonviolence is made, many have honestly believed that running away from danger every time was a virtue compared to offering resistance, especially when it was fraught with danger to one's life. As a teacher of nonviolence I must, so far as it is possible for me, guard against such an unmanly belief. (H, 20-7-1935, pp180-1)

Self-defence....is the only honourable course where there is unreadiness for self-immolation. (ibid, p181)

Though violence is not lawful, when it is offered in self-defence or for the defence of the defenseless, it is an act of bravery far better than cowardly submission. The latter befits neither man nor woman. Under violence, there are many stages and varieties of bravery. Every man must judge this for himself. No other person can or has the right. (H, 27-10-1946, pp369-70)

Resistance To Aggression

I MUST live. I would not be a vassal to any nation or body. I must have absolute independence or perish. To seek to win in a clash of arms would be pure bravado. Not so if, in defying the might of one who would deprive me of my independence, I refuse to obey his will and perish unarmed in the attempt. In so doing, though I lose the body, I save my soul, i.e., my honour. (H, 15-10-1938, p290)

Duty of Resistance

The true democrat is he who with purely nonviolent means defends his liberty and therefore, his country's and ultimately, that of the whole of mankind...But the duty of resistance accrues only to those who believe in nonviolence as a creed-not to those who will calculate and will examine the merits of each case and decide whether to approve of or oppose a particular war. It follows that such resistance is a matter for each person to decide for himself and under the guidance of the inner voice, if he recognizes its existence. (H, 15-4-1939, p90)

The true meaning of non-resistance has often been misunderstood or even distorted. It never implies that a nonviolent man should bend before the violence of an aggressor. While not returning the latter's violence by violence, he should refuse to submit to the latter's illegitimate demand even to the point of death. That is the true meaning of nonresistance....

He is not to return violence by violence, but neutralize it by withholding one's hand and, at the same time, refusing to submit to the demand. This is the only civilized way of going on in the world. Any other course can only lead to a race for armaments interspersed by periods of peace which is by necessity and brought about by exhaustion, when preparations would be going on for violence of a superior order. Peace through superior violence inevitably leads to the atom bomb and all that it stands for. It is the completes negation of nonviolence and of democracy which is not possible without the former. (H, 30-3-1947, pp85-86)

To answer brutality with brutality is to admit one's moral and intellectual bankruptcy and it can only start a vicious circle.... (H, 1-6-1947, p174)

Resistance both forms [passive resistance and non violent resistance] are, but you have to pay a very heavy price when your resistance is passive, in the sense of the weakness of the resister. Europe mistook the bold and brave resistance, full of wisdom, by Jesus of Nazareth for passive resistance, as if it was of the weak. As I read the New Testament for the first time, I detected no passivity, no weakness about Jesus as depicted in the four gospels, and the meaning became clearer to me when I read Tolstoy's Harmony of the Gospels and his other kindred writings.

Has not the West paid heavily in regarding Jesus as a Passive Resister? Christendom has been responsible for the wars which put to shame even those described in the Old Testament and other records, historical or semi-historical. I know that I speak under correction, for I can but claim very superficial knowledge of history-modern or ancient. (H, 7-12-1947, p453)

To die without killing requires more heroism [than to die in the act of killing]. There is nothing very wonderful in killing and being killed in the process. But the man who offers his neck to the enemy for execution, but refuses to bend to his will, shows courage of a far higher type. (H, 21-4-1946, p95)

The Way of Ahimsa

Ahimsa is one of the world's great principles which no power on earth can wipe out. Thousands like myself may die in trying to vindicate the ideal, but ahimsa will never die. And the gospel of ahimsa can be spread only through believers dying for the cause. (H, 17-5-1946, p140)

Ahimsa is the highest ideal. It is meant for the brave, never for the cowardly. To benefit by others' killing, and delude oneself into the belief that one is being very religious and nonviolent is sheer self-deception. (H, 9-6-1946, p172)

No power on earth can subjugate you when you are armed with the sword of Ahimsa. It ennobles both the victor and vanquished. (ibid, p174)

The proper way to view the present outburst of violence throughout the world is to recognize that the technique of unconquerable nonviolence of the strong has not been at all fully discovered as yet. Not an ounce of nonviolent strength is ever wasted. (H, 11-1-1948, p504)

I do not say 'eschew violence in you dealing with robbers or thieves or with nations that may invade India'. But, in order that we are better able to do so, we must learn to restrain ourselves. It is a sign not of strength but of weakness to take up the pistol on the slightest pretext. Mutual fisticuffs are a training not in violence but in emasculation. (YI, 29-5-1924, p176)

Whilst all violence is bad and must be condemned in the abstract, it is permissible for, it is even the duty of, a believer in ahimsa to distinguish between the aggressor and the defender. Having done so, he will side with the defender in a nonviolent manner, i.e., give his life in saving him. His intervention is likely to bring a speedier end to the duel, and may even result in bringing about peace between the combatants. (H, 21-10-1939, p309)

My nonviolence does recognize different species of violence-defensive and offensive. It is true that in the long run the difference is obliterated, but the initial merit persists. A nonviolent person is bound, when the occasion arises, to say which side is just. Thus I wished success to the Abyssinians, the Spaniards, the Czechs, the Chinese and the Poles, though in each case I wished that they could have offered nonviolent resistance. (H, 9-12-1939, p371)

If war is itself a wrong act, how can it be worthy of moral support or blessings? I believe all war to be wholly wrong. But, if we scrutinize the motives of two warring parties, we may find one to be in the right and the other in the wrong. For instance, if A wishes to seize B's country, B is obviously the wronged one. Both fight with arms. I do not believe in violent warfare, but all the same, B, whose cause is just, deserves my moral help and blessings. (H, 18-8-1940, p250)

You can return blow for blow if you are not brave enough to follow the path of nonviolence. But there is a moral code for the use of violence also. Otherwise, the very flames of violence will consume those who light them. I do not care if they are all destroyed. But I cannot countenance the destruction of India's freedom. (H, 17-11-1946, p402)

India's Way

I have recognized that the nation has the right, if it so wills, to vindicate her freedom even by actual violence. Only, then India ceases to be the land of my love, even though the land of my birth, even as I should take no pride in my mother if she went astray. (YI, 20-11-1924, p382)

When India becomes self-supporting, self-reliant, and proof against temptations and exploitation, she will cease to be the object of greedy attraction for any power in the West or the East and will then feel secure without having to carry the burden of expensive armaments. Her internal economy will be the strongest bulwark against aggression. (YI, 2-7-1931, p161)

Nonviolent Resistance

History has no record of a nation having adopted nonviolent resistance. If Hitler is unaffected by my suffering, it does not matter. For I shall have lost nothing worth. My honour is the only thing worth preserving. That is independent of Hitler's pity. But as a believer in nonviolence, I may not limit its possibilities. Hitherto he and his likes have built upon their invariable experience that men yield to force. Unarmed men, women and children offering nonviolent resistance without any bitterness in them will be a novel experience for them. Who can dare say that it is not in their nature to respond to the higher and finer forces? They have the same soul that I have....

I have a call I must answer. I must deliver my message to my people. This humiliation has sunk too deep in me to remain without an outlet. I, at least, must act up to the light that has dawned on me.

....When I first launched out on Satyagraha, I had no companion. We were thirteen thousand men, women and children against a whole nation, capable of crushing the existence out of us. I did not know who would listen to me. It all came as in a flash. All the 13,000 did not fight. Many fell back. But the honour or the nation was saved. New history was written by the South African Satyagraha....

My purpose will be fulfilled if I succeed in reaching these men's hearts and making them see that, if their nonviolence does not make them feel much braver than the possession of arms and the ability to use them, they must give up their nonviolence, which is another name for cowardice, and resume their arms which there is nothing but their own will to prevent them from taking back.

I present...a weapon not of the weak but of the brave. There is no bravery greater than a resolute refusal to bend the knee to an earthly power, no matter how great, and that without bitterness of spirit and in the fullness ot faith that the spirit alone lives, nothing else does. (H, 15-10-1938, pp290-1)

Basic Assumptions

I have argued from the analogy of what we do in families or even clans. The humankind is one big family. And if the love expressed is intense enough, it must apply to all mankind. If individuals have succeeded even with savages, why should not a group of individuals succeed with a group, say, of savages?

If we can succeed with the English, surely it is merely an extension of faith to believe that we are likely to succeed with less cultured or less liberally-minded nations. I hold that, if we succeed with the English with unadulterated nonviolent effort, we must succeed with the others, which is the same thing as saying, that, if we achieve freedom with nonviolence, we shall defend it also with the same weapon. If we have not achieved that faith, our nonviolence is a mere expedient; it is the alloy, not pure gold.

In the first place, we shall never achieve freedom with doubtful nonviolence; and in the second, even if we do—we shall find ourselves wholly unprepared to defend the country against an aggressor. If we have doubt about the final efficacy of nonviolence, it would be far better for the Congress to revise its policy and invite the nation to training in arms. A mass organization like the Congress will be untrue to its charge if, not knowing its own mind, it misled the people into a false belief. It would be an act of cowardice.... Because we cease to pin our faith to nonviolence, we do not necessarily become violent. We merely throw off the mask and be natural. It would be a perfectly dignified course to adopt. (H, 22-10-1938, p298)

However small a nation or even a group may be, it is able, even as the individual, provided that it has one mind as also the will and the grit, to defend its honour and self-respect against a whole world in arms. Therein consists the matchless strength and beauty of the unarmed. That is nonviolent defence which neither knows nor accepts defeat at any stage. Therefore, a nation or a group which has made nonviolence its final policy cannot be subjected to slavery even by the atom bomb. (H, 18-8-1946, p265)

The Congress has declared that she would carry out the struggle for India's independence through the method of nonviolence. But she has not yet decided whether she would adhere to that method for the protection of that freedom against possible foreign aggression.

To me it is a self-evident truth that, if freedom is to be shared equally by all—even physically the weakest, the lame and the halt—they must be able to contribute an equal share in its defence. How that can be possible when reliance is placed on armaments my plebian mind fails to understand. I, therefore, swear and shall continue to swear by nonviolence, i.e., by Satyagraha or soul force. In it physical incapacity is no handicap and even a frail woman or a child can pit herself or himself on equal terms against a giant, armed with the most powerful weapon. (H, 21-4-1946, p94)

My ahimsa forbids me from denying credit where it is due, even though the creditor is a believer in violence. Thus, though I did not accept Subhash Bose's belief in violence and his consequent action, I have not refrained from giving unstinted praise to his patriotism, resourcefulness and bravery. Similarly, though I did not approve of the use of arms by the Union Government for aiding the Kashmiries, and though I could not approve of Sheikh Abdullah's resort to arms, I cannot possibly withhold admiration for either for their resourceful and praiseworthy conduct, especially if both the relieving troops and the Kashmiri defenders die heroically to a man. I know that if they can do so, they will perhaps change the face of India. But if the defence is purely nonviolent in intention and action, I will not use the word 'perhaps', for I will be sure of change in the face of India even to the extent of converting to the defender's view the Union Cabinet, if not even the Pakistan Cabinet.

The nonviolent technique, I will suggest, will be no armed assistance to the defenders. Nonviolent assistance can be sent from the Union without stint. But the defenders, whether they get such assistance or not, will defy the might of the raiders or even a disciplined army in overwhelming numbers. And defenders dying at their post of duty without malice and without anger in their hearts against the assailants, and without the use of any arms including even their fists will mean an exhibition of heroism as yet unknown to history. Kashmir will then become a holy land shedding its fragrance not only throughout India, but the world. (H, 16-11-1947, p413)

THE CHOICE BEFORE INDIA

I am not pleading for India to practice nonviolence because it is weak. I want her to practice nonviolence being conscious of her strength and power. No training in arms is required for realization of her strength. We seem to need it because we seem to think that we are a lump of flesh. (YI, 11-8-1920, p3)

India has to make her choice. She may try, if she wishes, the way of war and sink lower than she has....If India can possibly gain her freedom by war, her state will be no better and will be, probably, much worse than that of France or England....

The Way of Peace

But the way of peace is open to her. Her freedom is assured if she has patience. That way will be found to be the shortest even though it may appear to be the longest to our impatient nature. The way of peace insures internal growth and stability. We reject it because we fancy that it involves submission to the will of the ruler who has imposes himself upon us. But the moment we realize that the imposition is only so called and that, through our unwillingness to suffer loss of life or property, we are party to the imposition, all we need do is to change that negative attitude of passive endorsement. The suffering to be undergone by the change will be nothing compared to the physical suffering and the moral loss we must insure in trying the way of war. And the sufferings of war harm both the parties. The sufferings in following the way of peace must benefit both. They will be like the pleasurable travail of a new birth....

The way of peace is the way of truth. Truthfulness is even more important than peacefulness. Indeed, lying is the mother of violence. A truthful man cannot long remain violent. He will perceive in the course of his search that he has no need to be violent, and he will further discover that, so long as there is the slightest trace of violence in him, he will fail to find the truth he is searching. (YI, 20-5-1926, p154)

Nonviolence is not an easy thing to understand, still less to practice, weak as we are. We must all act prayerfully and humbly and continually asking God to open the eyes of our understanding, being ever ready to act according to the light as we daily receive it. My task as a lover and promoter of peace, therefore, today consists in unflinching devotion to nonviolence in the prosecution of the campaign for regaining our liberty. And if India succeeds in so regaining our liberty. And if India succeeds in so regaining it, it will be the greatest contribution to the world peace. (YI, 7-2-1929, p46)

No Imitation of West

The fashion nowadays is to take for granted that whatever America and England are doing is good enough for us.....War has become a matter of money and resourcefulness in inventing weapons of destruction. It is no longer a matter of personal bravery or endurance. To compass the destruction of men, women and children, it might be enough for me to press a button and drop poison on them in a second.

Do we wish to copy this method of defending ourselves? Even if we do, have we the financial ability? We complain of ever-growing military expenditure. But if we would copy America or England, we would have to increase the burden tenfold....

The nation cannot be kept on the nonviolent path by violence. It must grow from within to the state it may aspire to. The question, therefore, for us to consider is, "What is our immediate aspiration?" Do we first want to copy the western nations and then, in the demand.distant future, after having gone through the agony, retrace our steps? Or do we want to strike out an original path, or rather retain what to me is our own predominantly peaceful path and there through win and assert our freedom?

Here there is no question of compromise with cowardice. Either we train and arm ourselves for destruction, be it in self-defence, and in the process train for suffering too, or we merely prepare ourselves for suffering for defending the country or delivering it from domination. In either case bravery is indispensable. In the first case personally bravery is not of such importance as in the second. In the second case, too, we shall perhaps never be able to do without violence altogether. But violence then will be subservient to nonviolence and will always be a diminishing factor in national life.

At the present moment, though the national and is nonviolence, in thought and word at least, we seem to be drifting towards violence. Impatience pervades the atmosphere. We are restrained from violence through our weakness. What is wanted is a deliberate giving up of violence out of strength. To be able to do this requires imagination coupled with a penetrating study of the world drift. Today the superficial glamour of the West dazzles us, and we mistake for progress the giddy dance which engages us from day to day. We refuse to see that it is surely leading us to death. Above all, we must recognize that to compete with the Western nations on their terms is to court suicide.

Whereas, if we realize that, notwithstanding the seeming supremacy of violence, it is the moral force that governs the universe, we should train for nonviolence with the fullest faith in its limitless possibilities. Everybody recognizes that, if a nonviolent atmosphere had been maintained in 1922, we could have completely gained our end. Even as it is, we had a striking demonstration of the efficacy of nonviolence crude though it was, and the substance of Swaraj then gained has never been lost. The paralyzing fear that had possessed the nation before the advent of Satyagraha has gone once for all. In my opinion, therefore, nonviolence is a matter of patient training. If we are to be saved and are to make a substantial contribution to the world's progress, ours must emphatically and predominantly be the way of peace. (YI, 22-8-1929, pp276-7)

Alternative to War

I feel in the innermost recesses of my heart, after a political experience extending over an unbroken period of close upon thirty-five years, that the world is sick unto death of blood-spilling. The world is seeking a way out, and I flatter myself with the belief that, perhaps, it will be the privilege of the ancient land of India to show that way out to the hungering world.

I have, therefore, no hesitation whatsoever in inviting all the great nations of the earth to give their hearty cooperation to India in her mighty struggle. (ICS, p209)

I venture to suggest, in all humility, that if India reaches her destiny through truth and nonviolence, she will have made no small contribution to the world peace for which all the nations of the earth are thirsting and she would also have, in that case, made some slight return for the help that those nations have been freely giving to her. (YI, 12-3-1931, p31)

If in the glow of freedom, India could live up to that creed [of nonviolence, non-dependence on physical force], no power on earth would ever case an evil eye upon her. This would be India's crowning glory and her contribution to the world's progress. (H, 14-4-1946, p90)

Nonviolence of the Brave

Our nonviolence has brought us to the gate of independence. Shall we renounce it after we have entered that gate? I for one am firmly convinced that nonviolence of the brave, such as I have envisaged, provides the surest ad most efficacious means to face foreign aggression and internal disorder just as it has done for winning independence.

A truly nonviolent India will have nothing to fear from any foreign power, nor will it look to British navy and air force for her defence. I know that we have not as yet the nonviolence of the brave. (H, 21-4-1946, p95)

I see clearly that, if the country cannot be turned to nonviolence, it will be bad for it and the world. It will mean goodbye to freedom. It might even mean a military dictatorship. I am day and night thinking how nonviolence of the brave can be cultivated. I said at the Asiatic Conference that I hoped the fragrance of the nonviolence of India would permeate the whole world. I often wonder if that hope will materialize. (H, 27-7-1947, p253)

India's Duty

India is now free, and the reality is now clearly revealed to me. Now that the burden of subjection has been lifted, all the forces of good have to be marshaled in one great effort to build a country which forsook the accustomed method of violence in order to settle human conflicts, whether it is between two States or between two sections of the same people. I have yet the faith that India will rise to the occasion and prove to the world that the birth of two new States will be not a menace, but a blessing to the rest of mankind. It is the duty of Free India to perfect the instrument of nonviolence for dissolving collective conflicts, if its freedom is going to be really worth while. (H, 31-8-1947, p302)

[Nonviolence] has enabled a mighty nation of forty cores to shake off the foreign yoke without bloodshed. It is the freedom of India that has brought freedom to Burma and Ceylon. A nation that has won freedom without the force of arms should be able to keep it, too, without the force of arms. This in spite of the fact that India has an army, a navy in the making and an air force, and these are being developed still further. I am convinced that, unless India develops her nonviolent strength, she has gained nothing either for herself or for the world. Militarization of India will mean her own destruction as well as the whole world. (H, 14-12-1947, p471)

INDIA AND THE NONVIOLENT WAY

While I admit my impotency regarding the spread of the ahimsa of the brave and the strong, as distinguished from that of the weak, the admission is not meant to imply that I do not know how she inestimable virtue is to be cultivated....It is truer (if it is a fact) to say that India is not ready for the lesson of the ahimsa of the strong than that no programme has been devised for the teaching. It will be perfectly just to say that the programme....for the ahimsa of the strong is not as attractive as that devised for the nonviolence of the weak has proved to be. (H, 29-6-1947, pp209-10)

Mere Passive Resistance

Passive resistance, unlike nonviolence, has no power to change men's hearts....What is to be done to convert the poison into nectar? Is the process possible? I know that it is, and I think I know the way too. But whereas the Indian mind is ready to respond to the effort at passive resistance, it is not receptive enough to imbibe the lesson of nonviolence which, and perhaps which alone, is capable of turning the poison into nectar.

Many admit that it is the way, but they have not the heart to adopt the golden path. I can proclaim from the house-top that nonviolence has not, has never failed. The people failed to rise to it.

I do not mind being told that I do not know the technique of propagating nonviolence. My critics even go so far as to suggest that I have no nonviolence in myself. God alone knows men's hearts. (H, 20-7-1947, p243)

It was not nonviolent resistance, but passive resistance which only the weak offer because they are unable, not unwilling, to offer armed resistance.

Let me make one thing clear. I have frankly and fully admitted that what we practiced during the past thirty years

If we knew the use of nonviolent resistance which only those with hearts of oak can offer, we would present to the world a totally different picture of free India instead of an India cut in twain, one part highly suspicious of the other and the two too much engaged in mutual strife to be able to think cogently of the food and clothing of the hungry and naked millions, who know no religion but that of the one and only God who appears to them in the guise of the necessaries of life. (H, 27-7-1947, p251)

....It was the passivity of the weak and not the nonviolence of the stout in heart, who will never surrender their sense of human unity and brotherhood even in the midst of conflict of interests, who will ever try to convert and not coerce their adversary.

If India can discover a way of sublimating the force violence...and turning it into constructive, peaceful ways whereby differences of interests can be liquidated, it will be a great day indeed. (H, 31-8-1947, p302)

No one has a right to say that what could not be achieved during the struggle for independence is unachievable at all times. On the contrary, today there is a real opportunity to demonstrate the supremacy of ahimsa. True, our people have been sucked into the whirlpool of universal militarization. If even a few can keep out of it, it will be their privilege to set an example of ahimsa of the brave and be reckoned as the first servants of India. This cannot be demonstrated by intellect. Therefore, till it can be realized through experience, it must be accepted in faith. (H, 1-2-1948, p6)

Police Force

Throughout my life it has been part of my creed not to avoid the police but to assist them in prying into all my work; for I have always abhorred of secrecy and it has made my life and work easy because of my indifference to this kind of surveillance. This indifference and invariable courtesy shown to the police result in the silent conversion of several amongst them.

My indifference, however, is one thing and personal to me. As a system the police surveillance cannot but be described as a despicable thing, unworthy of a good government. It is a useless burden upon an already over-burdened tax-payer. For, the whole of this extraordinary expenditure, it must be remembered, comes from the pockets of the toiling millions. (YI, 16-5-1929, p159)

Even in a nonviolent State a police force may be necessary. This, I admit, is a sign of my imperfect ahimsa. I have not the courage to declare that we can carry on without a police force, as I have in respect of an army. Of course, I can and do envisage a State where the police will not be necessary; but whether we shall succeed in realizing it the future alone will show.

The police of my conception will, however, be of a wholly different pattern from the present-day force. Its ranks will composed of believers in nonviolence. They will be servants, not masters, of the people. The people will instinctively render them every help, and through mutual cooperation they will easily deal with the ever-decreasing disturbances.

The police force will have some kind of arms, but they will be rarely used, it at all. In fact the policemen will be reformers. Their police work will be confined primarily to robbers and dacoits.

Quarrels between labour and capital and strikes will be few and far between in a nonviolent State, because the influence of the nonviolent majority will be so great as to command the respect of the principal elements in society. Similarly there will be no room for communal disturbances. (H, 1-9-1940, p265)

Under Swaraj you and I shall have a disciplined, intelligent police force that would keep order within and fight raiders from without, if by that time I or someone else does not show a better way of dealing with either. (H, 25-1-1942, p15)

Crime and Punishment

In Independent India of the nonviolent type, there will be crime but no criminals. They will not be punished. Crime is a disease like any other malady and is a product of the prevalent social system. Therefore, all crime including murder will be treated as a disease. Whether such an India will ever come into being is another question. (H, 5-5-1946, p124)

What should our jails be like in free India? All criminals should be treated as patients and the jails should be hospitals admitting this class of patients for treatment and cure. No one commits crime for the fun of it. It is a sign of a diseased mind. The causes of a particular disease should be investigated and removed. They need not have palatial buildings when their jails becomes hospitals. No country can afford that, much less can a poor country like India. But the outlook of the jail staff should be that of physicians and nurses in a hospital. The prisoners should feel that the officials are their friends. They are there to help them to regain their mental health and not to harass them in any way. The popular governments have to issue necessary orders, but meanwhile the jail staff can do not a little to humanize their administration.

What is the duty of the prisoners?....They should behave as ideal prisoners. They should avoid breach of jail discipline. They should put their heart and soul into whatever work is entrusted to them. For instance, the prisoners' food is cooked by themselves. They should clean the rice, dal or whatever cereal is used so that there are no stones and grit or weevils in them.

Whatever complaints the prisoners might have should be brought to the notice of the authorities in a becoming manner. They should so behave in their little community as to become better men when they leave the jail than when they entered it. (H, 2-11-1947, p395)

INDIA AND THE VIOLENT WAY

If India takes up the doctrine of the sword, she may gain momentary victory. Then India will cease to be the pride of my heart. I am wedded to India because I owe my all to her. I believe absolutely that she has a mission for the world. She is not to copy Europe blindly.

India's acceptance of the doctrine of the sword will be the hour of my trial. I hope I shall not be found wanting. My religion has no geographical limits. If I have a living faith in it, it will transcend my love for India herself. My life is dedicated to service of India through the religion of nonviolence.... (YI, 11-8-1920, p4)

If India makes violence her creed, and I have survived, I would not care to live in India. She will cease to evoke any pride in me. My patriotism is subservient to my religion. I cling to India like a child to its mother's breast because I feel that she gives me the spiritual nourishment I need. She has the environment that responds to my highest aspirations. When that faith is gone, I shall feel like an orphan without hope of ever finding a guardian. (YI, 6-4-1921, p108)

Unarmed Victory

This I know that, if India comes to her own demonstrably through nonviolent means, India will never want to carry a vast army, an equally grand navy and a grander air force. If her self-consciousness rises to the height necessary to give her a nonviolent victory in her fight for freedom, the world values will have changed and most of the paraphernalia of war would be found to be useless. Such an India may be a mere day-dream, a childish folly. But such, in my opinion, is undoubtedly the implication of an India becoming free through nonviolence....Hers will be the voice of a powerful nation seeking to keep under restraint all the violent forces of the world. (YI, 9-5-1929, p148)

What policy the National Government will adopt I cannot say. I may not even survive it much as I would love to. If I do, I would advise the adoption of nonviolence to the utmost extent possible and that will be India's great contribution to the peace of the world and the establishment of a new world order. I expect that, with the existence of so many martial races in India, all of whom will have a voice in the government of the day, the national policy will incline towards militarism of a modified character. I shall certainly hope that all the effort...to show the efficacy of nonviolence as a political force will not have gone in vain and a strong party representing true nonviolence will exist in the country. (H, 21-6-1942, p197)

Path of Militarization

What place will India have in the comity of nations? Will she be satisfied with being a fifth-rate power...? India will have long to wait before she can become a first-class military power. And for that she will have to go under the tutelage of some Western power. (H, 21-4-1946, p95)

....India will have to decide whether, attempting to become a military power, she would be content to become, at least for some years, a fifth-rate power in the world without a message...or whether she will, by further refining and continuing her nonviolent policy, prove herself worthy of being the first nation in the world using her hard-won freedom for the delivery of the earth from the burden [of violence] which is crushing her in spite of the so-called victory [of the Allies]. (H, 5-5-1946, p116)

A free India wedded to truth and nonviolence will teach the lesson of peace to the inhabitants of South Africa. But it will be for us and the Congress to decide whether a free India will follow the way of peace or the sword. It is bad enough tnat she small nations of the earth should denude humanity of its precious heritage; it will be awful if a sub-continent of some four hundred millions were to take to gun-powder and live dangerously. (H, 30-6-1946, pp206-7)

Will the war-weary Asiatic countries follow in the footsteps of Japan and turn to militarization? The answer lies in what direction India will throw its weight....Will a free India present the world a lesson of peace of hatred and violence of which the world is already sick unto death? (H, 8-6-1947, p177)

I am only hoping and praying [that....there] will rise a new and robust India-not warlike, basely imitating the West in all its hideousness, but a new India learning the best that the West has to give and becoming the hope not only of Asia and Africa, but the whole of aching world....

In spite, however, of the madness and the vain imitation of the tinsel of the West, the hope lingers in me and many others that India shall survive this death dance and occupy the moral height that should belong to her after the training, however imperfect, in nonviolence for an unbroken period of thirty-two years since 1915. (H, 7-12-1947, p453)

An India reduced in size but purged in spirit may still be the nursery of the nonviolence of the brave and take up the moral leadership of the world, bringing a message of hope and deliverance to the oppressed and exploited races. But an unwieldy, soul-less India will merely be an imitation, and a third-rate imitation at that, of the Western military States, utterly powerless to stand up against their onslaught. I have no desire to outlive the India of my dreams. (H, 18-1-1948, p513)

SATYAGRAHA

The Gospel of Satyagraha

Passive Resistance

Passive resistance is an all-sided sword; it can be used anyhow; it blesses him who uses it and him against whom it is used. Without drawing a drop of blood it produces far-reaching results. It never rusts and cannot be stolen. (Hs, p. 82)

I am quite sure that the stoniest heart will be melted by passive resistance...This is a sovereign and most effective remedy...It is a weapon of the purest type. It is not the weapon of the weak. It needs far greater courage to be a passive resister than a physical resister.

It is the courage of a Jesus, a Daniel, a Crammer, a Latimer and a Ridley who could go calmly to suffering and death, and the courage of a Tolstoy who dared to defy the Czars of Russia, that stands out as the greatest.

Indeed, one PERFECT resister is enough to win the battle of Right against Wrong. (YI, 10-11-1921, p. 362)

I claim...that the method of passive resistance...is the clearest and safest, because, if the cause is not true, it is the resisters and they alone who suffer.

Jesus Christ, Daniel and Socrates represented the purest form of passive resistance or soul force. All these teachers counted their bodies as nothing in comparison to their soul.

Tolstoy was the best and brightest (modern) exponent of the doctrine. He not only expounded it, but lived according to it. In India, the doctrine was understood and commonly practiced long before it came into vogue in Europe.

It is easy to see that soul force is infinitely superior to body force. If people in order to secure redress of wrongs resort to soul force, much of the present suffering will be avoided.

In any case, the wielding of the force never causes suffering to others. So that whenever it is misused, It only injures the users and not those against whom it is used. Like virtue it has its own reward. There is no such thing as failure in the use of this kind of force. (SW, p. 165)

The Buddha fearlessly carried the war into the enemy's camp and brought down on its knees an arrogant priesthood. Christ drove out the money-changers from the temple of Jerusalem and drew down curses from Heaven upon he hypocrites and the Pharisees. Both were for intensely direct action.

But even as the Buddha and Christ chastised, they showed unmistakable gentleness and love behind every act of theirs. They would not raise a finger against their enemies, but would gladly surrender themselves rather than the truth for which they lived. The Buddha would have died resisting the priesthood, if the majesty of his love had not proved to be equal to the task of bending the priesthood. Christ died on the cross with a crown of thorns on his head, defying the might of a whole empire. And if I raise resistances of a nonviolent character, I simply and humbly follow in the footsteps of the great teachers... (YI, 12-5-1920, p. 3)

Civil Disobedience

Disobedience to be civil must be sincere, respectful, restrained, never defiant, must be based upon some well-understood principle, must not be capricious and, above all, must have no ill-will or hatred behind it. (YI, 24-3-1920, p. 4)

I hold the opinion firmly that civil disobedience is the purest type of constitutional agitation. Of course, it becomes degrading and despicable, if its civil, i.e., nonviolent character is a mere camouflage. If the honesty of nonviolence be admitted, there is no warrant for condemnation even of the fiercest disobedience, because of the likehood of its leading to violence.

No big or swift movement can carried on without bold risks, and life will not be worth living if it is not attended with large risks. Does not the history of the world show that there would have been no romance in life if there had been no risks? (YI, 15-12-1921, p. 419)

Civil disobedience is the inherent right of a citizen. He dare not give it up without ceasing to be a man. Civil disobedience is never followed by anarchy. Criminal disobedience can lead to it. Every state puts down criminal disobedience by force. It perishes if it does not. (YI, 5-1-1922, p. 5). A Satyagrahi obeys the laws of society intelligently and of his own free will, because he considers it to be his sacred duty to do so. It is only when a person has thus obeyed the laws of society scrupulously that he is in a position of judge as to which particular laws are good and just and which unjust and iniquitous. Only when does the right accrue to him of civil disobedience of certain laws in well-defined circumstances. (A, p. 347)

Condition Precedent

The first indispensable condition precedent to any civil resistance is that there should be surety against any outbreak of violence, whether on the part of those who are identified with civil resistance or on the part of the general public. It would be no answer in the case of an outbreak of violence that it was instigated by the State or other agencies hostile to civil resisters.

It should be obvious that civil resistance cannot flourish in an atmosphere of violence. This does not mean that the resources of a satyagrahi have come to an end. Ways other than civil disobedience should be found out. (H, 18-3-1939, p. 53)

Character of Satyagraha

That is the beauty of Satyagraha. It comes up to oneself, one has not to go out in search for it. That is a virtue inherent in the principle itself.

A dharmayuddha, in which there are no secrete to be guarded, no scope for canning and no place for untruth, comes unsought; and a man of religion is ever ready for it. A struggle which has to be previously planned is not and it is only when the Satyagrahi feels quite helpless, is apparently on his last legs and finds utter darkness all around him, that God comes to the rescue. (SSA, p. xiv)

In the application of Satyagraha, I discovered, in the earliest stages, that pursuit of Truth did not admit of violence being inflicted on one's opponent, but that he must be weaned from error by patience and sympathy. For, what appears to be truth to the one may appear to be error to the other. And patience means self-suffering. So the doctrine came to mean vindication of Truth, not by infliction of suffering on the opponent but one's own self. (RCPS)

Satyagraha and its off-shoots, noncooperation and civil resistance, are nothing but new names for the law of suffering. (YI, 11-8-1920, p. 3)

With satya combined with ahimsa, you can bring the world to your feet. Satyagraha in its essence is nothing but the introduction of truth and gentleness in the political, i.e., the national, life. (YI, 10-3-1920, p. 3)

Satyagraha is utter self-effacement, greatest humiliation, greatest patience and brightest faith. It is its own reward. (YI, 26-2-1925, p. 73)

Satyagraha is a relentless search for truth and a determination to reach truth. (YI, 19-3-1925, p. 95)

It is a force that works silently and apparently slowly. In reality, there is no force in the world that is so direct or so swift in working. (YI, 4-6-1925, p. 189)

The word Satyagraha is often most loosely used and is made to cover veiled violence. But, as the author of the word, I may be allowed to say that it excludes every form of violence, direct or indirect, veiled or unveiled, and whether in thought, word or deed. It is breach of Satyagraha to with ill to an opponent or to say a harsh word to him or of him with the intention of harming him... Satyagraha is gentle, it never wounds. It must not be the result of anger or malice. It is never fussy, never impatient, never vociferous. It is the direct opposite of compulsion. It was conceived as a complete substitute for violence. (H, 15-4-1933, p. 8)

The fight of Satyagraha is for the strong in spirit, not the doubter or the timid. Satyagraha teaches us the art of living as well as dying. Birth and death are inevitable among mortals. What distinguishes the man from the brute is his conscious striving to realize the spirit within. (H, 7-4-1946, p. 74)

Evolving Science

I am myself daily growing in the knowledge of Satyagraha. I have no text-book to consult in time of need, not even the Gita which I have called my dictionary. Satyagraha as conceived by me is a science may prove to be no science at all and well prove to be the musings and doings of a fool, if not a madman.

It may be that what is true in Satyagraha is as ancient as the hills. But it has not yet been acknowledged to be of any value in the solution of world problems or, rather, the one supreme problem or war. It may be that what is claimed to be new in it will prove to be really of no value in terms of that supreme problem. It may be that what are claimed to be victories of Satyagraha i.e., ahimsa, were really victories not of truth and nonviolence but of fear of violence. These possibilities have always been in front of me. I am helpless. All I present to the nation for adoption is an answer to prayer or, which is the same thing, constantly waiting on God. (H, 24-9-1938, p. 266)

The Technique of Satyagraha

Not to yield your soul to the conqueror means that you will refuse to do that which your conscience forbids you to do. Suppose the 'enemy' were to ask you to rub your nose on the ground or to pull your ears or to go through such humiliating performances, you would not submit to any of these humiliations. But if he robs you of your possessions, you will yield them because, as a votary of ahimsa, you have from the beginning decided that earthly possessions have nothing to do with your soul. That which you look upon as your own you may keep only so long as the world allows you to own it.

Not to yield your mind means that you will not give way to any temptation. Man is oftentimes weak-minded enough to be caught in the snare of greed and honeyed words. We see this happening daily in our social life. A weak-minded man can never be a Satyagrahi. The latter's 'no' is invariably a 'no' and his 'yes' an eternal 'yes'. Such a man alone has the strength to be a devotee of truth and ahimsa. But here one must know the difference between steadfastness and obstinacy. If, after having said 'yes' or 'no', one finds out that the decision was wrong and in spite of that knowledge clings to it, that is obstinacy and folly. It is necessary to think things out carefully and thoroughly before coming to any decision.

The meaning of refusal to own allegiance is clear. You will not bow to the supremacy of the victor, you will not help him to attain his object. Herr Hitler has never dreamt of possessing Britain. He wants the British to admit defeat. The victor can then demand anything he likes from the vanquished, and the latter has perforce to yield. But if defeat is not admitted, the enemy will fight until he has killed his opponent. A Satyagrahi, however, is dead to his body even before the enemy attempts to kill him, i.e., he is free from attachment to his body ana only lives in the victory of the soul.

Therefore, when he is already thus dead, why would be yearn to kill anyone? To die in the act of killing is in essence to die defeated. Because, if the enemy is unable to get it after killing you. If, on the other hand, he realizes that you have not the remotest thought in your mind of raising your hand against him even for the sake of your life, he will lack the zest to kill you. Every hunter has had this experience. No one has ever heard of anyone hunting cows. (H, 18-8-1940, pp. 253-4)

Power of Suffering

The hardest heart and the grossest ignorance must disappear before the rising sun of suffering without anger and without malice. (YI, 19-2-1925, p. 61)

Suffering has its well-defined limits. Suffering can be both wise and unwise, and when the limit is reached, to prolong it would be not unwise but the height of folly. (YI, 12-3-1931, p. 30)

True suffering does not know itself and never calculates. It brings its own joy which surpasses all other joys. (YI, 19-3-1931, p. 41)

The conviction has been growing upon me that things of fundamental importance to the people are not secured by reason alone, but have to be purchased with their suffering. Suffering is the law of human beings; war is the law of the jungle. But suffering is infinitely more powerful than the law of the jungle for converting the opponent and opening his ears, which are otherwise shut, to the voice of reason. (YI, 5-11-1931, p. 341)

Code of Satyagraha

A Satyagrahi bids good-bye to fear. He is therefore, never afraid of trusting the opponent. Even if the opponent plays him false twenty times, the Satyagrahi is ready to trust him the twenty-first time, for an implicit trust in human nature is the very essence of his creed. (SSA, p. 159)

A Satyagrahi is nothing if not instinctively law-abiding, and it is his law-abiding nature which exacts from him implicit obedience to the highest law, that is the voice of conscience which overrides all other laws. (SW, p. 465)

Since Satyagraha is one of the most powerful methods of direct action, a Satyagrahi exhausts all other means before he resorts to Satyagraha. He will, therefore, constantly and continually approach the constituted authority, he will appeal to public opinion, educate public opinion, state his case calmly and coolly before everybody who wants to listen to him, and only after he has exhausted all these avenues will he resort to Satyagraha. But when he has found the impelling call of the inner voice within him and launches out upon Satyagraha, he has burnt his boats and there is no receding. (YI, 20-10-1927, p. 353)

The Satyagrahi, whilst he is ever ready for fight, must be equally eager for peace. He must welcome any honourable opportunity for peace. (YI, 19-3-1931, p. 40)

My advice is Satyagraha first and Satyagraha last. There is no other or better road to freedom. (H, 15-9-1946, p. 312)

In the code of the Satyagrahi there is no such thing as surrender to brute force. Or the surrender then is the surrender of suffering and not to the wielder of the bayonet. (YI, 30-4-1931, p. 93)

As a Satyagrahi I must always allow my cards to be examined and re-examined at all times and make reparation if an error is discovered. (H, 11-3-1939, p. 44)

Qualifications of a Satyagrahi

...The following qualifications....I hold are essential for every Satyagrahi in India:

He must have a living faith in God, for He is his only Rock

He must believe in truth and nonviolence as his creed and, therefore, have faith in the inherent goodness of human nature which he expects to evoke by his truth and love expressed through his suffering.

He must be leading a chaste life and be ready and willing, for the sake of his cause, to give up his life and his possessions.

He must be a habitual Khadi-wearer and spinner. This is essential for India.

He must be a teetotaler and be free from the use of other intoxicants in order that his reason may be always unclouded and his mind constant.

He must carry out with a willing heart all the rules or discipline as may be laid down from time to time.

He should carry out the jail rules unless they are specially devised to hurt his self-respect.

The qualifications are not to be regarded as exhaustive. They are illustrative only. (H, 25-3-1939, p. 64)

A Satyagrahi may not even ascend to heaven on the wings of Satan. (H, 15-4-1939, p. 86)

In Satyagraha there is no place for fraud or falsehood, or any kind of untruth. (BC, 9-8-1942)

A Satyagrahi never misses, can never miss, a chance of compromise on honourable terms, it being always assumed that, in the event of failure, he is ever ready to offer battle. He needs no previous preparation, his cards are always on the table. (YI, 16-4-1931, p. 77)

It is often forgotten that it is never the intention of a Satyagrahi to embarrass the wrongdoer. The appeal is never to his fear; it is, must, always to his heart. The Satyagrahi's object is to convert, not to coerce, the wrongdoer. He should avoid artificiality in all his doings. He acts naturally and from inward conviction. (H, 25-3-1939, p. 64)

Satyagraha is essentially a weapon of the truthful. A Satyagrahi is pledged to nonviolence and, unless people observe it in thought, word and deed, I cannot offer Satyagraha. (A, p. 345)

I have always held that it is only when one sees one's own mistakes with a convex lens, and does just the reverse in the case others, that one is able to arrive at a just relative estimate of the two. I further believe that a scrupulous and conscientious observance of this rule is necessary for one who wants to be a Satyagrahi. (ibid, p. 346)

A Satyagrahi relies upon God for protection against the tyranny of brute force... (H, 7-4-1946, p. 73)

No confirmed Satyagrahi is dismayed by the dangers, seen or unseen, from his opponent's side. What he must fear, as every army must, is the danger from within. (H, 14-7-1946, p. 220)

Satyagraha and Repression

Repression itself affords a training in Satyagraha, even as an unsought war affords a training for the soldier. Satyagrahis should discover the causes repression. They will find that repressed people are easily frightened by the slightest show of force and are unprepared for suffering and self-sacrifice. This is then the time for learning the first lessons of Satyagraha.

Those who know anything of this matchless force should teach their neighbours to bear repression not weakly and helplessly, but bravely and knowingly.....

And yet they [the unexciting rules of preparation] are much the most important part of Satyagraha training.

Potent and active nonviolence cannot be cultivated unless the candidate goes through the necessary stages which require a lot of plodding. (H, 8-4-1939, p. 80)

POWER OF SATYAGRAHA

Victory of Satyagraha

A clear victory of Satyagraha is impossible so long as there is ill-will. But those who believe themselves to be weak are incapable of loving. Let, then, our first act every morning be to make the following resolve for the day: 'I shall not fear any one on earth. I shall fear God only; I shall not bear ill-will towards any one. I shall not submit to injustice from any one.

I shall conquer untruth by truth and in resisting untruth I shall put up with all suffering. (SL NO. 14, 4-5-1919)

There is no time-limit for a Satyagrahi nor is there a limit to his capacity for suffering. Hence there is no such thing as defeat in Satyagraha. (YI, 19-2-1925, p.61)

It is not because I value life low that I countenance with joy thousands voluntarily losing their lives for Satyagraha, but because I know that it results, in the long run, in the least loss of life and, what is more, it ennobles those who lose their lives and morally enriches the world for their sacrifice. (YI, 8-10-1925, p. 345)

And when once it is set in motion, its effect, if it is intensive enough, can overtake the whole universe. It is the greatest force because it is the highest expression of the soul. (YI, 23-9-1926, p. 332)

My experience has taught me that a law of progression applies to every righteous struggle. But in the case of Satyagraha the law amounts to an axiom. As a Satyagraha struggle progresses onward, many another element helps to swell its current and there is a constant growth in the results to which it leads. This is really inevitable, and is bound up with the first principles of Satyagraha.

For in Satyagraha the mininum is also the maximum, and as it is the irreducible minimum, there is no question of retreat, and the only movement possible is an advance. In other struggles, even when they are righteous, the demand is first pitched a little higher so as to admit of future reduction, and hence the law of progression does not apply to all of them without exception. (S, p. 319)

To me it is one of the most active forces in the world, It is like the sun that rises upon us unfailingly from day to day. Only if we would but understand it, it is infinitely greater than a million suns put together. It radiates life and light and peace and happiness. (YI, 18-4-1929, p. 126)

One True Satyagrahi

If a single Satyagrahi holds out to the end, victory is certain. (SSA, p. xiv)

Self-sacrifice of one innocent man is a million times more potent than the sacrifice of a million men who die in the act of killing others. The willing sacrificed of the innocent is the most powerful retort to insolent tyranny that has yet been conceived by God or man. (YI, 12-2-1925, p. 60)

I have maintained that, even if there is one individual who is almost completely nonviolent, he can put out the conflagration...In this age of democracy, it is essential that desired results are achieved by the collective effort of the people. It will no doubt be good to achieve an objective through the effort of a supremely powerful individual, but it can never make the community conscious of its corporate strength. (H, 8-9-1940, p. 277)

I believe in walking alone. I came alone in this world, I have walked alone in the valley of the shadow of death and I shall quit alone when the time comes. I know I am quite capable of launching Satyagraha even if I am all alone. I have done so before. (YI, 21-7-1946, p. 227)

Application of Satyagraha

It is a force that may be used by individuals as well as by communities. It may be used as well in political as in domestic affairs. Its universal applicability is a demonstration of its permanence and invincibility. It can be used alike by men, women and children.

It is totally untrue to say that it is a force to be used only by the weak so long as they are not capable of meeting violence by violence....

This force is to violence and, therefore, to all tyranny, all injustice, what light is to darkness. In politics, its use is based upon the immutable maxim that government of the people is possible only so long as they consent either consciously or unconsciously to be governed. (YI, 3-11-1927, 369)

I have never claimed to be the one original Satyagrahi. What I have claimed is the application of that doctrine on an almost universal scale, and it yet remains to be seen and demonstrated that it is a doctrine which is capable of assimilation by thousands upon thousands of peoples in all ages and climes. (YI, 22-9-1927, p. 317)

The Nonviolent Sanction

Satyagraha is a law of universal application. Beginning with the family, its use can be extended to every other circle.

Supposing a landowner exploits his tenants and mulcts them of the fruit of their toil by appropriating it to his own use. When they expostulate with him he does not listen and raises objections that he requires so much for his wife, so much for his children and so on. The tenants or those who have espoused their cause and have influence will make an appeal to his wife to expostulate with her husband. She would probably say that for herself she does not need his exploited money. The children will say likewise that they would earn for themselves what they need.

Supposing further that he listens to nobody or that his wife and children combine against the tenants, they will not submit. They will quit if asked to do so, but they will make it clear that the land himself and he will have to give in to their just demands.

It may, however, be that the tenants are replaced by others. Agitation short of violence will then continue till the replacing tenants see their error and make common cause with the evicted tenants.

Thus Satyagraha is a process of educating public opinion, such that it covers all elements of society and in the end makes itself irresistible. Violence interrupts the process and prolongs the real revolution of the whole social structure.

The conditions necessary for the success of Satyagraha are: (1) The Satyagrahi should not have any hatred in his heart against the opponent. (2) The issue must be true and substantial. (3) The Satyagrahi must be prepared to suffer till the end for his cause. (H, 31-3-1946, p. 64)

Training for Self-defence

I believe that every man and woman should learn the art of self-defence in this age. This is done through arms in the

West. Every adult man is conscripted for army training for a definite period. The training for Satyagraha is meant for all, irrespective of age or sex. The more important part of the training here is mental, not physical. There can be no compulsion in mental training. The surrounding atmosphere no doubt acts on the mind, but that cannot justify compulsion...

Satyagraha is always superior to armed resistance. This can only be effectively proved by demonstration, not by argument. It is the weapon that adorns the strong. It can never adorn the weak. By weak is meant the weak in mind and spirit, not in body. That limitation is a quality to be prized and not defect to be deplored.

One ought also to understand one of its other limitations. It can never be used to defend a wrong cause.

Satyagraha brigades can be organized in every village and in every block of buildings in the cities. Each brigade should be composed of those persons who are well-known to the organizers. In this respect Satyagraha differs from armed defence. For the latter the State impresses the service of everybody. For a Satyagraha brigade only those are eligible who believe in ahimsa and satya. Therefore, an intimate knowledge of the persons enlisted is necessary for the organizers. (H, 17-3-1946, pp. 45-46)

Duragraha

I can see nothing but catastrophe for India from methods of violence. Workmen would be committing suicide and India would have to suffer indescribable misery if workingmen were to vent their anger by criminal disobedience of the laws of the land....

When I began to preach Satyagraha and civil disobedience, it was never meant to cover criminal disobedience. My experience teaches me that truth can never be propagated by doing violence.

Those who believe in the justice of their cause need to possess boundless patience, and those alone are fit to offer civil disobedience who are above committing criminal disobedience or doing violence.

A man cannot commit both civil and criminal disobedience at the same time, even as he cannot be both temperate and furious at the same time, and just as self-restraint is acquired only after one has been able to master his passions, so is the capacity for civil disobedience acquired after one has disciplined oneself in complete and voluntary obedience of the laws of the land.

Again, just as he alone can be said to be proof against temptations who, having been exposed to them, has succeeded in resisting them, so may we be said to have conquered anger when, having sufficient cause for it, we have succeeded in controlling ourselves. (YI, 28-4-1920, pp. 7-8)

Some students have revived the ancient form of barbarity in the form of 'sitting dhurna'...I call it 'barbarity' for it is a crude way of using coercion. It is also cowardly, because one who sits dhurna knows that he is not going to be trampled over. It is difficult to call the practice violent, but it is certainly worse.

If we fight our opponent, we at least enable him to return the blow. But when we challenge him to walk over us, knowing that he will not, we place him in a most awkward and humiliating position. I know that the over-zealous students who sat dhurna never thought of the barbarity of the deed. But one who is expected to follow the voice of conscience and stand even single-handed in the face of odds cannot afford to be thoughtless.

There must be no impatience, no barbarity, no insolence, no undue pressure. If we want to cultivate a true spirit of democracy, we cannot afford to be intolerant. Intolerance betrays want of faith in one's cause. (YI, 2-2-1921, p. 33)

I have not been able to understand the cause of so much excitement and disturbance that followed my detention. It is not Satyagraha. It is worse than Durgraha.

Those who join Satyagraha demonstrations were bound one and all to refrain at all hazard from violence, not to throw stones or in anyway whatever to injure anybody. But in Bombay we have been throwing stones. We have obstructed tram-cars by putting obstacles in the way. This is not Satyagraha. We have demanded the release of about 50 men who had been arrested for deeds of violence. Our duty is chiefly to get ourselves arrested. It is breach of religious duty to endeavour to secure the release of those who have committed deeds of violence. (SW, p. 474)

I have said times without number that Satyagraha admits of no violence, no pillage, no incendiarism; and still, in the name of Satyagraha, we have burnt buildings, forcibly captured weapons, extorted money, stopped trains, cut off telegraph wires, killed innocent people and plundered shops and private houses. If deeds such as these could save me from the prison-house or the scaffold, I should not like to be so saved. (ibid, p. 476). ....Heroism and sacrifice in a bad cause are so much waste of splendid energy and hurt the good cause by drawing away attention from it by the glamour of the misused heroism and sacrifice in a bad cause. (YI, 12-12-1925, p. 60)

....Indiscriminate resistance to authority must lead to lawlessness and unbridled license and consequent self-destruction. (YI, 2-4-1931, p. 58)

NON-COOPERATION

Non-co-operations is an attempt to awaken the masses to a sense of their dignity and power. This can only be by enabling them to realize that they need not fear brute force if they would but know the soul within. (YI, 1-12-1920, p. 3)

Noncooperation is a protest against an unwitting and unwilling participation in evil....Non-cooperation with evil is as much a duty as cooperation with good. (YI, 1-6-1921, p. 172)

Noncooperation is not a passive state, it is an intensively active state, more active than physical resistance or violence. Passive resistance is a misnomer. Noncooperation in the sense used by me must be nonviolent and therefore, neither punitive nor based on malice, ill-will or hatred. (YI, 25-8-1920, p. 322)

Religious Basis

I venture to submit that the Bhagvad Gita is a gospel of noncooperation between the forces of darkness and those of light. If it is to be literally interpreted, Arjuna representing a just cause was enjoined to engage in bloody warfare with the unjust Kauravas.

Tulasidas advises the sant (the good) to shun the asant (the evil doers).

The Zend Avesta represents a perpetual duel between Ormuzd and Ahriman, between whom there is no compromise. To say of the Bible that it taboos noncooperation is not to know Jesus, a prince among passive resisters, who uncompromisingly challenged the might of the Sadducees and the Pharisees and, for the sake of truth, did not hesitate to divide sons from their parents.

And what did the Prophet of Islam do? He non-co-operated in Mecca in a most active manner so long as his life was not in danger, and wiped the dust of Mecca off his faith when he found that he and his followers might have uselessly to perish, and fled to Medina and returned when he was strong enough to give battle to his opponents.

The duty of noncooperation with unjust men and kings is as strictly enjoined by all the religions as is the duty of cooperation with just men and kings. Indeed, most of the scriptures of the world seem even to go beyond noncooperation and prefer violence to effeminate submission to a wrong. The Hindu religious tradition.....clearly proves the duty of noncooperation. Prahlad dissociated from his father, Meerabai from her husband, Bibhishan from his brutal brother. (YI, 4-8-1920, p. 4)

Basic Principle

The basic principle on which the practice of nonviolence rests is that what holds good in respect of oneself equally applies to the whole Universe. All mankind in essence are alike. What is therefore possible for me, is possible for everybody....

This is essence is the principle of nonviolent noncooperation. It follows therefore that it must have its root in love. Its object should not be to punish the opponent or to inflict injury upon him. Even while non-co-operating with him, we must make him feel that in us he has a friend and we should try to reach his heart by rendering him humanitarian service whenever possible.

In fact, it is the acid test of nonviolence that in a nonviolent conflict there is no rancour left behind and, in the end, the enemies are converted into friends. That was my experience in South Africa with General Smuts. He started with being my bitterest opponent and critic. Today he is my warmest friend.....

Enduring Quality

Times change and systems decay. But it is my faith that, in the result, it is only nonviolence and things that are based on nonviolence that will endure. Nineteen hundred years ago Christianity was born. The ministry of Jesus lasted for only three brief years. His teaching was misunderstood even during his own time and today Christianity is a denial of his central teaching [: "Love your enemy." But what are nineteen hundred years for the spread of the central doctrine of a man's teaching?]

Six centuries rolled by and Islam appeared on the scene. Many Musalmans will not even allow me to say that Islam, as the word implies, it unadulterated peace. My reading of the Koran has convinced me that the basis of Islam is not violence.

But, here again, thirteen hundred years are but a speck in the cycle of Time. I am convinced that both these great faiths will life only to the extent that their followers imbibe the central teaching of nonviolence. But it is not a thing to be grasped through mere intellect, it must sink into our hearts. (H, 12-11-1938, p. 327)

Although noncooperation is one of the main weapons in the armoury of Satyagraha, it should not be forgotten that it is after all only a means to secure the cooperation of the opponent consistently with truth and justice. The essence of nonviolent technique is that it seeks to liquidate antagonisms but not the antagonists themselves. In nonviolent fight you have, to a certain measure, to conform to the tradition and conventions to the system you are pitted against. Avoidance of all relationship with the opposing power, therefore, can never be a Satyagrahi's object, but transformation or purification of that relationship. (H, 29-4-1939, p. 101)

Ethics of Noncooperation

I consider noncooperation to be such a powerful and pure instrument that, if it is enforced in an earnest spirit, it will be like seeking first the Kingdom of God and everything else following as a matter of course. People will then have realized their true power. They would have learnt that value of discipline, self-control, joint action, nonviolence, organization and everything else that goes to make a nation great and good, and not merely great. (YI, 2-6-1920, p. 3). There is no instrument so clean, so harmless and yet so effective as noncooperation. Judiciously handled, it need not produce any evil consequences. And its intensity will depend purely on the capacity of the people for sacrifice. (YI, 30-6-1920, p. 3)

We had lost the power of saying 'no'. It had become disloyal, almost sacrilegious to say 'no' to the Government. This deliberate refusal to co-operate is like the necessary weeding process that a cultivator has to resort to before he sows. Weeding is as necessary to agriculture as sowing. Indeed, even whilst the crops are growing, the weeding fork, as every husbandman knows, is an instrument almost to daily use.

The nation's noncooperation is an invitation to the Government to co-operate with it on its own terms, as is every nation's right and every good government's duty. Noncooperation is the nation's notice that it is no longer satisfied to be in tutelage. (YI, 1-6-1921, p. 173). The movement of nonviolent noncooperation has nothing in common with the historical struggles for freedom in the west. It is not based on brute force or hatred. It does not aim at destroying the tyrant. It is a movement of self-purification. It therefore seeks to convert the tyrant. It may fail because India was not ready for mass nonviolence. But it would be wrong to judge the movement by false standards. My own opinion is that the movement has in no wise failed. It has found an abiding place in India's struggle for freedom. (YI, 11-2-1926, 59)

A Duty

At times noncooperation becomes as much a duty as cooperation. No one is bound to co-operate in one's own undoing or slavery. Freedom received through the effort of others, however benevolent, cannot be retained when such effort is withdrawn. In other words, such freedom is not real freedom. But the lowliest can feel its glow as soon as they learn the art of attaining it through nonviolent no-co-operation....

I am quite sure that nonviolent noncooperation can secure what violence never can, and this by ultimate conversion of the wrong-doers. We in India have never given nonviolence the trial it has deserved. The marvel is that we have attained so much even with our mixed nonviolence. (YI, 20-4-1920, p. 97)

I have presented noncooperation in terms of religion, because I enter politics only in so far as it develops the religious faculty in me. (YI, 19-1-1921, p. 19)

Behind my noncooperation there is always the keenest desire to co-operate on the slightest pretext even with the worst of opponents. To me, a very imperfect moral, ever in need of God's grace, no one is beyond redemption. (YI, 4-6-1925, p, 193)

....Nothing crooked will have countenance from me. For me, the law of Satyagraha, the law of love, is an eternal principle. I co-operate with all that is good. I desire to non-co-operate with all that is evil... (YI, 18-6-1925, p. 213)

No Hatred

By a long course of prayerful discipline, I have ceased for over forty years to hate anybody. I know that this is a big claim. Nevertheless, I make it in all humility. But I can and I do hate evil wherever it exists.

My noncooperation has its root not in hatred, but in love. My personal religion peremptorily forbids me to hate anybody. I learnt this simple yet grand doctrine when I was twelve years old through a school book, and the conviction has persisted up to now. It is daily growing on me. It is a burning passion with me. (YI, 6-8-1925, p. 272)

It is not that I harbour disloyalty towards anything whatsoever, but I do so against all untruth, all that is unjust, all that is evil.....I remain loyal to an institution so long as that institution conduces to my growth, to the growth of the nation.

Immediately I find that the institution, instead of conducing to its growth, impedes it, I hold it to be my bounden duty to be disloyal to it. (YI, 13-8-1925, p. 277)

My noncooperation, though it is part of my creed, is a prelude to cooperation. My noncooperation is with methods and systems, never with men. I may not harbour ill-will even against a Dyer. I regard ill-will as beneath the dignity of man. (YI, 12-9-1929, p. 300)

Some have called me the greatest revolutionary of my time. It may be false, but I believe myself to be a revolutionary, a nonviolent revolutionary. My means are noncooperation. No person can amass wealth without the cooperation, willing or forced, of the people concerned. (YI, 26-11-1931, p. 369)

I am by instinct a co-operator; my very noncooperation is intended to purge cooperation of all meanness and falsity, for I hold such so-operation is not worth the name. (EF, p. 84)

FASTING AND SATYAGRAHA

Weapon of Satyagraha

Fasting is a potent weapon in the Satyagraha armoury. It cannot be taken by every one. Mere physical capacity to take it is no qualification for it. It is of no use without a living faith in God. It should never be a mechanical effort or a mere limitation. It must come from the depth of one's soul. It is, therefore, always rare. (H, 18-3-1939, p. 56)

There can be no room for selfishness, anger, lack of faith or impatience in a pure fast....Infinite patience, firm resolve, single-mindedness of purpose, perfect calm, and no anger must of necessity be there. But since it is impossible for a person to develop all these qualities all at once, no one who has not devoted himself to following the laws of ahimsa should undertake a Satyagrahi fast. (H, 13-10-1940, p. 322)

[Fasting] is...fierce and not altogether free from danger. I myself have before condemned fasting when it seemed to me to be wrong or morally unjustified. But to shirk a fast where there is a clear moral indication is a dereliction of duty. Such a fast has to be based on unadulterated truth and ahimsa. (H, 28-7-1946, p. 235)

Fasting and Death

Fasting unto death is the last and the most potent weapon in the armoury of Satyagraha. It is a sacred thing. But it must be accepted with all its implication. It is not the fast itself, but what it implies that matters. (H, 18-8-1846, p. 262)

Fasting and the Way of Christ

Fasting cannot be undertaken mechanically. It is a powerful thing but a dangerous thing, if handled amateurishly. It requires complete self-purification, much more than what is required in facing death with retaliation even in mind. One such act of perfect sacrifice would suffice for the whole world. Such is held to be Jesus' example. (H, 27-10-1946, p. 272)

Of course, it is not to be denied that fasts can be really coercive. Such are fasts to attain a selfish object. A fast undertaken to wring money from a person or for fulfilling some such personal end would amount to the exercise of coercion or undue influence. I would unhesitatingly advocate resistance of such undue influence. I have myself successfully resisted it in the fasts that have been undertaken or threatened against me.

And if it is argued that the dividing line between a selfish and unselfish end is often very thin, I would urge that a person who regards the end of a fast to be selfish or otherwise base should resolutely refuse to yield to it, even though the refusal may result in the death of the fasting person.

If people will cultivate the habit of disregarding fasts which, in their opinion, are taken for unworthy ends, such fasts will be robbed of the taint of coercion and undue influence. Like all human institutions, fasting can be both legitimately and illegitimately used. (H, 9-9-1931, p. 5)

If a man, however popular and great he may be, takes up an improper cause and fasts in defence of the impropriety, it is the duty of his friends (among whom I count myself), fellow-workers and relatives to let him die rather than that an improper cause should triumph so that he may live. Fairest means cease to be fair when the end sought is unfair. (H, 17-3-1946, p. 43)

Last Resort

One general principle, however, I would like to enunciate: A Satyagrahi should fast only as a last resort when all other avenues of redress have been explored and have failed. There is no room for imitation in fasts. He who has no inner strength should not dream of it, and never with attachment to success.

But if a Satyagrahi once undertakes a fast from conviction, he must stick to his resolve whether there is a chance of his action bearing fruit or not. This does not mean that fasting cannot or can bear fruit. He who fasts in the expectation of fruit generally fails. And even if he does not seemingly fail, he loses all the inner joy which a true fast holds...

Ridiculous fasts spread like plague and are harmful. But, when fasting becomes a duty, it cannot be given up. Therefore, I do fast when I consider it to be necessary and cannot abstain from it on any score. What I do myself I cannot abstain from it on any score. What I do myself I cannot prevent others from doing under similar circumstances. It is common knowledge that the best of good things are often abused. We see this happening every day. (H, 21-4-1946, p. 93)

...When human ingenuity fails, the votary fasts. This fasting quickens the spirit of prayer, that is to say, the fasting is a spiritual act, and therefore, addressed to God. The effect of such action on the life of the people is that, where the person fasting is at all known to them, their sleeping conscience is awakened. But there is the danger that the people through mistaken sympathy may act against their will in order to save the life of the loved one. This danger has got to be faced. One ought not to be deterred from right action when one is sure of the rightness. It can best promote circumspection. Such a fast is undertaken in obedience to the dictates of the inner voice and, therefore, prevents haste. (H, 21-12-1947, p. 476)

NON-POSSESSION

The Gospel of Non-Possession

Key to Service: When I found myself drawn into the political coil, I asked myself what was necessary for me in order to remain absolute untouched by immorality, by untruth, by what is known as political gain... it was a difficult struggle in the beginning and it was wrestle with my wife and-as I can vividly recall-with my children also. But be that as it may, I came definitely to the conclusion that, if I had to serve the people in whose midst my life was cast and of whose difficulties I was a witness from day to day, I must discard all wealth, all possession....

I cannot tell you with truth that, when this belief came to me, I discarded everything immediately. I must confess to you that progress at first was slow. And now, as I recall those days of struggle, I remember that it was also painful in the beginning. But, as days went by, I saw that I had to throw overboard many other things which I used to consider as mine, and a time came when it became a matter of positive joy to give up those things. And one after another, then, by almost geometric progression, the things slipped away from me.

And, as I am describing my experiences, I can say a great burden fell off my shoulders, and I felt that I could now walk with ease and do my work also in the service of my fellow-men with great comfort and still greater joy. The possession of anything then became a troublesome thing and a burden.

Exploring the cause of that joy, I found that, If I kept anything as my own, I had to defend it against the whole world. I found also that there were many people who did not have the thing, although they wanted it; and I would have to seek police assistance also if hungry, famine-stricken people, finding me in a lonely place, wanted not merely to divide the thing with me but to dispossess me. And I said to myself, if they want it and would take it, they do so not from any malicious motive, but they would do it because theirs was a greater need than mine. (SW, pp. 1066-7)

It is open to the world...to laugh at my dispossessing myself of all property. For me the dispossession has been a positive gain. I would like people to complete with me in my contentment. It is the richest treasure I own. Hence it is perhaps right to say that, though I preach poverty, I am a rich man! (YI, 30-4-1925, p. 149)

Voluntary Self-denial

Our civilization, our culture, our Swaraj depend not upon multiplying our wants—self-indulgence, but upon restricting our wants—self-denial. (YI, 23-2-1921, p. 59)

Non-possession is allied to non-stealing. A thing not originally stolen must nevertheless be classified as stolen property, if we possess it without needing it. Possession implies provision for the future. A seeker after Truth, a follower of the law of Love, cannot hold anything against tomorrow. God never stores for the morrow. He never creates more than what is strictly needed for the moment. If, therefore, we repose faith in His Providence, we should rest assured that He will give us every day our daily bread, meaning everything that we require....

Our ignorance or negligence of the Divine Law, which gives to man from day to day his daily bread and no more, has given rise to inequalities with all the miseries attendant upon them. The rich have superfluous store of things which they do not need and which are, therefore, neglected and wasted, while millions are starved to death for want of sustenance. If each retained possession of only what he needed, no one would be in want, and all would live in contentment. As it is, the rich are discontented no less than the poor. The poor man would fain become a millionaire, and the millionaire a multi-millionaire.

The rich should take the initiative in dispossession with a view to a universal diffusion of the spirit of contentment. If only they keep their own property within moderate limits, the starving will be easily fed, and will learn the lesson of contentment along with the rich. Perfect fulfilment of the ideal of non-possession requires that man should, like the birds, have no roof over his head, no clothing and no stock of food for the morrow. He will indeed need his daily bread, but it will be God's business, and not his, to provide it. Only the fewest possible, if any at all, can reach this ideal. We ordinary seekers may not be repelled by the seeming impossibility. But we must keep the ideal constantly in view, and in the light thereof, critically examine our possessions and try to reduce them.

Civilization, in the real sense of the term, consists not in the multiplication, but in the deliberate and voluntary reduction of wants. This alone promotes real happiness and contentment, and increases the capacity for service.

From the standpoint of pure truth, the body too is a possession. It has been truly said that desire for enjoyment creates bodies for the soul. When this desire vanishes, there remains no further need for the body, and man is free from the vicious cycle of births and deaths. The soul is omnipresent; why should she care to be confined within the cage-like body, or do evil and even kill for the sake of the cage?

Ideal of Renunciation

We thus arrive at the ideal of total renunciation, and learn to use the body for the purpose of service so long as it exists, so much so that service and not bread becomes with us the staff of life. We eat and drink, sleep and wake for service alone. Such an attitude of mind brings us real happiness, and the beatific vision in the fullness of time. Let us all examine ourselves from this standpoint.

Needless to say, this is not a plea for inertia. Every moment of our life should be filled with mental or physical activity, but that activity should be sattvika, tending to truth. One who has consecrated his life to service learn to distinguish between good activity and evil activity. This discernment goes naturally with a single-minded devotion to service. (FYM, pp. 23-6)

Moral Purpose

Why should all of us possess property? Why should not we, after a certain time, dispossess ourselves of all property? Unscrupulous merchants do this for dishonest purpose. Why may we not do it for a moral and a great purpose?

For a Hindu it was the usual thing at a certain stage. Every good Hindu is expected, after having lived the household life for a certain period, to enter upon a life of non-possession of property. Why may we not revive the noble tradition? In effect it merely amounts to this that for maintenance we place ourselves at the mercy of those to whom we transfer our property. To me the idea is attractive. In the innumerable cases of such honourable trust there is hardly one case in a million of abuse of trust.

...How such a practice can be worked without giving handle to dishonest persons can only be determined after long experimenting. No one, however, need be deterred from trying the experiment for fear of the example being abused. The divine author of Gita was not deterred from delivering the message of he 'Song Celestial' although he probably knew that it would be tortured to justify every variety of vice including murder. (YI, 3-7-1924, p. 221)

The highest fulfilment of religion...requires a giving up of all possession. Having ascertained the law of our being, we must set about reducing it to practice to the extent of our capacity and no further. That is the middle way. (YI, 5-2-1925, p. 48)

Golden Rule

The golden rule...is resolutely to refuse to have what the millions cannot. This ability to refuse will not descend upon us all of a sudden. The first thing is to cultivate the mental attitude that will not have possessions or facilities denied to millions, and the next immediate thing is to re-arrange our lives as fast as possible in accordance with that mentality. (YI, 24-6-1926, p. 226)

Love and exclusive possession can never go together. Theoretically, where there is perfect love, there must be perfect non-possession. The body is our last possession. So, a man can only exercise perfect love and be completely dispossessed if he is prepared to embrace death and renounce his body for the sake of human service.

But that is true in theory only. In actual life we can hardly exercise perfect love, for the body as possession will always remain imperfect and it will always be his part to try to be perfect. So that perfection in love or non-possession will remain an unattainable ideal as long as we are alive, but towards which we must ceaselessly strive. (MR, October 1935, p. 412)

Jesus, Mahomed, Buddha, Nanak, Kabir, Chaitanya, Shankara, Dayanand, Ramakrishna were men who exercised an immense influence over and moulded the character of thousands of men. The world is the richer for their having lived in it. And they were all men who deliberately embraced poverty as their log....In so far as we have made the modern materialistic craze our goal, so far are we going downhill in the path of progress. (SW, p. 353)

How heavy is the toll of sins and wrongs that wealth, power and prestige exact from man! (A, p. 168)

To take something from another without his permission is theft of course. But it is also theft to use a thing for a purpose different from the one intended by the lender or to use it for a period longer than that which has been fixed with him. The profound truth upon which this observance is based is that God never creates more than what is strictly needed for the moment. Therefore, whoever appropriates more than the minimum that is really necessary for him is guilty of theft. (AOA, p. 58)

Secret of Life

Renounce all and dedicate it to God and then live. The right of living is thus derived from renunciation. It does not say, 'When all do their part of the work, I too will do it.' It says, 'Don't bother about others, do your job first and leave the rest to Him. (H, 6-3-1937, p. 27)

You may have occasion to possess or use material things, but the secret of life lies in never missing them. (H, 10-12-1938, p. 371)

The secret of happy life lies in renunciation. Renunciation is life. Indulgence spells death. Therefore, everyone has a right and should desire to live 125 years while performing service without an eye on result. Such life must be wholly and solely dedicated to service. Renunciation made for the sake of such service is an ineffable joy of which none can deprive one, because that nectar springs from within and sustains life. In this there can be no room for worry or impatience. Without this joy, long life is impossible and would not be worth while even if possible. (H, 24-2-1946, p. 19)

This does not mean that, if one has wealth, it should be thrown away and wife and children should be turned out of doors. It simply means that one must give up attachment of these things and dedicate one's all to God and make use of His gifts to serve Him only. (H, 28-4-1946, p. 111)

POVERTY AND RICHES

Avoidance of Strife

I cannot picture to myself a time when no man shall be richer than another. But I do picture to myself a time when the rich will spurn to enrich themselves at the expense of the poor and the poor will cease to envy the rich. Even in a most perfect world, we shall fail to avoid inequalities, but we can and must avoid strife and bitterness. (YI, 7-10-1926, p. 348)

I have heard many of our countrymen say that we will gain American wealth, but avoid its methods. I venture to suggest that such an attempt, if it were made, is foredoomed to failure. We cannot be 'wise, temperate and furious' in a moment. (SW, pp. 353-4)

Every palace that one sees in India is a demonstration, not of her riches, but of the insolence of power that riches give to the few, who owe them to the miserably requited labours of the millions of the paupers of India. (YI, 28-4-1927, p. 137)

Duty of the rich

The rich should ponder well as to what their duty is today. They who employ mercenaries to guard their wealth may find those very guardians turning on them. The moneyed classes have got to learn how to fight either with arms or with the weapon of nonviolence.

For those who wish to follow the latter way, the best and most effective mantra is: (Enjoy the wealth by renouncing it). Expanded it means: "Earn your cores by all means. But understand that your wealth is not yours; it belongs to the people. Take what you require for your legitimate needs, and use the remainder for society."

This truth has hitherto not been acted upon; but, if the moneyed classes do not even act on it in these times of stress.

they will remain the slaves of their riches and passions and, consequently, of those who overpower them.

...I see coming the day of the rule of the poor, whether that rule be through force of arms or of nonviolence. Let it be remembered that physical force is transitory even as the body is transitory. But the power of the spirit is permanent, even as the spirit is everlasting. (H, 1-2-1942, p. 20)

I have no hesitation in endorsing the opinion that generally rich men and, for that matter, most men are not particular as to the way they make money. In the application of the method of nonviolence, one must believe in the possibility of every person, however depraved, being reformed under humane and skilled treatment. We must appeal to the good in human beings and expect response.

Good of All

It is not conducive to the well-being of society that every member uses all his talents, only not for personal aggrandizement but for the good of all? We do not want to produce a dead equality where every person becomes or is rendered incapable of using his ability to the utmost possible extent. Such a society must ultimately perish. I therefore suggest that my advice, that moneyed men may earn their cores (honestly only, of course) but so as to dedicate them to the service of all, is perfectly sound is a mantra based on uncommon knowledge. It is the surest method to evolve a new order of life of universal benefit in the place of the present one where each one lives for himself without regard to what happens to his neighbour. (H, 22-2-1942, p. 49)

Beggary

The grinding poverty and starvation with which our country is afflicted is such that it drives more and more every year into the ranks of the beggars, whose desperate struggle for bread renders them insensible to all feelings of decency and self-respect. And our philanthropists, instead of providing work for them and insisting on their working for bread, give them alms. (A, p. 320)

My ahimsa would not tolerate the idea of giving a free meal to a healthy person who has not worked for it in some honest way, and if I had the power, I would stop every Sadavrat where free meals are given. It has degraded the nation and has encouraged laziness, idleness, hypocrisy and even crime. Such misplaced charity adds nothing to the wealth of the country, whether material or spiritual, and gives a false sense of meritoriousness to the donor.

Work, Not Charity

How nice and wise it would be if the donors were to open institutions where they would give meals under healthy, clean surroundings to men and women who would work for them. I personally think that the spinning wheel or any of the processes that cotton has to go through will be an ideal occupation. But if they will not have that, they may choose any other work; only the rule should be, "No labour, no meal."....

I know that it is easier to fling free meals in the faces of idlers, but much more difficult to organize an institution where honest work has to be done before meals are served. From a pecuniary standpoint, in the initial stages at any rate, the cost of feeding people after taking work from them will be more than the cost of the present free kitchen. But I am convinced that it will be cheaper in the long run, if we do not want to increase in geometrical progression the race of loafers which is fast over-running this land. (YI, 13-8-1925, p. 282)

To people famishing and idle, the only acceptable form in which God can dare appear is work and promise of food as wages. (YI, 13-10-1921, p. 325)

I must refuse to insult the naked by giving them clothes they do not need, instead of giving them work which they sorely need. I will not commit the sin of becoming their patron but, on learning that I had assisted in impoverishing them, I would give them neither crumbs nor cast off clothing, but the best of my food and clothes and associate myself with them in work. (ibid)

I do feel that, whilst it is bad to encourage begging, I will not send away a beggar without offering him work and food.

If he will not work, I should let him go without food. Those who are physically disabled like the halt and the maimed have got to be supported by the State.

There is, however, a lot of fraud going on under cover of pretended blindness or even genuine blindness. So many blind have become rich because of ill-gotten gains. It would be a good thing if they were taken to an asylum, rather than be exposed to his temptation. (H, 11-5-1935, p. 99)

Dependence on Servants

I hold that a man who desires the cooperation of and wishes of co-operate with others should not be dependent on servants. If anyone has to have one at a time of scarcity of servants, he will have to pay what is demanded and accept all other conditions with the result that he will instead of being master, become the servant of his employee. This is good for neither the master nor the servant.

But if what an individual seeks is not slavery, but the cooperation of a fellow-being, he will not only serve himself but also him whose cooperation he needs. Through the extension of this principle, a man's family will become co-terminus with the world and his attitude towards his fellow-beings will also undergo a corresponding change. There is no other way of reaching the desired consummation. (H, 10-3-1946, p. 40)

DARIDRANARAYAN

God of the Poor

Daridranarayan is one of the millions of names by which humanity knows God who is unnamable and unfathomable by human understanding, and it means God of the poor, God appearing in the hearts of the poor. (YI, 4-4-1929, p. 110)

For the poor the economic is the spiritual. You cannot make any other appeal to those starving millions. It will fall flat on them. But you take food to them and they will regard you as their God. They are incapable of any other thought. (YI, 5-5-1927, p. 142)

With this very hand I have collected soiled pies from them, and tied tightly in their rags. Talk to them of modern progress.

Insult them by taking the name of God before them in vain. They will call you and me friends if we talk about God to them. They know if they know any God at all, a God of terror, vengeance, a pitiless tyrant. (YI, 15-9-1927, p. 313)

I am working for winning Swaraj...for those soiling and unemployed millions who do not get even a square meal a day and have to scratch along with a piece of stale roti and a pinch of salt. (YI, 26-3-1931, p. 53)

Message of God

I dare not take before them the message of God. I may as well place before the dog over there the message of God as before those hungry millions, who have no luster in their eyes and whose only God is their bread. I can take before them a message of God only by taking the message of sacred work before them.

It is good enough to talk of God whilst we are sitting here after a nice breakfast and looking forward to a nicer luncheon. But how am I to talk of God to the millions who have to go without two meals a day? To them God can only appear as bread and butter. Well, the peasants of India were getting their bread from their soil. I offered them the spinning wheel in order that they may get butter and, if I appear today...in my loin-cloth, it is because I come as the sole representative of those half-starved, half-naked dumb millions. (YI, 15-10-1931, p. 310)

I claim to know my millions. All the 24 hours of the day I am with them. They are my first care and last because I recognize no God except that God that is to be found in the hearts of the dumb millions. They do not recognize His presence; I do. And I worship the God that is Truth or Truth which is God through the service of these millions. (H, 11-3-1939, p. 44)

5

Gandhi on Social Issues

RELIGION AND MORALS

710. You must watch my life, how I live, eat, sit, talk, behave in general. The sum total of all those in me is my religion. –H, 22-9-46, 321.

True Religion

711. There is no religion higher than Truth and Righteousness. –ER, 49.

712. Let me explain what I mean by religion. It is not the Hindu religion which I certainly prize above all other religions, but the religion which transcends Hinduism, which changes one's very nature, which binds one indissoluble to the truth within and which ever purifies. It is the permanent element in human nature which counts no cost too treat in order to find full expression and which leaves the soul utterly restless until it has found itself, known its Maker and appreciated the true correspondence between the Maker and itself. –YI, 12-5-20, Tagore, 1070.

True Morality

713. True morality consists, not in following the beaten track, but in finding out the true path for ourselves and in fearlessly following it. –ER, 38.

714. No action which is not voluntary can be called moral. So long as we act like machines, there can be no question of morality. If we want to call an action moral, it should have been done consciously and as a matter of duty. Any action that is

dictated by fear or by coercion of any kind ceases to be moral. It also follows that all good deeds that are prompted by hope of happiness in the next world cease to be moral. –ER, 43.

715. How can I, the champion of ahimsa, compel anyone to perform even a good act? Has not a well-known Englishman said that to make mistakes as a free man is better than being in bondage in order to avoid them? I believe in the truth of this. The reason is obvious. The mind of a man who remains good under compulsion cannot improve, in fact it worsens. And when compulsion is removed all the defects will up to the surface with even greater force. –H, 29-9-46, 333.

Religion and Morality

716. True religion and true morality are inseparably bound up with each other. Religion is to morality what water is to the seed that is sown in the soil. –ER, 49.

717. I reject any religious doctrine that does not appeal to reason and is in conflict with morality. I tolerate unreasonable religious sentiment when it is not immoral.–YI, 21-7-20, Tagore, 173.

718. As soon as we lose the moral basis, we cease to be religious. There is no such thing as religion overriding morality. Man for instance cannot be untruthful, cruel and incontinent and claim to have God on his side. –YI, 24-11-21, 385.

719. Our desires and motives may be divide into two classes—selfish and unselfish. All selfish desires are immoral, while the desire to improve ourselves for the sake of doing good to others is truly moral. The highest moral law is that we should unremittingly work for the good of mankind. –ER, 36.

Religion and Practical Affairs

720. Swaraj is synonymous with Rama Raj—the establishment of the Kingdom of Righteousness on earth. –YI, 4-5-21, 143.

721. Hanuman tore open his heart and showed that there was nothing there but Ramanama. I have none of the power of Hanuman to tear open my heart, but if any of you feel inclined to do it I assure you will find nothing there but love

for Rama whom I see face to face in the starving millions of India. –YI, 24-3-27, 93.

722. Religion which takes no account of practical affairs and does not help to solve them, is no religion. And that is why I am putting a religious matter before you in a practical form. –YI, 7-5-25, 164.

723. If any action of mine claimed to he spiritual is proved to be unpractical it must be pronounced to be a failure. I do believe that the most spiritual act is the most practical in the true sense of the term. –H, 1-7-39, 181.

724. Q. In your autobiography you have said that you cannot think of politics apart from religion. Bo you still hold that view? If so, how is it that in a country of many diverse religions like India you expect a common political policy to be adopted?

Yes, I still hold the view that I cannot conceive politics as divorces from religion. Indeed religion should evade every one of our actions. Here religion does not mean sectarianism. It means a belief in ordered moral government of the universe. It is not less real because it is unseen. This religion transcends Hinduism, Islam, Christianity, etc. It does not supersede them. It harmonizes them and gives them reality.–H, 10-2-40, 445.

725. To practice nonviolence in mundane matters is to know its true value. It is to bring heaven upon earth. There is no such thing as the other world. All worlds are one. There is no 'here' and no 'there'. As Jeans has demonstrated, the whole universe including the most distant stars, invisible even through the most powerful telescope in the world, is compressed in an atom. I hold it therefore to be wrong to limit the use of nonviolence to cave-dwellers and for acquiring merit for a favoured position in the other world. All virtue ceases to have use if it serves no purpose in every walk of life. –H, 26-7-42, 248.

The Various Religious Creeds

726. Religions are different roads converging to the same pint. What does it matter that we take different roads, so long as we reach the same goal? In reality, there are as many religions as there are individuals. –IHR, 24, 23.

727. If a man reaches the heart of his own religion, he has reached the heart of the others too. –Polak, 41.

728. So long as there are different religions, every-one of them may need some distinctive symbol. But when the symbol is made into a fetish and an instrument of proving the superiority of one's religion over other's it is fit only to be discarded. –Auto, 480.

Missionary Effort and the State

729. The State should undoubtedly be secular. Everyone living in it should be entitled to profess his religion without let or hindrance, so long as the citizen obeyed the common law of the land. There should be no interference with missionary effort, but no mission could enjoy the patronage of the State as it did during the foreign regime. –H, 24-8-47, 292.

730. 'If I were a dictator, religion and State would be separate. I swear by my religion. I will die for it. But it is my personal affair. The State has nothing to do with it,' remarked Gandhiji sometime back in answer to a question by a missionary friend who asked whether in Free India there would be complete religious freed and whether religion will be separate from the State. 'The State would look after your secular welfare, health, communications, foreign relations, currency and so on, but not your or my religion. That is everybody's personal concern.' He then went on to describe his conception of religion. 'You must watch my life, how I live, eat, sit, talk, behave in general. The sum total of all those in me is my religion,' he said. –H, 22-9-46, 321.

Tolerance

731. I do not like the word tolerance, but could not think of a better one. Tolerance may imply a gratuitous assumption of the inferiority of other faiths to one's own, whereas ahimsa teaches us to entertain the same respect for he religious faiths of others as we accord to lour own, thus admitting the imperfection of the latter. This admission will be readily made by a seeker of Truth, who follows the law of Love. If we had attained the full vision of Truth, we would no longer be mere seekers, but have become one with God, for truth is God. But

being only seekers, we prosecute our quest, and are conscious of our imperfection.

And if we are imperfect ourselves, religion as conceived by us must also be imperfect. We have not realized religion in its perfection, even as we have not rallied God. Religion of our conception, being thus imperfect, is always subject to a process of evolution and reinterpretation. Progress towards Truth, towards God, is possible only because of such evolution. And if all faiths outlined by men are imperfect, the question of comparative merit does not arise. All faiths constitute a revelation of Truth, but all are imperfect, and liable to error. Reverence for other faiths need not blind us to their faults. We must be keenly alive to the defects of our own faith also, yet not leave it on that account, but try to overcome those defects. Looking at all religions with an equal eye, we would not only not hesitate, but would think it our duty, to blend into our faith every acceptable feature of other faiths.

Even as a tree has a single trunk, but many branches and leaves, so there is one true and perfect Religion, but it becomes many, as it passes through the human medium. The one Religion is beyond all speech. Imperfect men put it into such language as they can command, and their words are interpreted by other men equally imperfect. Imperfect. Whose interpretation is to be held to be the right one? Everybody is right from his own standpoint, but it is not possible that everybody is wrong. Hence the necessity of tolerance, which does not mean indifference to one's own faith, but a more intelligent and purer love for it. Tolerance gives us spiritual insight, which is as far from fanaticism as the north pole from the south. True knowledge of religion breaks down the barriers between faith and faith. –YM, 55.

732. There is one rule, however, which should always be kept in mind while studying all great religions and that is that one should study them only through the writings of known votaries of the respective religions. For instance, if one wants to study the Bhagavata, one should do so not through a translation of it made by a hostile critic but one prepared by a lover of the Bhagavata. Similarly to study the Bible one

should study it through the commentaries of devoted Christians. This study of other religions besides one's own will give one a grasp of the rock-bottom unity of all religions and afford a glimpse also of the universal and absolute truth which lies beyond the 'dust of creeds and faiths'.

Let no one even for a moment entertain the fear that a reverent study of other religions is likely to weaken or shake one's faith in one's own. The Hindu system of philosophy regards all religions as containing the elements of truth in them and enjoins an attitude of respect and reverence towards them all. This of course presupposes regard for one's own religion. Study and appreciation of other religions need not cause a weakening of that regard; it should mean extension of that regard to other religions. –YI, 6-13-28, 406.

733. Religion does not teach us to bear ill-will towards one another. It is easy enough to be friendly to one's friends. But to befriend the one who regards himself as your enemy, is the quintessence of true religion. The other is mere business. –H, 11-5-47, 146.

Gandhi's Personal Attitude

734. After long study and experience, I have come to the conclusion that (1) all religions are true; (2) all religions have some error in them (3) all religions are almost as dear to me as my own Hinduism, in as much as all human beings should be as dear to one as one's own close relatives. My own veneration for other faiths is the same as that for my own faith; therefore no thought of conversion is possible. The aim of the Fellowship should be to help a Hindu to become a better Hindu, a Muscleman to become a better Mussalman, and a Christian a better Christian, The attitude of patronizing toleration is false to the spirit of International Fellowship. If I have a suspicion in my mind that my religion is more or less true, and that others' are more or less false, instead of being more or less true, then, though I may have some sort of fellowship with them, it is of an entirely different kind from the one we need in the International Fellowship. Our prayer for other must be NOT 'God, give him the light that Thou has given me, ' BUT' Give him all the light and truth he needs for his highest development.'

Pray merely that your friends may become better men, whatever their form of religion.

Nevertheless, your experience may become a part of their experience, without your knowing it. –Sabarmati, 1928, 17-19.

To Christian Friends

735. Your work will be all the richer if you accept as settled fact the faiths of the people you come to serve, faiths which, however crude, are valuable to them. I want you to complement the faith of the people instead of undermining it. Make us better Hindus, i.e. better men and women. Why should a man, even if he becomes a Christian, be torn from his surroundings?

Superstitions and undesirable things go as soon as we begin to live the correct life. I concern myself not with belief but with asking to do the right thing. As soon as they do it, their belief rights itself. –YI, 11-8-27, 250, 251.

True Preaching

736. It is better to allow our lives to speak for us than our words. God did not bear the Cross only 1900 years ago, but He bears it today, and He dies and is resurrected from day to day. It would be poor comfort to the would if it had to depend upon a historical God who died 2000 years ago. Do not then preach the God of history, but show Him as He lives today through you. –YI, 11-8-27, 251.

737. God has created different faiths just as He has the votaries thereof. How can I even secretly harbour the thought that my neighbour's faith is inferior to mine and wish that he should give up his faith and embrace mine? As a true and loyal friend, I can only wish and pray that he may live and grow perfect in his own faith. In God's houses there are many mansions and they are equally holy. —H, 20-4-34, 73.

738. I do not believe in people telling others of their faith, especially with a view to conversion. Faith does not admit of telling. It has to be lived and then it becomes self-propagating. –YI, 20-10-27, 352.

739. Even a lofty utterance, that has not the backing of sincerity and experience, will be inert and lifeless, and will

utterly fail to penetrate and quicken the hearts of men,. While the speech that springs from self-realization and genuine experience is always fruitful. –H, 21-11-36, 322.

740. Learning takes us through many stages in life but it fails us utterly in the hour of danger and temptation. Then faith alone saves. –YI, 22-1-25, 27.

741. Divine knowledge is not borrowed from books. It has to be realized in oneself. Books are at best an aid, often ever a hindrance. –YI, 17-7-24, 238.

742. Religion is a very personal matter. We should by living the life according to our lights share the best with one another, thus adding to the sum total of human effort to reach God. –H, 28-11-36, 330.

The Acid Test

743. I would reject all authority if it is in conflict with sober reason or the dictates of the heart. Authority sustains and ennobles the weak when it is the handiwork of reason, but it degrades them when it supplants reason sanctified by the still small voice within.—YI, 8-12-20, Tagore, 616.

744. Scriptures cannot transcend reason and truth. They are intended to purify reason and illuminate truth. –YI, 19-1-21, 22.

745. Error can claim no exemption even if it can be supported by the scriptures of the world. –YI, 26-2-25, 74.

746. An error does not become truth by reason of multiplied propagation, nor does truth become error because nobody sees it. –YI, 26-2-25, 75.

747. I do not hold that everything ancient is good because it is ancient. I do not advocate surrender of God-given reasoning faculty in the face of dancing tradition. Any tradition, however ancient, if inconsistent with morality, is fit to be banished from the land. Untouchability may be considered to be an ancient traction, the institution of child widowhood and child marriage may be considered to be an ancient tradition, and even so many an ancient horrible belief and superstitious practice. I would sweep them out of existence if I had the power. When, therefore,

I talk of respecting the ancient tradition, you now understand what I mean. –YI, 22-9-27, 319.

-748. We should cease to grow the moment we cease to discriminate between virtue and vice, and slavishly copy the past which we do not fully know. We are proud heirs to all that was noblest and best in the bygone age. We must not dishonour our heritage by multiplying past errors. –YI, 15-9-21, 292.

749. Intolerance of criticism even of what one may prize as life itself is not conducive to the growth of public corporate life. –YI, 5-3-25, 82.

On Hinduism

750. I can no more describe my feeling for Hinduism than for my wife. She moves me as no other woman in the world can. Not that she has no faults. I dare say she has many more than I see myself. But the feeling of an indissoluble bond is there. Even so I feel about Hinduism with all its faults and limitations. Nothing elates me so much as the music of the Gita or he Ramayana of Tulsidas, the only two books in Hinduism I may be said to know. I know the vice that is going on today in all the great Hindu shrines, but I love them in spite of their unspeakable failings. I am a reformer through and through. But my zeal never takes me to the rejection of any of the essential things in Hinduism. –YI, 6-10-21, 318.

751. Hinduism is a living organism liable to growth and decay, and subject to the laws of nature. One and indivisible at the root, it has grown into a vast tree with innumerable branches. The changes in the seasons affect it. It has its autumn and summer, its winter and spring. The rains nourish and fructify it too. Hinduism is like the Ganges, pure and unsullied at its source, but taking in its course the impurities in the way. Even like the Ganges it is beneficent in its total effect. –YI, 8-4-26, 131.

(A) GURUVADA

752. I believe in the Hindu theory of guru and its importance in spiritual realization. I think there is a great deal of truth in the doctrine that true knowledge is impossible without a guru. An imperfect teacher in mundane affairs may be tolerable,

but not so in spiritual matters. Only a perfect gnani (a knowing one, a seer) deserves to be enthroned as guru. –Auto, 113.

753. I must therefore warn all against accepting imperfect ones as gurus. It is better to grope in the dark and wade through a million errors to Truth than to entrust oneself to one who 'knows not that he knows not'. –YI, 3-12-25, 422.

(B) IDOL WORSHIP

754. I do not disbelieve in idol worship An idol does not excite any feeling of veneration in me. But I think that idol worship part of human nature. We hanker after symbolism. –YI, 6-1 -21, 318.

755. Should we forget our humanity and return a blow for a blow? If some misdirected individual took it into his head to desecrate a temple or break idols, should a Hindu in return desecrate a mosque on that account? Did it in any way help to protect the temple or to save the cause of Hinduism? Personally, he was as much an idol-worshipper as an idol-breaker, and he suggested that the whole of the audience, whether Hindu, Muslim or any other, were also so, whether they admitted it or not. He knew that mankind thirsted for symbolism. Were not masjids or churches in reality the same as mandirs? God resided everywhere, no less in stock or stone than in a single hair on the body of man. But men associated sacredness with particular places and things more than with others. Such sentiment was worthy of respect when it did not mean restrictions on similar freedom for others. To every Hindu and Mussulman, Gandhiji's advice was if there was compulsion anywhere, they should gently but firmly refuse to submit to it. Personally, he himself would hug an idol and lay down his life to protect it rather than brook any restriction upon his freedom of worship. –H, 30-3-47, 86.

(C) INCARNATION

756. In Hinduism, incarnation is ascribed to one who has performed some extraordinary service of mankind. All embodied life is in reality an incarnation of God, but it is not usual to consider every living being as an incarnation. Future generations pay this homage to one who, in his own generation, has been

extraordinarily religious in his conduct. I can see nothing wrong in this procedure; it takes nothing from God's greatness and there is no violence done to truth. There is an Urdu saying which means 'Adam is not God but he is a spark of the Divine.' And therefore he who is the most religiously behaved has most of the divine spark in him. It is in accordance with this train of thought that Krishna enjoys, in Hinduism, the status of the most perfect incarnation. –YI, 6-8-31, 205.

(D) BELIEF IN THE HEREDITARY TRANSMISSIBILITY OF CHARACTER

757. Children inherit the qualities of the parents, no less than their physical features. Environment does play an important part, but the original capital on which a child starts in life is inherited from its ancestors. –Auto, 381.

758. I believe that just as every one inherits a particular form so dies he inherit the particular characteristics and qualities of his progenitors, and to make this admission is to conserve one's energy. That frank admission, if he will act up to it, would put a legitimate curb upon our ambitions, and thereby our energy is set free for extending the field of spiritual research and spiritual evolution. It is this doctrine of Varnashrama Dharma which I have always adopted. –YI, 29-9-27, 329.

(E) VARNA

759. I regard Varnashrama as a healthy division of work based on birth. The present ideas of caste are a perversion of the original. There is no question with me of superiority or inferiority. It is purely a question of duty. I have indeed stated that varna is based on birth. But I have also said that it is possible for a shudra, for instance, to become a Vaishya. But in order to perform the duty of a Vaishya he does not need the label of a Vaishya. He who performs the duty of a Brahman will easily become one in the next incarnation. –YI, 23-4-25, 145.

760. So far as I know anything at all of Hinduism, the meaning of varna is incredibly simple. It simply means the following on the part of us all the hereditary calling of our

forefathers, in so far as that traditional calling is not inconsistent with fundamental ethics, and this only for the purpose of earning one's livelihood. You will realize that if all of us follow this law of varna we would limit our material ambition, and our energy would be set free for exploring those vast fields whereby and where through we can know God. –YI, 20-10-27, 355.

761. Varnashrama Dharma defines man's mission on this earth. He is not born day after day to explore avenues for amassing riches and to explore different means of livelihood; on the contrary man is born in order that he may utilize every atom of his energy for the purpose of knowing his Maker. It restricts him therefore, for the purpose of holding body and soul together, to the occupation of his forefathers. That and nothing more or nothing less is Varnashrama Dharma. –YI, 27-10-27, 357.

762. Numerous verses from the shastras unmistakably show that mere birth counts for nothing. A person must show corresponding works and character to establish his claim by birth. Such verses also enforce the argument that:

(i) a person loses varna by failing to exhibit its peculiar characteristics;

(ii) inter-varna marriage or interdining, whatever virtue the restrictions on them may have, does not affect a person's varna, at least not so much as the failing to live up to one's varna;

(iii) birth, while it gives a start and enables the parents to determine the training and occupation of their children, does not perpetuate the varna of one's birth, if it is not fulfilled by works. –H, 15-4-33, 2.

(F) CASTE AS VARNA

763. Our existing caste organizations are really trade guilds.

–YI, 13-4-231, 114.

764. From the economic point of view, its value was once very great. It ensured hereditary skill; it limited competition. It was the best remedy against pauperism. And it had all the advantages of trade guilds. Although it did not foster adventure or invention there, it is not known to have come in the way

either. Historically speaking, caste may be regarded as man's experiment or social adjustment in the laboratory of Indian society. If we can prove it to be a success, it can be offered to the world as a leaven and as the best remedy against heartless competition and social disintegration born of avarice and greed. –YI, 5-1-21, 2.

765. The vast organization of caste answered not only the religious wants of the community but it answered its political needs. The villagers managed their internal affairs through the caste system, and through it they dealt with any oppression from the ruling power or powers. It is not possible to deny of a nation that was capable of producing the caste system its wonderful power of organization. –Nat, 339.

766. I believe that every man is born in the would with certain natural tendencies. Every person is born with certain definite limitations which he cannot overcome. From a careful; observation of those limitations the law of varna was deduced. It establishes certain spheres of action for certain people with certain tendencies. This avoided all unworthy competition. Whilst recognizing limitations the law of varna admitted of no distinctions of high and low; on the one hand it guaranteed to each the fruits of his labours and on the other it prevented him from pressing upon his neighbour. This great law has been degraded and fallen into disrepute. But my conviction is that an ideal social order will only be evolved when the implications of this law are fully understood and given effect to.

Q. Do you not think that in ancient India there was much difference in economic status and social privileges between the four varnas?

A. That may be historically true. But misapplication or an imperfect understanding of the law must not lead to the ignoring of the law itself. By constant striving we have to enrich the inheritance left to us. This law determines the duties of man. Rights follow from a due performance of duties. –MR., 414.

(G) CASTE IN SO FAR AS IT IS DIFFERENT FROM VARNA

767. I consider the four divisions alone to be fundamental, natural, and essential. The innumerable subcastes are

sometimes a convenience, often a hindrance. The sooner there is fusion the better. –YI, 8-12-20, Tagore, 613.

768. The existing innumerable divisions with the attendant artificial restrictions and elaborate ceremonial are harmful to the growth of a religious spirit, as also to the social wellbeing of the Hindus and therefore also their neighbours. –YI, 25-2-26,77.

769. Varnashrama of the shastras is today nonexistent in practice. The present caste system is the very antithesis of varna-shrama. The sooner public opinion abolishes it the better. __H,I6-11-35,3i6.

770. Caste has nothing to do with religion. It is harmful both to spiritual and national growth.—H.

771. Today Brahmans and kshatriyas, vaishyas and shudras are mere labels. There is utter confusion of varna as I understand it and I wish that all the Hindus will voluntarily call themselves shudras. That is the only way to demonstrate the truth of Brahmanism and to revive Varna Dharma in its true state. – H, 25-3-33, 3.

(H) INTERDINING AND INTERMARRIAGE

772. I do not believe that interdining and even intermarriage necessarily deprives man of his status that his birth has given him. The four divisions define a man's calling, they do not restrict or regulate social intercourse. The divisions define duties, they confer no privileges. All are born to serve God's creation, a Brahmans with his knowledge, a kshatriya with his power of protection, a Vaishya with his commercial ability and a shudra with bodily labour. This however does not mean, that a Brahman for instance is absolved from bodily labour, or the duty of protecting himself and others. His birth makes a Brahman predominantly a man of knowledge, the fittest by heredity and training to impart it to others. There is nothing, again, to prevent the shudra from acquiring all the knowledge he wishes. Only, he will best serve with his body and need not envy others their special qualities for service. Varnashrama is self-restraint and conservation and economy of energy. Though therefore Varnashrama is not affected by interdining and

intermarriage, Hinduism does most emphatically discourage interdining and intermarriage between divisions. Hinduism is undoubtedly a religion of the renunciation of the flesh so that the spirit may be set free. It is no part of a Hindu's duty to dine with his son. And by restricting his choice of a bride to a particular group, he exercises rare self-restraint. Prohibitiobn against intermarriage and interdining is essential for the rapid evolution of the soul. But this self-denial is no test of varna. A Brahmans may remain a Brahman, though he may dine with his shudra brother, if he has not left off his duty of service by knowledge. It follows from what I have said above, that restraint in matters of marriage and dining is not based upon notions of superiority. –YI, 6-10-21, 317.

773. Correspondents have asked whether inter-dining and intermarriage are a part of the movement of untouchability. In my opinion they are not. They touch the caste men equally with the outcastes. It is, therefore, not obligatory on an anti-untouchability worker to devote himself or herself to inter-dining and intermarriage reform. Personally I am of opinion that the reform is coming sooner than we expect. Restriction on inter-caste dining and inter-caste marriage is no part of Hindu religion. It is a social custom which crept into Hinduism when perhaps it was in its decline, and was then probably meant to be a temporary protection against disintegration of Hindu society. Today those two prohibitions are weakening Hindu society, and the emphasis on them has turned the attention of the mass mind from the fundamentals which alone are vita to life's growth. Wherever, therefore, people voluntarily take part in functions where 'touchables' and 'untouchables', Hindus and non-Hindus are invited to joint dinner parties, I welcome them as a healthy sing,. But I should never dream of making this reform, however desirable in itself it may be, part of an all-India reform which is long overdue. Untouchability, in the form we all know it, is a canker eating into the very vitals of Hinduism. Dining and marriage restrictions stunt Hindu society. I think the distinction is fundamental. It would be unwise in a hurricane campaign to overweight and thus endanger the main issue. It may even amount to a breach of faith with the masses to call upon them suddenly to view the

removal of untouchability in a light different from what they have been taught to believe it to be. On the one hand, therefore, whilst inter-dining may go on where the public itself is ready for it, it should not be a part of an India-wide campaign. (Press statement of 4-11-32)—My Soul's Agony, 5*

774. The question of food and drink has or ought to have no social value. –YI, 29-12-20, Tagore, 619.

775. In Varnashrama there was and there should be no prohibition of intermarriage or interdining.

Though there is in Varnashrama no prohibition against intermarriage and interdining, there can be no compulsion. It must be left to the unfettered choice of the individual as to where he or she will marry or dine. If the law of Varnashrama was observed there would naturally be a tendency, so far as marriage is concerned, for people to restrict the marital relations to there own varna. –H, 16-11-35, 316.

*Regarding the above two passages and their apparent inconsistency, Gandhiji wrote in answer to a correspondent's question:

As I read them with a detached mind, I find no contradiction between the two statements especially if they are read in their full context. I still believe that restriction imposed by oneself upon interdining and intermarriage is an act of renunciation of the flesh. There is one word that perhaps I would change if I was writing the article of 1921 today. Instead of 'prohibition', I should repeat the expression used in the same article just a few lines before and say 'self-imposed restriction against intermarriage and interdining is essential for a rapid evolution of the soul'. –H, 29-4-33, 2.

776. When I said that removal of untouchability did not include the removal of restrictions on interdining and intermarriage, I had the general Hindu public in mind, not the congress workers or Congressmen. These have to abolish untouchability from every part of their life. –H, 1-2-42, 23.

777. There should be a breach in the double wall of caste and province. If India is one and indivisible, surely there should be no artificial divisions creating innumerable little groups

which would neither interdine nor intermarry. There is no religion in this cruel custom. It would not do to plead that individuals can not make the commencement and that they must wait till the whole society is ripe for change. No reform has ever been brought about except through intrepid individuals breaking down inhuman customs or usages. And after all what hardships can the schoolmaster suffer if he and his daughters refused to treat marriage as a marketable transaction instead of a status or sacrament, which it undoubtedly is I would, therefore, advise my correspondent courageously to give up the idea of borrowing or begging and to save the four hundred rupees he can get on his life policy by choosing in consultation with his daughter a suitable husband no matter to what caste or province he belongs. –H, 25-7-36, 192.

778. Q. Does the congress programme for the abolition of untouchability include interdining and intermarriage with Harijans?

A. So far as I know the Congress mind today there is no opposition to dining with Harijans. But speaking for myself, I have said that we have all to become Harijans today or we will not be able to purge ourselves completely of the taint of untouchability. I, therefore, tell all boys and girls who want to marry that they cannot be married sat Sevagram Ashram unless one of the parties is a Harijan. I am convinced that there is no real difficulty in this. All that is needed is a change of outlook. –HS, 5-1-46.

(I) UNTOUCHABILITY

779. Hinduism has sinned in giving sanction to untouchability. It has degraded us, made us pariahs. Even the Mussalman have caught the sinful contagion from us. –YI, 27-4-21, 136.

780. The 'touch-me-not'-ism that disfigures the present-day Hinduism is morbid growth. It only betrays a woodenness of mind, a blind self-conceit. It is abhorrent alike to the spirit of religion and morality. –H, 20-4-34, 73.

781. Untouchability is not only not a part and parcel of Hinduism, but a plague, which it is the bounden duty of every

Hindu to combat. It has received religious sanction in India, and reduced lakhs and crores of human beings to a state bordering on slavery.

The observance (of the vow of the removal of untouchability) is not fulfilled, merely by making friends with 'untouchables', but by loving all life as one's own self. Removal of untouchability means love for, and service of, the whole world, and it thus merges into ahimsa. –YM, 47, 49.

782. I do not want to be reborn. But if I have to be reborn, I should be born an untouchable, so that I may share their sorrows, sufferings, and affronts levelled at them, in order that I may endeavour to free myself and them from that miserable condition. I, therefore, pray that if I should be born again, I should do so not as a Brahmans, kshatriya, Vaishya or shudra, but as an atishudra. –YI, 4-5-21, 144.

783. Q. How can the cast-Hindus look after the interests of the Untouchables? How can they realize the feelings of the classes who have suffered so long at their hands? Is it not then better to entrust the interests of the Untouchables to men of their own caste?

A. Gandhiji was of opinion that the caste-Hindu owed a sacred duty to the so-called Untouchables. He must become a bhangi (sweeper) in name and action. When that happened the Untouchables would rise at a bound and Hinduism would leave a rich legacy to the would. If that happened, the system of cleaning closets would undergo transformation. In England real bhangis were famous engineers; and sanitarians. That could not happen in India so long as society was sluggish and slothful. –H, 23-3-47, 78.

(J) ANIMAL SACRIFICE

784. It does not matter, that animal sacrifice is alleged to find a place in the Vedas. It is enough for us, that such sacrifice cannot stand the fundamental tests of truth and nonviolence. I readily admit my incompetence in Vedic scholarship. But the incompetence, so far as this subject is concerned does not worry me, because even if the practice of animal sacrifice be proved to have been a feature of Vedic society, it can form no precedent for a votary of ahimsa. –YM, 77.

(K) RELIGIOUS INSTITUTIONS

785. The hoards rotting in the name of religion in the various parts of India have made many of these religious institutions a shame, where they have not become hot-beds of corruption. –YI, 6-7-25, 209.

(L) REINTERPRETATION OF TERMS

786. As the world progresses the same terms acquire new values. –YI, 7-5-25, 161.

787. I have come to feel that like human beings words have their evolution from stage to stage in the contents they hold. For instance, the contents of the richest word—God—are not the same to every lone of us. They will vary with the experience of each. –YI, 11-8-27, 250.

788. Yajna is a word full of beauty and power. Hence with the growth of knowledge and experience and with the change of time, its meaning is likely to grow and change. Yajna literally means worship; hence sacrifice; hence any sacrificial act or any act of service. And in this sense every age may and should have its own particular Yajna. The principles of religion are one thing, and practices based on them are another. The principles are absolute and irrespective of space and time. Practices change with place and time. –YI, 13-5-26, 179.

789. 'Satyam bruyat priyam bruyat ma bruyat satyam apriyam':-In my opinion the Sanskrit text means that one should speak the truth in gentle language. One had better not speak it, if one cannot do so in a gentle way; meaning thereby that there is not truth in a man who cannot control his tongue. –YI, 17-9-25, 318.

WOMEN'S PROBLEMS

Women and India's Future

790. I am firmly of opinion that India's salvation depends on the sacrifice and enlightenment of her women.-H,27-6-36,i53.

791. I had flattered myself that my contribution to the women's cause definitely began with the discovery of satyagraha. But the writer of the letter is of opinion that the fair sex requires treatment different from men. It is so, I do not think

any man will find the correct solution. No matter how much he tries, he must fail because nature has made him different from woman. Only the toad under the harrow knows where it pinches him. Therefore ultimately woman will have to determine with authority what she needs. My own opinion is that, just as fundamentally man and woman are one, their problem must be one in essence. The soul in both is the same. The two live the same life, have the same feelings. Each is a complement of the other. The one cannot live without the other's active help.

But somehow or other man has dominated woman from ages past., and so woman has developed an inferiority complex. She has believed in the truth of man's interested teaching that she is inferior to him. But the seers among men have recognized her equal status.

Nevertheless there is no doubt that at some point there is bifurcation. Whilst both are fundamentally one, it is also equally true that in the form there is a vital difference between the two. Hence the vocations of the two must also be different. The duty of motherhood, which the vast majority of women will always undertake, requires qualities which man need not possess. She is passive, he is active. She is essentially mistress of the house. He is the breadwinner. She is the keeper and distributor of the bread. She is the caretaker in every sense of the term. The art of bringing up the infants of the race is her special and sole prerogative. Without her care the race must become extinct.

In my opinion it is degrading both for man and woman that woman should be called upon or induced to forsake the hearth and shoulder the rifle for the protection of that hearth. It is a reversion to barbarity and the beginning of the end. In trying to ride the horse that man rides, she brings herself and him down. The sin will be on man's head for tempting or compelling his companion to desert her special calling. There is as much bravery in keeping one's home in good order and condition as there is in defending it against attack from without.

As I have watched millions of peasants in their natural surroundings and as I watch them daily in little Segaon, the natural division of spheres of work has forced itself on my attention. There are no women blacksmiths and carpenters. But men and women work on the fields, the heaviest work being done by the males. The women deep and manage the homes. They supplement the meagre resources of the family, but man remains the main breadwinner.

The divisions of the spheres of work being recognized, the general qualities and culture required are practically the same for both the sexes.

My contribution to the great problem lies in my presenting for acceptance truth and ahimsa in every walk of life, whether for individuals or nations. I have hugged the hope that in this woman will be the unquestioned leader and, having thus found her place in human evolution, she will shed her inferiority complex. If she is able to do this successfully, she must resolutely refuse to believe in the modern teaching that everything is determined and regulated by the sex impulse. I fear I have put the proposition rather clumsily. But I hope my meaning is clear. I do not know that the millions of men who are taking an active part in the war are obsessed by the sex specter. Nor are the peasants working together in their fields worried or dominated by it. This is not to say or suggest that they are free from the instinct implanted in man and woman. But it most certainly does not dominate their lives as it seems to dominate the lives of those who are saturated with the modern sex literature. Neither man nor woman has time for such things when he or she is faced with the hard fact of living life in its grim reality.

I have suggested in these columns that woman is the incarnation of ahimsa. Ahimsa means infinite love, which again means infinite capacity for suffering. Who but woman, the mother of man, shows this capacity in the largest measure? She shows it as she carries the infant and feeds it during nine months and derives joy in the suffering involved. What can beat the suffering caused by the pangs of labour? But she forgets them in the joy of creation. Who again suffers daily so that her babe may wax from day to day? Let her transfer that love to the whole of humanity, let her forget that she ever was or can be the object of man's lust. And she will occupy her proud position by the side on man as his mother, maker and silent leader. It is given to her to teach the art of peace to the warring would thirsting for that nectar. She can become the leader in satyagraha which does not require the learning that books give but does require the stout heart that comes from suffering and faith.

My good nurse in the Sassoon Hospital, Poona, as I was lying on a sick bed years ago, told me the story of a woman who refused to take chloroform because she would not risk the life of the babe she was carrying. She had to undergo a painful operation. The only anesthetic she had was her love for the babe, to save whom no suffering was too great. Let not women, who can count many such heroines among them, ever despise their sex or deplore that they were not born men. The contemplation of that heroine often makes me envy woman the status that is hers, if she only knew. There is as much reason for man to with that he was born a woman as for woman to do otherwise. But the wish is fruitless. Let us be happy in the state to which we are born and do the duty for which nature has destined us. –H, 24-2-40, 13.

The Problem

792. I passionately desire the utmost freedom for our women. I detest child marriages. I shudder to see a child widow, and shiver with rage when a husband just widowed contracts with brutal indifference another marriage. I deplore the criminal indifference of parents who deep their daughters utterly ignorant and illiterate and bring them up only for the purpose of marrying them off to some young man of means. Notwithstanding all this grief and rage, I realize the difficulty of the problem. Women must have votes and an equal legal status. But the problem does not end there. It only commences at the point where women begin to affect the political deliberations of the nation. –YI, 21-7-21, 229.

The Ideal of Marriage

793. The ideal that marriage aims at is that of spiritual union through the physical. The human love that it incarnates is intended to serve as a stepping stone to divine or universal love. S.F.G-18

794. The wife is not the husband's bond slave, but his companion and his helpmate, and an equal partner in all his joys and sorrows—as free as the husband to choose her own path—Auto, 38.

Child Marriage

795. What is kanaka in the case of little children? Has a father any rights of property over his children? He is their protec·. r not owner. And he forfeits the privileg^ of protection when he abuses it by seeking to garter away the liberty of the ward.

The least that a parent, who has so abused his trust as to give in marriage an infant to an old man in his dotage or to a boy hardly in his teens, can do, is to purge himself of his sin by remarrying his daughter when she becomes widowed. As I have said in a previous note, such marriages should be declared null and void from the beginning. –YI, 11-11-26, 388.

796. You must be able surely to control your lust to this extent, that you are not going to marry a girl that is under 16 years age. If I could do so I would lay down 20 as the minimum. Twenty years is early enough even in India. It is we who are responsible for the precocity of the girls, not even the Indian climate, because I know girls of the age of twenty who are pure and undefiled and able to stand the storm that may rage round. Let us not hug that precocity to ourselves. Some Brahman students tell me that they cannot follow this principle, that they cannot get Brahman girls sixteen years old, very few Brahmans keep their daughters unmarried till that age, the Brahman girls are married mostly before 10, 12 and 13 years. Then I say to the Brahman youth, "Cease to be a Brahman, if you cannot possibly control yourself. Choose a grown up girl of 16 who became a widow when she was a child. If you cannot get a Brahman widow who has reached that age, then go and take any girl you like. And I tell you that the God of the Hindus will pardon that boy who has preferred to marry out of his caste rather than ravish a girl of twelve. When your heart is not pure and you cannot master your passions, you cease to an educated man. You have called your institution a premier institution. I want you to leave up to the name of the premier institution

which must produce boys who will occupy the front rank in character. And what is education without character and what is character without elementary personal purity? Brahmanism I adore. I have defended Varnashrama Dharma. But Brahmanism that can tolerate untouchability, virgin widowhood, spoliation of virgins, stinks in my nostrils. It is a parody of Brahmanism. There is no knowledge of Brahman therein. There is no true interpretation of the scriptures. It is undiluted animalism, Brahmanism is made of sterner stuff. –YI, 15-9-27, 314.

The Dowry System

797. The system has to go. Marriage must cease to be a matter of arrangement made by parents for money. The system is intimately connected with caste. So long as the choice is restricted to a few hundred-young men or young women of a particular caste, the system, will persist no matter what is said against it. The girls or boys or their parents will have to break the bonds of caste if the evil is to be eradicated. All this means education of a character that will revolutionize the mentality of the youth of the nation. –H, 23-5-36, 117.

798. There should be work done in the schools and colleges and amongst the parents of girls. The parents should so educate their daughters that they would refuse to marry a young man who wanted a price for marrying and would rather remain spinsters than be party to the degrading terms. The only honourable terms in marriage are mutual love and mutual consent. –YI, 27-12-28, 431.

799. Q. Namashudra girls are generally married at the age of 12 or 13; formerly the usual age was 8 or 9. The bridegroom has to pay a dowry of Rs. 150 for the bride. The average difference of age between the two is about 12 to 15 years. As a result of this the number of widows in namashudra society is rather large. Among one section of the caste, widow remarriage was prevalent. But in imitation of another section which was looked upon as superior, the former are giving up that practice. What is your advice regarding child marriage and widow remarriage?

A. Dealing with the question Gandhiji said that his opinion was definite. In the first instance there should be no possibility of child widows. He was averse to child marriages. It was an evil custom which unfortunately the namashudras had perhaps taken from the so-called higher castes.

Gandhiji was also against the system of dowry. It was nothing but the sale of girls. That there should be castes even amongst namashudras was deplorable and he would strongly advise them to abolish all caste-distinctions amongst themselves. And in this they should bear in mind the opinion the speaker had often expressed that all caste-distinctions should be abolished, and there should be only one caste, namely, bhangis and all Hindus should take pride in being called bhangis and nothing else. This applied to the namashudras as well.

When child marriages were abolished, naturally there would be few, if any, young widows. As a general rule he was for one man one wife for life, and one woman one husband for life. Custom had familiarized women in the so-called higher castes with enforced widowhood. Contrary was the rule with men. He called it a disgrace, but whilst society was in that pitiable condition, he advocated widow remarriage for all young widows. He believed in equality of the sexes and, therefore, he could only think of the same rights for women as men.-16-3-47, 67.

The Choice of Mates and Social Interference

800. (Referring to a case of suicide, Gandhiji wrote:)

In my opinion such marriages as are interdicted in a particular society cannot be recognized all at once or at the will of the individual. Nor has society or relatives of parties concerned any right to impose their will upon and forcibly curtail the liberty of action of the young people who may want to contract such marriages. In the instance cited by the correspondent both the parties had fully attained maturity. They could well think for themselves. No one had a right forcibly to prevent them from marrying each other if they wanted to. Society could at the most refuse to recognize the marriage, but it was the height of tyranny to drive them to suicide. Marriage taboos are not universal and are largely based on social usage. The usage varies from province to province and as between different divisions. This does not mean that the youth may ride roughshod over all established social custqms and inhibitions. Before they decide to do so, they must convert public opinion to their side. In the meantime, the individuals concerned ought patientlyto bide their time, or if they cannot do that calmly and quietly to face the consequences of social ostracism. At the same time it is equally the duty of society not to take up a heartless, step-motherly attitude towards those who might disregard or break the established conventions. In the instance described by my correspondent the guilt of driving the young couple to suicide certainly rests on the shoulders of society if the version that is before me is correct. –H, 29-5-37. 125.

801. Q. You advocate inter-caste marriages. Do you also favour marriages between Indians professing different religions? Should they declare themselves as belonging to no denomination, or can they continue their old religious practices and yet intermarry? If so, what form should the marriage ceremony take? Is it to be a purely civil function or a religious function?

Do you consider religion to be exclusively a personal matter?

A. Though Gandhiji admitted that he had not always held the view, he had come to the conclusion long ago that an inter-religious marriage was a welcome event whenever it took place. His stipulation was that such connection was not a product of lust. In his opinion it was no marriage. It was illicit intercourse. Marriage in his estimation was a sacred institution. Hence there must be mutual friendship, either party having equal respect for the religion of the other. There was no question in this of conversion. Hence the marriage ceremony would be performed by the priests belonging to either faith. This happy event could take place when the communities shed mutual enmity and had regard for the religions of the world. –H, 16-3-47, 63.

802. Q. You say that you are in favour of inter religious marriages, but at the same time you say that each arty should retain his or her own religion and, therefore, you said, you tolerated even civil marriages. Are there any instances of parties belonging to different religions keeping up their own religions

to the end of their lives? And is not the institution of civil marriage a negation of religion and does it not tend towards laxity of religion?

A. Gandhiji said that the questions were appropriate. He had no instances in mind where the parties had clung to their respective faiths up to death, because these friends whom he knew had not yet died. He had, however, under his observation men and women professing different religions and each clinging to his or her own faith without abatement. But he would go so far as to say that they need not wait for the discovery of past instances. They should create new ones so that timid ones may shed their timidity.

As to civil marriages, he did not believe in them, but he welcomed the institution of civil marriage as a much needed reform for the sake of reform. –H, 16-3-47, 67.

Marriage and Love

803. A correspondent laid down the following conditions of marriage : (I) Mutual attraction or love; (2) Eugenic fitness; (3) Approval and consent of the respective families concerned; and consideration for the interest of the social order to which one belongs; (4) Spiritual development.

I accept generally the conditions for an ideal marriage enumerated by my correspondent. But I would change their order of importance and put 'love' last in the list. By giving it the first place, the other conditions are liable to be overshadowed by it altogether and rendered more or less nugatory. Therefore, spiritual development ought to e given the first place in the choice for marriage. Service should come next, family considerations and the interest of the social order should have the third place, and mutual attraction or 'love' the fourth and the last place. This means that 'love' alone, where the other three conditions are not fulfilled, should not be held as a valid reason for marriage. At the same time, marriage where there is no love should equally be ruled out even though all the other conditions are fully complied with. I should score out the condition of eugenic fitness, because the begetting of offspring being the central purpose of marriage, eugenic fitness cannot be treated as a 'condition'; it is the sine qua non of marriage. –H, 5-6-37, 131.

The Married Estate

804. A sister, who is a good worker, and was anxious to remain celibate in order to serve better the country's cause, has recently married having met the mate of her dreams. But she imagines that in doing so she has done wrong and fallen from the high ideal which she had set before herself. I have tried to rid her mind of this delusion. It is no doubt an excellent thing for girls to remain unmarried for the sake of service, but the fact is that only one in a million is able to do so. Marriage is a natural thing in life, and to consider it derogatory in any sense is wholly wrong. When one imagines any act a fall it is difficult, however hard one tries, to raise oneself. The ideal is to look upon marriage as a sacrament and therefore to lead a life of self-restraint in the married estate. Marriage in Hinduism is one of the four ashrams. In fact the other three are based on it.

The duty of the above-mentioned and other sisters wh think like her is, therefore, not to look down upon marria but to give it its due place and make of it the sacrament it . If they exercise the necessary self-restraint, they will fin growing within themselves a greater strength for service. She who wishes to serve will naturally choose a partner in life who is of the same mind, and their joint service will be the country's gain. –H, 22-3-42, 88.

Divorce

805. Marriage confirms the right of union between two partners to the exclusion of all the others when in their joint opinion they consider such union to be desirable, but it confers no right upon one partner to demand obedience of the other to one's wish for union. What should be done when one partner on moral or other grounds cannot conform to the wishes of the other is a separate question. Personally, if divorce was the only alternative, I should not hesitate to accept it, rather than interrupt my moral progress,-assuming that I want to restrain myself on purely moral grounds. –YI, 8-10-25, 346.

Widow Remarriage

806. The total of 1921 is a trifle higher than for the two (previous) decades They only demonstrate still further the enormity of the wrong done to the Hindu girl widows. We cry out for cow-protection in the name of religion, but we refuse protection to the girl widow. In the name of religion we force widowhood upon our three lakhs of girl widows who could not understand the import of the marriage ceremony. To force widowhood upon little girls is a brutal crime for which we Hindus are daily paying dearly. If our conscience was truly awakened there would be no marriage before 15, let alone widowhood, and we would declare that these three lakhs of girls were never married. Voluntary widowhood cons: ously adopted by a woman who has felt the affection of a partner adds grace and dignity to life, sanctifies the home and uplifts religions itself. Widowhood imposed by religion or custom is an unbearable yoke and defiles the home by secret vice and degrades religion.

If we would be pure, if we would save Hinduism, we must rid ourselves of this poison of enforced widowhood. The reform must begin by those who have girl widows taking courage in both their hands and seeing that the child widows in their charge are duly and well married –not remarried. They were never really married. –YI, 5-8-26, 276.

807. Widow-remarriage is no sin—if it be, it is as much a sin as the marriage of a widower is all widowhood is not holy. It is an adornment to her who can observe it. If this sister has the courage, then let her speak out her mind to her uncle and brothers and seek their help. It they cannot assist in the marriage, then the sister will have to quit their house and take refuge in some widow-remarriage institution. –(Translated from the Hindi Navajivan of 9-5-29.)

808. Some Brahman students told me that they cannot follow this principle, that they cannot get Brahman girls sixteen years old, very few Brahmans keep their daughters unmarried till that age, the Brahman girls are married mostly before 10, 12 and 13 years. Then I say to the Brahman youth, 'Cease to be Brahman if you cannot possibly control yourself. Choose a grown up girl of 16 who became a widow when she was a child.

If you cannot get a Brahman widow who has reached that age, then go and take any girl you like. And I tell you that the God of the Hindus will pardon that boy who has preferred to marry out of his caste rather than ravish a girl of twelve.' –YI, 15-9-27, 314.

The Purdah

809. Chastity is not a hot-house growth. It cannot be protected by the surrounding wall of the purdah. It must grow from within, and to be worth anything it must be capable of withstanding every unsought temptation. –YI, 3-2-27, 37.

810. And why is thee all this morbid anxiety about female purity? Have women any say in the matter of male purity? We hear nothing of women's anxiety about men's chastity. Why should men arrogate to themselves the right to regulate female purity? It cannot be superimposed from without. It is a matter of evolution from within and therefore of individual self-effort. –YI, 25-11-26, 415.

811. Q. Do you not think that a strict enforcement of the purdah system would improve the moral condition of women?

A. Gandhiji was warned by some Muslim critics against speaking on the purdah. He had therefore some hesitation in speaking about it. But he took heart when he turned round and saw that many Hindu women observed it and that numerous Malaya Muslim women of whom he had many friends did not observe the purdah. He also knew many distinguished Muslim women of India who did not observe it. Lastly the real purdah was of the heart. A woman who peeped through the purdah and contemplated a male on whom her gaze fell violated the spirit behind it. If a woman observed it in spirit, she was truly carrying out what the great Prophet had said. –H, 23-3-47, 78.

Coeducation

812. I cannot definitely state as yet whether it will be successful or not. It does not seem to have succeeded in the West. I tried it myself years ago when I even made boys and girls sleep in the same verandah with no partition between them, Mrs. Gandhi and myself sharing the verandah with them. I must say it brought undesirable results.

Q. But do not worse things happen in purdah-ridden communities?

A. Yes, of course, but coeducation is still in an experimental stage and we cannot definitely say one way or the other as to its results. I think we should begin with the family first. There boys and girls should grow together freely and naturally. Then coeducation will come of itself. –ABP, 12-1-35.

Contraception

813. If it is contended that birth control is necessary for the nation because of overpopulation, I dispute the proposition. It has never been proved. In my opinion, by a proper land-system, better agriculture and a supplementary industry, this country is capable of supporting twice as many people as there are today. But I have joined hands with the advocates of birth control in India from the standpoint of the present political condition of the country. –YI, 2-4-125, 118.

814. *Q. For the sake of the mother whose health is drained away by too many children and for the sake of children themselves, may not birth control through contraceptives be resorted to as the next best thing to self-control?*

A. Women should have to resist their husbands. If contraceptives are resorted to, frightful results will follow. Men and women will be living for sex alone. They will become soft-brained, unhinged, in fact mental and moral wrecks.

Q. Even in exceptional cases where women are too weak for childbearing or where either of the parents is diseased can't this method be resorted to?

A. No. In cases stated above it is better that husband and wife should live apart.

I consider it inhuman to impose sterilization law on the people. But in cases of individuals with chronic diseases, it is desirable to have them sterilized if they are agreeable to it. Sterilization is a sort of contraceptive and though I am against the use of contraceptives in case of women, I do not mind voluntary sterilization in case of man since he is the aggressor.

(Mrs. Nair asked if contraceptives were not permitted, how the population problem could be solved; to which Gandhiji replied that nature would solve the problem. If people multiplied like rabbits, they will die like rabbits.) ABP, 12-1-35.

815. *Q. Is the reason you object to artificial means of birth control because of the means or the act?*

A: Yes. I object for the latter reason. I have felt that during the years still left to me if I can drive home to women's minds the truth that they are free, we shall have no birth control problem in India. If they will only learn to say 'no' to their husbands when they approach them carnally..... The real problem is that they do not want to resist them.

Q. You are giving them advice which they cannot accept. Would it not make their condition worse?

A. Not if they learn the art of resistance. It boils down to education. I want woman to learn the primary right of resistance. She thinks now that she has now got it. Among the women of India it is most difficult to drive home this truth. If I were to devote myself to birth control I would miss this primary education.

The case for birth control is not hopelessly weak, otherwise these brilliant men would not be aligned with it. If you eliminate birth control there would be other methods. As soon as you agree to eliminate certain methods as harmful, you are bound to find others. In the cases you tell of, as soon as I made the discovery I would have seen to it that the men and women were separated.

Q. But what about the woman's economic condition? She has had no preparation to support herself, especially in India. She has depended upon marriage and her husband for maintenance and her bread and butter. Who is to take care of the children? You must think of these things when you suggest separation.

A. You must devise means. I might suggest that the State take care of them. Or the law might be called in to give a divorce. At present, divorce is granted on grounds of infidelity. In the future it may be granted on grounds of health. Even then some hard cases will occur.

Q. Mr. Gandhi, there are thousands, millions, who regard your word as that of a saint. How can you ask them who are so humble, so weak, to follow, when you who are so much stronger and wiser, have taken years to bring about that self-control in your life?

Mr. Gandhi just smiled. -Mrs. Margaret Sanger in Asia, November 1936, pp. 698-702.

On Education

816. Real education consists in drawing the best out of yourself. What better book can there be than the book of humanity?-*H, 30-3-34, 55.*

National Education

817. So many strange things have been said about my views on national education, that it would perhaps not be out of place to formulate them before the public.

In my opinion the existing system of education is defective, apart from its association with an utterly unjust Government, in three most important matters:

(1) It is based upon foreign culture to the almost entire exclusion of indigenous culture.

(2) It ignores the culture of the heart and the hand, and confines itself simply to the head.

(3) Real education is impossible through a foreign medium.

Let us examine the three defects. Almost from the commencement, the textbooks deal, not with things the boys and the girls have always to deal with in their homes, but things to which they are perfect strangers. It is not through the textbooks, that a lad learns what is right and what is wrong in the home life. He is never taught to have any pride in his surroundings. The higher he goes, the farther he is removed from his home, so that at the end of his education he becomes estranged from his surroundings. He feels no poetry about the home life. The village scenes are all a sealed book to him. His own civilization is presented to him as imbecile, barbarous, superstitious and useless for all practical purposes. His education is calculated to wean him from his traditional culture.

And if the mass of educated youths are not entirely denationalized, it is because the ancient culture is too deeply embedded in them to be altogether uprooted even by an education adverse to its growth. If I had my way, I would certainly destroy the majority of the present textbooks and cause to be written textbooks which have a bearing on and correspondence with the home life, so that a boy as he learns may react upon his immediate surroundings.

Secondly, whatever may be true of other countries, in India at any rate where more than eighty par cent of the population is agricultural and another ten per cent industrial, it is a crime to make education merely literary and to unfit boys and girls for manual work in afterlife. Indeed I hold that as the larger part of our time is devoted to labour for earning our bread, our children must from their infancy be taught the dignity of such labour. Our children should not be so taught as to despise labour. There is no reason, why a peasant's son after having gone to a school should become useless as he does become as agricultural labourers.

It is a sad thing that our school boys look upon manual labour with disfavour, if not contempt. Moreover, in India, if we expect, as we must every boy and girl of school-going age to attend public schools, we have not the means to finance education in accordance with the existing style, nor are million of parents able to pay the fees that are at present imposed. Education to be universal must therefore be free. I fancy that even under an ideal system of government, we shall not be able to devote two thousand million rupees which we should require for finding education for all the children of school-going age. It follows, therefore, that our children must be made to pay in labour partly or wholly for all the education they receive. Such universal labour to be profitable can only be (to my thinking) hand-spinning and hand-weaving. But for the purposes of my proposition, it is immaterial whether we have spinning or any other form of labour, so long as it can be turned to account. Only, it will be found upon examination, that on a practical, profitable and extensive scale, there is no occupation other than the processes connected with cloth-production which can be introduced in our schools throughout India. The introduction of manual training will serve a double purpose in a poor country like ours. It will pay for the education of our children and teach them an occupation on which they can fall back in afterlife, if they choose, for earning a living. Such a system must make our children self-reliant. Nothing will demoralize the nation so much as that we should learn to despise labour.

One word only as to the education of the heart. I do not believe, that this can be imparted through books. It can only be done through the living touch of the teacher. And, who are the teachers in the primary and even secondary schools? Are they men and women of faith and character? Have they themselves received the training of the heart? Are they ever expected to take care of the permanent element in the boys an girls placed under their charge? Is not the method of engaging teachers for lower schools an effective bar against character? Do the teachers get even a living wage? And we know, that the teachers of primary schools are not selected for their patriotism. They only come who cannot find any other employment.

Finally, the medium of instruction. My views on this point are too well known to need restating. The foreign medium has caused brain-fag, put an undue strain upon the nerves of our children, made them crammers and imitators, unfitted them for original work and thought, and disabled them for filtrating their learning to the family or the masses. The foreign medium has made our children practically foreigners in their own land. It is the greatest tragedy of the existing system. The foreign medium has prevented the growth of our vernaculars. If I had the powers of a despot, I would today stop the tuition of our boys and girls through a foreign medium, and require all the teachers and professors on pain of dismissal to introduce the change forthwith. I would not wait for the preparation of textbooks. They will follow the change. It is an evil that needs a summary remedy.

My uncompromising opposition to the foreign medium has resulted in an unwarranted charge being levelled against me of being hostile to foreign culture or the learning of the English language. No reader of Young India could have missed the statement often made by me in these pages, that I regard English as the language of international commerce and diplomacy, and therefore consider its knowledge on the part of some of us as essential. As it contains some of the richest treasures of thought and literature, I would certainly encourage its careful study among those who have linguistic talents and expect them to translate those treasures for the nation in its vernaculars.

Nothing can be farther from my thought than that we should become exclusive or erect barriers. But I do respectfully contend that an appreciation of other cultures can fitly follow, never precede, an appreciation and assimilation of our own. It is my firm opinion that no culture has treasures so rich as ours has. We have not known it, we have been made even to deprecate its study and depreciate its value. We have almost ceased to live it. An academic grasp without practice behind it is like an embalmed corpse, perhaps lovely to look at but nothing to inspire or ennoble. My religion forbids me to belittle or disregard other cultures, as it insists under pain *of* civil suicide upon imbibing and living my own.—*YI, 1-9-21, 276*

The Cause of the Vernaculars

818. It is evident that unless we advance this cause, we shall not be able to remove the growing intellectual and cultural gulf between our men and women and between the classes and the masses. It is also equally certain that the vernacular medium alone can stimulate originality in thought in the largest number of persons.—*YI, 21-4-20, Tagore, 465.*

Religious Instruction and the State

819. Q. Should religious instruction form part of the school curriculum as approved by the state? Do you favour separate schools for children belonging to different denominations for facility of religious instruction? Or, should religious instruction be left in the hands of private bodies? If so, do you think it is right for the state to subsidize such bodies?

A. As to this question Gandhiji said that he did not believe in state religion even though the whole community had one religion. The state interference would probably always be unwelcome. Religion was purely a personal matter. There were in reality as many religions as minds. Each mind had a different conception of God from that of the other.

He was also opposed to state aid, partly or wholly, to religious bodies. For he knew that an institution or group, which did not manage to finance its own religious teaching, was a stranger to true religion. This did not mean that the state schools would not give ethical teaching. The fundamental ethics were common to all religions. *–H, I6-3-47, 63.*

820. I do not believe that the state can concern itself or cope with religious instruction. I believe that religious education must be the sole concern of religious associations. Do not mix up religion and ethics. I believe that fundamental ethics is common to all religions. Teaching of fundamental ethics is undoubtedly a function of the state. By religion I have not in mind fundamental ethics but what goes by the name of denominationalism. We have suffered enough from state-aided religion and a state church. A society or a group, which depends partly or wholly on state aid for the existence of its religion, does not deserve or, better still, does not have any religion worth the name. I do not need to give any illustrations in support of this obvious truth as it is to me. *—H, 23-3-47, 76.*

821. Religion was a personal matter and if we succeeded in confining it the personal plane, all would be well in our political life. *–H,31-8-47, 303.*

Character-building, First

822. Q. What is your goal in education when India obtains self-rule?

A. Character-building. I would try to develop courage, strength, virtue, to ability to forget oneself in working towards great aims. This is more important than literacy, academic learning is only a means to this greater end. That is why India's great lack of literacy, deplorable as it is, does not appeal to me nor make me feel that India is unfit for self-rule.

Q. Would you try to bring about any specific kind of social organization through education?

A. I would feel that if we succeed in building the character of the individual, society will take care of itself. I would be quite willing to trust the organization of society to individuals so developed.

Q. In developing the new national spirit in India would you like to make patriotic feelings so strong that duty to one's country would be a higher good than obeying one's personal conscience?

A. I hope that will never be. One's own inner convictions come first always. But in a nation where character is developed in all individuals, there can be no conflict between the dictates of one's own conscience and those of the State.—Carlton Washburne: *Remakers of Mankind. (1932),PP.104-05.*

The Place of Literacy

823. Literary training by itself adds not an inch to one's moral height and character-building is independent of literary training.—*YI,1-6-21, 172.*

824. What is literary training worth if it cramp and confine us at a critical moment in national life? Knowledge and literary training are no recompense for emasculation. *-YI,21-6-28, 205.*

825. Let them (students) realize that learning without courage is like a waxen statue beautiful to look at but bound to melt at the least touch of a hot substance. *-YI,12-7-28,236.*

826. But although much good and useful work can be done without a knowledge of the three R's, it is my firm belief that we cannot always do without such knowledge. It develops and sharpens one's intellect, and it increases our capacity of doing good. I have never placed an unnecessarily high value on the knowledge of the three R's. I am only attempting to assign its proper place to it. I have pointed out from time to time that there is no justification for men to deprive women of, or to deny to them, equal rights on the ground of their illiteracy. But education is essential for enabling women to assert these natural rights, to exercise them wisely, and to work for their expansion; again, the true knowledge of self is unattainable by the millions who lack such education. Many a book is full of innocent pleasure, and this will be denied to us without education. It

is no exaggeration to say that a human being without education is not far removed from an animal. Education, therefore, is necessary for women as it is for men. —(Speech delivered on20-2-18)*WSI,3.*

827. I am not sure that it is not better for the children to have much of the preliminary instruction imparted to them vocally. To impose o children of tender age a knowledge of the alphabet and the ability to read before they can gain general knowledge is to deprive them, whilst they are fresh, of the power of assimilating instruction by word of mouth. —*YI, I6-9-26, 323.*

828. This utterly false idea that intelligence can be developed only through book-reading should give place to the truth that the quickest development of the mind can be achieved by artisan's work being learnt in a scientific manner. True development of the mind commences immediately the apprentice is taught at every step why a particular manipulation of the hand or a tool is required. The problem of the unemployment of students can be solved without difficulty, if they will rank themselves among the common labourers. —*H, 9-I-37, 386.*

Basic Education

839. I hold that true education of the intellect can only come through a proper exercise and training of the bodily organs, e.g. hands, feet, eyes, ears, nose, etc. In other words an intelligent use of the bodily organs in a child provides the best and quickest way of developing his intellect. But unless the development of the mind and body goes hand in hand with prove to be a prove to be a poor lopsided affair. By spiritual training I mean education of the heart. A proper and all-round development of the mind, therefore, can take place only when it proceeds pari passu with the education of the physical and spiritual faculties of the child. They constitute an indivisible whole. According to this theory, therefore, it would be a gross fallacy to suppose that they can be developed piecemeal or independently of one another.—H, 8-5-37, I04.

830. By education I mean an all-round drawing out of the best in child and man-body, mind and spirit. Literacy is not

the end of education nor even the beginning. It is only one of the means whereby man and woman can be educated. Literacy in itself is no education. I would therefore begin the child's education by teaching it a useful handicraft and enabling it to produce from the moment it begins its training. Thus every school can be made self-supporting, the condition being that the state takes over the manufactures of these schools.

I hold that highest development of the mind and the soul is possible under such a system of education. Only every handicraft has to be taught not merely mechanically as is done today but scientifically, i.e. the child should know the why and the wherefore of every process. I am not writing this without some confidence, because it has the backing of experience. This method is being adopted more or less completely wherever spinning is being taught to workers.

I have myself taught sandal-making and even spinning on these lines with good results. This method does not exclude o these lines with good results. This method does not exclude a knowledge of history and geography. But I find that this is best taught by transmitting such general information by word of mouth. One imparts ten times as much in this manner as by reading and writing. The signs of the alphabet may be taught later when the pupil has learnt to distinguish wheat from chaff and when he has somewhat developed his or her tastes. This is a revolutionary proposal but it saves immense labour and enables a student to acquire in one year what he may take much longer to learn. This means all-round economy. Of course the pupil learns mathematics whilst he is learning his handicraft.

I attach the greatest importance to primary education which according to my conception should be equal to the present matriculation less English. -H, 31-7-37, 197.

831. We have up to now concentrated on stuffing children's minds with all kinds of information, without ever thinking of stimulating and developing them. Let us now cry a halt and concentrate on education the child properly through manual work, not as a side activity, but as the prime means of intellectual training. You have to train the boys in one occupation or

another. Round this special occupation you will train up his mind, his body, his handwriting, his artistic sense, and so on. He will be master of the craft he learns. –H, 18-9-37, 261.

832. The scheme that I wish to place before you today is not the teaching of some handicraft side with so-called liberal education. I want that the whole education should be imparted through some handicraft or industry. It might be objected that in the middle ages only handicrafts were taught to the students; but the occupational training, then, was far from serving an educational purpose. The crafts were taught only for the sake of the crafts, without any attempt to develop the intellect as well. In this age those born to certain professions had forgotten them, had taken to clerical careers and were lost to countryside. The remedy lies in imparting the whole art and science of a craft through practical training and there through imparting the whole education.

I am very keen on finding the expenses of a teacher through the product of the manual work of his pupils, because I am convinced that there is no other way to carry education to crores of our children. We cannot wait until we have the necessary revenue and until the Viceroy reduces the military expenditure. You should bear in mind that this primary education would include the elementary principles of sanitation, hygiene, nutrition, of doing their won work, helping parents at home etc. The present generation of boys know no clean lines, no self-help, and are physically weak. I would therefore, give compulsory physical training through musical drill.—Ed, Rec., 61-63 or H, 30-10-37, 323.

833. I am a firm believer in the principle of free and compulsory primary education For India. I also hold that we shall realize this only by teaching the children useful vocation and utilizing it as a means for cultivating their mental, physical and spiritual faculties. Let no one consider these economic calculations in connection with education as sordid or out of place. There is nothing essentially sordid about economic calculations. True economics never militates against the highest ethical standard, just as true ethics to be worth its name must at the same time, be also good economics. –H, 9-10-37, 292.

834. What kinds of vocation are the fittest for being taught to children in urban schools? There is no hard and fast rule about it. But my reply is clear. I want to resuscitate the villages of India. Today our villages have become a mere appendage to the cities. They exist, as it were, to be exploited by the latter and depend on the latter's sufferance. This is unnatural. It is only when the cities realize the duty of making an adequate return to the villages for the strength and sustenance which they derive from them, instead of selfishly exploiting them, that a healthy and moral relationship between the two will spring up. And if the city children are to play their part in this great and noble work of social reconstruction, the vocations through which they are to achieve their education ought to be directly related to the requirements of the villages. So far as I can see, the various processes of cotton manufacture from ginning and cleaning of cotton to the spinning of yarn, answer this test as nothing else does. Even today the cotton is grown in the villages and is ginned and spun and converted into cloth in the cities. But the chain of processes which cotton undergoes in the kills from the beginning to the end constitutes a huge tragedy of waste in men, materials and mechanical power.

My plan to impart primary education through the medium of village handicrafts like spinning and carding, etc. is thus conceived as the spearhead of a silent social revolution fraught with most far-reaching consequences. It will provide a healthy and moral basis of relationship between the city and the village and thus go a long way towards eradicating some of the worst evils of the present social insecurity and poisoned relationship between the classes. It will check the progressive decay of our villages and lay the foundation of a just social order in which there is no unnatural division between the 'haves' and the 'have-nots' and everybody is assured of a living wage and the right to freedom. And all this would be accomplished without the horror of a bloody class war or a colossal capital expenditure such as would be involved in the mechanization of a vast continent like India. Nor would it entail a helpless dependence on foreign imported machinery of technical skill. Lastly, by obviating the necessity for highly specialized talent, it would place the destiny of the masses, as it were, in their own hands.

But who will bell the cat? Will the city-folk listen to me at all? Or, will mine remain a mere cry in the wilderness? Replies to these and similar questions will depend more on lovers of education like my correspondent living in cities than on me. —H, 9-10-37, 293.

Higher Education

835. I would revolutionize college education and relate it to national necessities. There would be degrees for mechanical and other engineers. They would be attached to the different industries which would pay for the training of the graduates they need. Thus the Tatas would be expected to run a college for training engineers under the supervision of the state, the mill associations would run among them a college for training graduates whom they need. Similarly for other industries that may be named. Commerce will have its college. There remain arts, medicine and agriculture. Several private arts colleges are today self-supporting. That State would. Therefore, cease to run its own. Medical colleges would be attached to certified hospitals. As they are popular among moneyed men they may be expected by voluntary contributions to support medical colleges. And agricultural colleges to be worthy of the name must be self-supporting. I have a painful experience of some agricultural graduates. Their knowledge is superficial. They lack practical experience. But if they had their apprenticeship on farms which are self-sustained and answer the requirements of the country, they would not have to gain experience after getting their degrees and at the expense of their employers. *—H, 31-7-37, 197.*

836. The Rt. Hon. Shri Srinivasa Shastri has criticized, as he had a perfect right to do, the views I timidly and very briefly expressed some time ago on higher education. I entertain a very high regard for him as man, patriot and scholar. It is therefore always painful to me when I find myself disagreeing with him. And yet duty compels me to re-express my views on higher education more fully than before, so that the reader may make out for himself the difference between his views and mine.

I admit my limitations. I have no university education worth the name. My high school career was never above the average, I was thankful if I could pass my examinations. Distinction in the school was beyond my aspiration. Nevertheless I do hold very strong views on education in general, including what is called higher education. And I own it to the country that my views should be clearly known and taken for what they may be worth. I must shed the timidity that has led almost to self-suppression. I must not fear ridicule and even loss of popularity or prestige. If I hide my belief, I shall never correct errors of judgment. I am always eager to discover them and more than eager to correct them.

Let me now state my conclusions held for a number of ears and enforced wherever I had opportunity of enforcing them:

(1) I am not opposed to education even of the highest type attainable in the world.

(2) The state must pay for it wherever it has definite use for it.

(3) I am opposed to all higher education being paid for from the general revenue.

(4) It is my firm conviction that the vast amount of the so-called education it arts, given in our colleges, is sheer waste and has resulted in unemployment among the educated classes. What is more, it has destroyed the health, both mental and physical, of the boys and girls who have the misfortune to go through the grind in our colleges.

(5) The medium of a foreign language through which higher education has been imparted in India has caused incalculable intellectual and moral injury to the nation. We are too near our own times to judge the enormity of the damage done. And we judges-an almost impossible feat. I must give my reasons for the conclusions set forth above. This I can best do, perhaps, by giving a chapter from my own experience.

Up to the age of 12 all the knowledge I gained was through Gujarati, my mother tongue. I knew then something of Arithmetic, History and Geography. Then I entered a High school. For the first three years the mother tongue was still the medium. But the school-master's business was to drive English into the pupil's head. Therefore more than half of our time was given to learning English and mastering its arbitrary spelling and pronunciation. It was a painful discovery to have to learn a language that was not pronounced as it was written. It was a strange experience to have to learn the spelling by heart. But that is by the way, and irrelevant to my argument. However, for the first three years, it was comparatively plain sailing.

The pillory began with the fourth year. Everything had to be learnt through English-Geometry, Algebra, Chemistry, Astronomy, History, and Geography. The tyranny of English was so great that even Sanskrit or Persian had to be learnt through English, not through the mother tongue. If any boy spoke in the class in Gujarati which he understood, he was punished. It did not matter to the teacher if a boy spoke bad English which he could neither pronounce correctly nor understand fully. Why should the teacher worry? His own English was by no means without blemish. It could not be otherwise. English was as much a foreign language to him as to his pupils. The result was chaos. We the boys had to learn many things by heart, though we could not understand them fully and often not at all. My head used to reel as the teacher was struggling to make his exposition on Geometry understood by us. I could make neither head nor tail of Geometry till we reached the 13th theorem of the first book of Euclid.

And let me confess to the reader that in spite of all my love for the mother tongue, I do not to this day know the Gujarati equivalents of the technical terms of Geometry, Algebra and the like. I know now that what I took four years to learn of Arithmetic, Geometry, Algebra, Chemistry and Astronomy, I should have learnt easily in one year, if I had not to learn them through English but Gujarati. My grasp of the subjects would have been easier and clearer. My Gujarati vocabulary would have been richer. I would have made use of such knowledge in my own home. This English medium created an impassable barrier between me and the members of my family, who had not gone through English schools. My father knew nothing of what I was doing. I could not, even if I had wished it, interest my father in what I was learning. For though he had ample intelligence, he knew not a word of English. I was fast becoming a strange in my own home. I certainly became a superior person. Even my dress began to undergo imperceptible changes. What happened to me was not an uncommon experience. It was common to the majority.

The first three years in the High School made little addition to my stock of general knowledge. They were a preparation for fitting the boys for teaching them everything through English. High schools were schools for cultural conquest by the English. The knowledge gained by the three hundred boys of my High School became a circumscribed possession. It was not for transmission to the masses.

A word about literature. We had to learn several books of English prose and English poetry. No doubt all this was nice. But that knowledge has been of no use to me in serving or bringing me in touch with the masses. I am unable to say that if I should have missed a rare treasure. If I had, instead, passed those precious seven years in mastering Gujarati and had learnt Mathematics, sciences and Sanskrit and other subjects through Gujarati, I could easily have shared the knowledge so gained with my neighbours. I would have enriched Gujarati, and who can say that I would not have, with my habit of application and my inordinate love for the country and mother tongue, made a richer and greater contribution to the service of the masses?

I must not be understood to decry English or noble literature. The columns of the Harijan are sufficient evidence of my love of English. But the nobility of its literature climate or the scenery of England can avail her. India has to flourish in her own climate and scenery and her own literature, even though all the three may be inferior to the English climate, scenery and literature. We and our children must build on our own heritage. If we borrow another, we impoverish our own. We can never grow on foreign victuals. I want the nation to have the treasures contained in that language, and for that matter in the other languages of the world, through its own vernaculars.

I do not need to learn Bengali in order to know the beauties of Rabindranath's matchless productions. I get them through good translations. Gujarati boys and girls do not need to learn Russian to appreciate Tolstoy's short stories. They learn them through good translations. It is the boast of Englishmen that the best of the world's literary output is in the hands of that nation in simple English inside of a week its publication. Why need I learn English to get at the best of what Shakespeare and Milton thought and wrote?

It would be good economy to set apart a class of students whose business would be to learn the best of what is to be learnt in the different languages of the world and give the translation in the vernaculars. Our masters chose the wrong way for us, and habit has made the wrong appear as right.

I find daily proof of the increasing and continuing wrong being dome to the millions by our false de-Indianizing education. Those graduates who are my valued associates themselves flounder when they have to give expression to their innermost thoughts. They are strangers in their own homes. Their vocabulary in the mother tongue is so limited that they cannot always finish their speech without having recourse to English words and even sentences. Nor can they exist without English books. I cite the case of my companions to show how deep the evil has gone. For we have made a conscious effort to mend ourselves.

It has been argued that the wastage that occurs in our colleges need not worry us if, out of the collegians, one Jagadish Bose can be produced by them. I should freely subscribe to the argument, if the wastage was unavoidable. I hope I have shown that it was and is even now avoidable. Moreover the creation of a Bose does not help the argument. For Bose was not a product of the present education. He rose in spite of the terrible handicaps under which he had to labour. And his knowledge became almost intransmissible to the masses. We seem to have come to think that no one can hope to be like a Bose unless he knows English. I cannot conceive a grosser superstition than this. No Japanese feels so helpless as we seem to do. Nothing but a heroic remedy can deal with the deep-seated evil which I have endeavoured to describe. The Congress Ministers can, if they will, mitigate it, if they cannot remove it.

Universities must be made self-supporting The State should simply educate those whose services it would need. For all other branches of learning it should encourage private effort. The medium of instruction should be altered at once and at any cost, the provincial languages being given their rightful place. I would prefer temporary chaos in higher education to the criminal waste that is daily accumulating.

In order to enhance the status and the market-value of the provincial languages, I would have the language of the law courts to be the language of the law courts to be the language of the province where the court is situated. The proceedings of the provincial legislatures must be in the language, or even in the languages, of the province where a province has more than one language within its borders. I suggest to the legislators that they could, by enough application, inside of a month, understand the languages of their provinces. There is nothing to prevent a Tamilian from easily learning the simple grammar and a few hundred words of Telugu, Malayalam and Kanarese, all allied to Tamil. At the centre Hindustani must reign supreme.

In my opinion this is not a question to be decided by academicians. They cannot decide through what language the boys and girls of a place are to be educated. That question is already decided for them in every free country. Nor can they decide the subjects to be taught. That depends upon the wants of the country to which they belong. Theirs is the privilege of enforcing the nation's will in the best manner possible. When this country becomes really free, the question of medium will be settled only one way. The academicians will frame the syllabus and prepare textbooks accordingly. And the products of the education of a free India will answer the requirements of the country as today they answer those of the foreign ruler. So long as we the educated classes play with this question, I very much fear we shall not produce the free and healthy India of our dream. We have to grow by strenuous effort out of our bondage, whether it is educational, economical, social or political. The effort itself is three-fourths of the battle.

Thus I claim that I am not an enemy of higher education. But I am an enemy of higher education as it is given in this country. Under my scheme there will be more and better libraries, more and better laboratories, more and better research institutes. Under it we should have an army of chemists, engineers and other experts who will be real servants of the nation, and answer the varied and growing requirements of a people who are becoming increasingly conscious of their rights and wants. And all these experts will speak, not a foreign tongue, but the language of the people. The knowledge gained by them will be the common property of the people. There will be truly original work instead of mere imitation. And the cost will be evenly and justly distributed. *–H, 9-7-38, 176.*

The Future Culture of India

837. The Indian culture of our times is in the making. Many of us are striving to produce a blend of all the cultures which seem today to be in clash with one another. No culture can live, if it attempts to be exclusive. There is no such thing as pure Aryan culture in existence today in India. Whether the Aryans were indigenous to India or were unwelcome intruders, does not interest me much. What does interest me is the fact that my remote ancestors blended with one another with the utmost freedom and we of the present generation are a result of that blend. Whether we are doing any good to the country of our birth and the tiny globe which sustains us or whether we are a burden, the future alone will show. –H, 9-5-36,100.

838. I do not want my house to be walled in on all sides and my windows to be stuffed. I want the cultures of all lands to be blown about my house as freely as possible. But I refuse to be blown off my feet by any. I would have our young men and women with literary tastes to learn as much of English and other world-languages as they like, and then expect them to give the benefits of their learning to India and to the world like a Bose, a Roy or the Poet himself. But I would not have a single Indian to forget, neglect or be ashamed of his mother tongue, or to feel that he or she cannot think or express the best thoughts in his or her own vernacular. Mine is not a religion of the prison-house. –YI, 1-6-21, 170.

839. The (Gujarat) Vidyapith does not propose merely to feed on, or repeat, the ancient cultures. It rather hopes to build a new culture based on the traditions of the past and enriched by the experience of later times. It stands for synthesis of the different cultures that have come to say in India, that have influenced Indian life, and that, in their turn, have themselves been influenced be the spirit of the soil. This synthesis will naturally be of the Swadeshi type, where each culture is assured its legitimate place, and not of the American pattern, where one dominant culture absorbs the rest, and where the aim is not towards harmony, but towards an artificial and forced unity. –YI, 17-11-20, Tagore, 45.

MISCELLANEOUS

Guide to Health

840. Our body has been given to us on the understanding that we should render devoted service to God with its aid. It is our duty to keep it pure and unstained from within as will as from without, so as to render it back to the Giver when the time comes for it, in the state of purity in which we got it. –*GH, 129.*

841. The relation between the body and the mind is so intimate that, if either of them got out of order, the whole system would suffer. Hence it follows that a pure character is the foundation of health in the real sense of the term; and we may say that all evil thoughts and evil passions are but different forms of disease. –*GH, 8.*

842. Perfect health can be attained only by living in obedience to the laws of God, and defying the power of Satan. True happiness is impossible without true health and true health is impossible without a rigid control of the palate. All the other senses will automatically come under control when the palate has been brought under control. And he who has conquered his senses has really conquered the whole world, and he becomes a part of God. –*GH, 131.*

Municipal Sanitation

843. The one thing which we can and must learn from the West is the science of municipal sanitation. The peoples of the

West have evolved a science of corporate sanitation and hygiene from which we have much to learn. We must modify Western methods of sanitation to suit our requirements. And as my patriotism is inclusive and admits of no enmity or ill-will, I do not hesitate, in spite of my horror of Western materialism, to take from the West what is beneficial for me. *–YI, 26-12-24, 430.*

Institutions and Public Support

844. It is my settled conviction that no deserving institution ever dies for want of support. Institutions that have died have done so either because there was nothing in them to commend them to the public or because those in control lost faith, or which is perhaps the same thing, lost stamina. I would therefore urge the conductors of such institutions not to give in because of the general depression. It is a time of test for worthy institutions. *–YI, 15-10-25, 351.*

845. Q. What is the outlook, in view of the precarious financial position of our Ashrams and institutions (for Harriman work) today?

A: It is not our financial position, but our moral position that is precarious. No movement or activity that has the sure foundation of the purity of character of its workers, is ever in danger to come to an end for want of funds. Then we in Gujarat have to realize that we must not always depend only on our moneyed men. We have to tap humbler resources. Our middle classes and even poor classes support so many beggars, so many temples, why will they not support a few good workers? We must beg from door to door, beg grain, beg copper coins, do as they do in Bihar and Maharashtra. In Maharashtra they have paisa funds and mushti funds. It will be the finest form of propaganda. But remember that everything will depend on the singleness of your purpose, your devotion to the task and the purity of your character. People won't give for such work unless they are sure of our selflessness.

Q. If it is impossible to get the caste Hindus' cooperation in anti-untouchability work, would it not be better to take up the village industries work?

A. That is a delusion. You may be sure that he who gives up Harijan work on a pretext like that will be able to do less for the village industries work. You can't settle down in a village and miss the Harijans who are the foundation of society. *–H, 28-11-36, 331.*

Running Institutions on Public Money

846. I had learnt at the outset not to carry on public work with borrowed money. One could rely on people's promise in most matters except in matters of money. *–Auto, 186.*

847. The public should be the bank for all public institutions, which should not last a day longer than the public wish. An institution run with the interest of accumulated capital ceases to be amenable to public opinion and becomes autocratic and self-righteous. *–SA, 202.*

848. Take the illustration of the new educational experiment. The experiment I said must go on without asking for monetary help. Otherwise, after my death the whole organization would go to pieces. The fact is that the moment financial stability is assured, spiritual bankruptcy is also assured. *–H, 10-12-38, 371.*

849. After considerable experience with the many public institutions which I have managed, it has become my firm conviction that it is not good to run public institutions on permanent funds. A permanent fund carries in itself the seed of the moral fall of the institution. A public institution means an institution conducted with the approval, and from the funds, of the public. When such an institution ceases to have public support, it forfeits its right to exist. Institutions maintained on permanent funds are often found to ignore public opinion, and are frequently responsible for acts contrary to it. In our country we experience this at every step. Some of the so-called religious trusts have ceased to render any accounts. The trustees have become the owners and are responsible to none. I have no doubt that the ideal is for public institutions to live, like nature, from day to day. The institution that fails to win public support has no right to exist as such. The subscriptions that an institution annually receives are a test of its popularity and the honesty

of its management, and I am of opinion that every institution should submit to that test. But let no one misunderstand me. My remarks do not apply to the bodies which cannot, by their very nature, be conducted without permanent buildings. What I mean to say is that the current expenditure should be found from subscriptions voluntarily received from year to year. – *Auto, 243.*

850. Because an institution happens to have plenty of funds it does not mean that it should anyhow spend away every pie that it possesses. The golden rule is not to hesitate to ask for or spend even a crore when it is absolutely necessary and when it is not, to hoard up every pie though one may have a crore of rupees at one's disposal. *–YI, 21-5-31, 118.*

Public Accounts

851. Public money belongs to the poor public of India than whom there is none poorer on earth. We have to be more wakeful, none cautious, more careful; and let us be ready to account for every pie that we receive from the public. *–YI, 16-4-31,74.*

852. Carefully kept accounts are a sine qua non for any organization. Without properly dept accounts it is impossible to maintain truth in its pristine purity. *–Auto, 188.*

853. If we do not account for every single pie we receive and do not make a judicious use of the funds, we shall deserve to be blotted out of public life. *–YI, 6-7-21, 209.*

On Journalism

854. The sole aim of Journalism should be service. *–Auto, 349.*

855. One of the objects of a newspaper is to understand the popular feeling and give expression to it; another is to arouse among the people certain desirable sentiments; and the third is fearlessly to expose popular defects. *–IHR, 1.*

865. Reference to abuses in the States is undoubtedly a necessary part of journalism and it is a means of creating public opinion. Only, my scope is strictly limited; I have taken up journalism not for its sake but merely as an aid to what I

have conceived to be my mission in life. My mission is to teach by example and precept under severe restraint the use of the matchless weapon of satyagraha which is as direct corollary of nonviolence and truth. I am anxious, indeed I am impatient, to demonstrate that there is no remedy for the many ills of life wave that of nonviolence. It is a solvent strong enough to melt the stoniest heart. To be true to my faith, therefore, I may not write merely to excite passion. The reader can have no idea of the restraint I have to exercise from week to week in the choice of topics and my vocabulary. It is training for me. It enables me to peep into myself and to make discoveries of my weaknesses. Often my vanity dictates a smart expression or my anger a harsh adjective. It is a terrible ordeal but a fine exercise to remove these weeds. The reader sees the pages of the Young India fairly well-dressed-up and sometimes, with Romain Rolland, he is inclined to say 'what a fine old man this must be'. Well, let the world understand that the fineness is carefully and prayerfully cultivated. And if it has proved acceptable to some whose opinion I cherish, let the reader understand that when that fineness has become perfectly natural, i.e. when I have become incapable of evil and when nothing harsh or haughty occupies, be it momentarily, my thought-world, then and not till then, my nonviolence will move all the hearts of all the world. I have placed before me and the reader no impossible ideal or ordeal. *–YI, 2-7-25, 232.*

857. Unfortunately, the newspapers had become more important to the average man than the scriptures. He would fain advise them to give up reading newspapers. They would lose nothing by so doing whereas real food for their minds and spirits lay in the scriptures and other good literature.

The press was called the Fourth Estate. It was definitely a power but to misuse that power was criminal. He was a journalist himself and would appeal to fellow journalists to realize their responsibility and to carry on their work with no idea other than that of upholding the truth. *–H, 27-4-47, 128.*

The Learned Professions

858. If you would spiritualize the practice of law, you must not make your profession subservient to the interests of your

purse, but use your profession for the service of your country. *–Ceylon, 36.*

859. Put your talents in the service of the country instead of converting them to f.s.d. If you are a medical man, there is disease enough in India to need all your medical skill. If you are a lawyer, there are differences and quarrels enough in India. Instead of fomenting more trouble, patch up those quarrels and stop litigation. If you are an engineer, build model houses suited to the means and needs of your people and yet full of health and fresh air. There is nothing that you have learnt which cannot be turned to account.

(The friend who had asked the question was an accountant and Gandhiji accordingly said to him): There is dire need everywhere for accountants to audit the accounts of the Congress and its adjunct associations. Cone to India—I will give you enough work and also hire—four annas per day which is surely more than millions in India get. *–YI, 5-11-31, 334.*

860. A medical practitioner from Kenya asks whether medical practitioners can engage in moneylending business or speculation. I have long held the opinion that professional men, whether medical or legal or other, should not seek to add to their income by speculation or other pursuits. It tends to make them careless in their special work, There have been cases in which doctors and lawyers have ruined their reputation by going outside their profession to make money.—*H, I6-I2-39, 379.*

On Art

861. There are two aspects of things-the outward and the inward. It is purely a matter of emphasis with me. The outward has no meaning except in so far as it helps the inward. All true art is thus the expression of the soul. The outward forms have value only in so far as they are the expression of the inner spirit in man. Art of that nature has the greatest possible appeal for me. But I know that many call themselves artists, and are recognized as such, and yet in their works there is absolutely no trace of the soul's upward urge and unrest. All true art must help the soul to realize its inner self. In my own case, I find

that I can do entirely without external forms in my soul's realization. My room may have blank walls; and I may even dispense with the roof, so that I may gaze out upon the starry heavens overhead that stretch in an unending expanse of beauty. What conscious art of man can give me the panoramic scenes that open out before me, when I look up to the sky above with all its shining stars? This, however, does not mean that I refuse to accept the value of productions of art, generally accepted as such, but only that I personally feel how inadequate these are compared with the eternal symbols of beauty in Nature. These productions of man's art have their value only so far as they help the soul onward towards self-realization.

All truths, not merely true ideas, but truthful faces, truthful pictures, or songs, are highly beautiful. People generally fail to see beauty in truth, the ordinary man runs away from it and becomes blind to the beauty in it. Whenever men begin to see beauty in truth, then true art will arise.

Truly beautiful creations come when right perception is at work. If these moments are rare in life they are also rare in art.—*YI, 13-11-24, 377.*

862. True art takes note not merely of form but also of what lies behind. There is an art that kills and an art that gives life. True art must be evidence of happiness, contentment and purity of its authors. —*YI, 11-821,253.*

863. We have somehow accustomed ourselves to the belief that art is independent of the purity of private life. I can say with all experience at my command that nothing could be more untrue. As I am nearing the end of my earthly life I can say that purity of life is the highest and truest art. The art of producing purity of life is the highest and truest art. The art of producing good music from a cultivated voice can be achieved by many, but the art of producing that music from the harmony of a pure life is achieved very rarely.—*H, 19-2-38, 10.*

Music

864. Music means rhythm, order. Its effect is electrical. It immediately soothes. Unfortunately like our shastras, music has been the prerogative of the few. It has never become

nationalized in the modern sense. If I had any influence with volunteer boy scouts and Seva Samiti organizations, I would make compulsory a proper singing in company of national songs. And to that end I should have great musicians attending every Congress or Conference and teaching mass music.—*YI, 8-9-20, Tagore, 763.*

Music and Education

865. In Pandit Khare's opirion, based upon widc experience, music should form part of the syllabus of primary education. I heartily endorse the proposition. The modulation of the voice is as necessary as the training of the hand. Physical drill, handicrafts, drawing and music should go hand in hand in order to draw the best out of the boys and girls and create in them a real interest in their tuition.

That this means a revolution in the system of training is admitted. If the future citizens of the State are to build a sure foundation for life's work, these four things are necessary. One has only to visit only primary school to have a striking demonstration of slovenliness, disorderliness and discordant speech. I have no doubt, therefore, that when the Education Ministers in the several provinces recast the system of education and make it answer the requirements of the country, they will not omit the essentials to which I have drawn attention. My plan of primary education certainly comprises these things which easily become possible the moment you remove from the children's shoulders the burden of having to master a difficult foreign language. *–H, 11-9-37, 250.*

Drill

866. The object of mass drill is to enable large bodies of people to perform any movement rhythmically and swiftly and with absolute precision. What a saving in national time and energy it would mean if we could do that in our public meetings and functions! There is a silent music in disciplined movement of masses of men and women. Just now I asked you to move a little towards me so that my low voice may reach you. Had you advanced far enough in your drill, you would have been able to perform that movement with ease, without any noise

or confusion. There is a rhythm and music in drill that makes action effort less and eliminates fatigue. If the whole nation of three hundred millions could be drilled so as to move together and act together and if necessary to die together as one man, we should attain independence without striking a blow and set an example of a peaceful revolution the whole world to emulate.—*H, 31-12-38, 411.*

Regarding Ancient Things

867. I do not subscribe to the superstition that everything is good because it is ancient. I do not believe either that anything is good because it is Indian. *-YI, 8-1-25, 11.*

868. I am no indiscriminate worshipper of all that goes under the name 'ancient'. I never hesitate to demolish all that is evil or immoral, no matter how ancient it may be, but with that reservation. I must confess to you that I am an adorer of ancient institutions and it hurts me to think that people in their rush for everything modern despise all their ancient traditions and ignore them in their lives. *-Ceylon, 107.*

869. I came by a process of examination to this irresistible conclusion that there was nothing so very ancient in this world as these two good old things—truth and nonviolence. I also discovered that I must not attempt to revive ancient practices if they were inconsistent with, call it if you will, modern life as it must be lived. Ancient practices may have been perfectly good and perhaps absolutely necessary at the time when those practices were adopted, but they mighty be entirely out of date with modern needs and still not be contrary to truth or nonviolence. *-Ceylon, 131.*

Swadeshi

870. I have never considered the exclusion of everything foreign under every conceivable circumstance as a part of Swadeshi. The broad definition of Swadeshi is the use of all home-made things to the exclusion of foreign things, in so far as such use is necessary for the protection of home-industry, more especially those industries without which India will become pauperized. In my opinion, therefore, Swadeshi which excludes the use of everything foreign, no matter how beneficent it may

be and irrespective of the fact that it impoverishes nobody, is a narrow interpretation of Swadeshi.-*YI, 17-6-26, 218.*

871. But even Swadeshi, like any other good thing, can be ridden to death if it is made a fetish. That is a danger that must be graded against. To reject foreign manufactures merely because they are foreign, and to go on wasting national time and money in the promotion in one's country of manufactures for which it is not suited would be criminal folly, and a negation of the Swadeshi spirit. A true votary of Swadeshi will never harbour ill-will towards the foreigner, he will not be moved by antagonism towards anybody on earth. Swadeshism is not a cult of hatred. It is a doctrine of selfless service, that has its roots in the purest ahimsa, i.e. love. –*YM, 95.*

872. I wish to utter a word of caution against your believing that I am an indiscriminate despiser of everything that comes from the West. There are many things which I have myself assimilated from the West. –Ceylon, 108.

True Swadeshi

873. If I have to use the adjective 'true' before Swadeshi, a critic may well ask, 'Is there also false Swadeshi?' Unfortunately I have to answer 'Yes'. As, since the days of Khadi, I am supposed to be an authority on Swadeshi, numerous conundrums are presented to me by correspondents. And I have been obliged to distinguish between the two kinds of Swadeshi. If foreign capital is mixed with indigenous, or if foreign talent is mixed with indigenous, is the enterprise Swadeshi? There are other questions too. But I had better reproduce the definition I gave to a Minister the other day. 'Any article is Swadeshi if it sub serves the interest of the millions, even though the capital and talent are foreign but under effective Indian control.' Thus Khadi of the definition of the A. I. S. A. would be true Swadeshi even though the capital may be all foreign and there may be Western specialists employed by the Indian Board. Conversely, Bata's rubber or other shoes would be foreign though the labour employed may be all Indian and the capital also found by India. The manufactures will be doubly foreign because the control will be in foreign hands and the article, no matter how cheap it is,

will oust the village tanner mostly and the village mochi always. Already the mochis of Bihar have begun to feel the unhealthy competition. The Bata shoe may be the saving of Europe; it will mean the death of our village shoemaker and tanner. I have given two telling illustrations, both partly imaginary. For in the A. I. S. A. the capital is all indigenous and the whole of the talent also. But I would love to secure the engineering talent of the West to give me a village wheel which will beat the existing wheels, though deep down in me I have the belief that the improvements that indigenous talent has made are by no means to be despised. But this is a digression. I do hope that those Ministers and others who guide or serve the public will cultivate the habit of distinguishing between true and false Swadeshi. *–H, 25-2-39, 25,*

European Civilization

874. European civilization is no doubt suited for the Europeans but it will mean ruin for India, if we endeavour to copy it. This is not to say that we may not adopt and assimilate whatever may be good and capable of assimilation by us as it does not also mean that even the Europeans will not have to part with whatever evil might have crept into it. The incessant search for material comforts and their multiplication is such an evil, and I make bold to say that the Europeans themselves will have to remodel their outlook, if they are not to perish under the weight of the comforts to which they are becoming slaves. It may be that my reading is wrong, but I know that for India to run after the Golden Fleece is to court certain death. Let us engrave in our hearts the motto of a Western philosopher, 'plain living and high thinking'. Today it is certain that the millions cannot have high living and we the few who profess to do the thinking for the masses run the risk, in a vain search after high living, of missing high thinking. –YI, 30-4-31, 88.

875. As to the habit of looking to the West for light, I can give little guidance of the whole of my life has not provided any. Light used to go out from the East. If the Eastern reservoir has become empty, naturally the East will have to borrow from the West. I wonder if light, if it is light and not a miasma, can

ever be exhausted. As a boy I learnt that it grew with the giving. Anyway I have acted in that belief and have, therefore, traded on the ancestral capital. It has never failed me. This, however, does not mean that I must act like a frog in the well. There is nothing to prevent me from profiting by the light that may come from the West. Only I must take care that I am not overpowered by the glamour of the West. I must not mistake the glamour for true light.-H, 13-1-40, 414.

To Foreigners in any Land

876. Even as a cup of milk which is full up to the brim does not overflow when sugar is gently added to it, the sugar accommodating itself in the milk, in the same way, I would like you to live in this island so as not to become interlopers, and so as to enrich the life of the people in whose midst you may be living. –*Ceylon, 116.*

Bibliography

Anthony, J. Parel : *Hind Swaraj or Indian Home Rule*, Cambridge University Press, 1925.

Atri, Ajit : *Gandhi's View of Legal Justice*, New Delhi, Deep and Deep Pub., 2007.

Bakshi, S.R. : *Gandhi and the Congress,* New Delhi, Sarup & Sons, 1996.

Biswas, C.C. : *Bengal's Response to Gandhi*, Kolkata, Minerva Associates, 2004.

Chakrabarti, Mohit : *Fire Sans Ire : A Critical Study of Gandhian Non-Violence,* New Delhi, Concept, 2005.

Dalton, Dennis : *Gandhi's Power : Nonviolence in Action*, New Delhi, OUP, 2001.

Das, Dipty Moyee : *Gandhi's Doctrine of Truth and Non-Violence: A Critical Study*, New Delhi, Dominant Pub., 2008.

Das, Ratan : *Gandhi and Mao*, New Delhi, Sarup & Sons, 2004.

Dash, Nibedita : *Life and Thoughts of Gandhi and Nehru*, New Delhi, Dominant, 2004.

Desai, Mahadev : *Gandhi and Indian Villages*, New Delhi, Mohit Pub., 2002.

Gandhi, M. K. : *Satyagraha In South Africa* Navjivan Publishing House, 1922.

George, Davis : *Dynamics of Power : The Gandhian Perspective*, New Delhi, Frank Bros. & Co., 2000.

Guha, Ramachandra : *India After Gandhi : The History of the World's Largest Democracy*, New Delhi, Picador, 2007.

Hardiman, David : *Gandhi : In His Time and Ours*, Delhi, Permanent Black, 2003.

Jain, P.C. : *Gandhi in Stamps : The Courier of Truth and Non-violence*, New Delhi, Aravali, 2002.

Kamath, M.V. : *Gandhi : A Spiritual Journey*, Mumbai, Indus Source Books, 2007.

Kibriya, Mazhar : *Gandhi and Indian Freedom Struggle*, 1999.

Maharajan, M. : *Mahatma Gandhi and the New Millennium*, New Delhi, Discovery Publishing, 2001.

McDonough, Sheila : *Gandhi's Responses to Islam*, New Delhi, D.K. Printworld, 1994.

Nauriya, Anil : *The African Element in Gandhi*, New Delhi, Gyan Pub., 2006.

Pandey, Janardan : *Gandhi and 21st Century*, 1998.

Pani, Narendar : *Inclusive Economics : Gandhian Method and Contemporary Policy*, New Delhi, Sage, 2001.

Radhakrishnan, N. : *Gandhi : The Quest for Tolerance and Survival*, New Delhi, Gandhi Media Centre, 1995.

Richards, Glyn : *Gandhi's Philosophy of Education*, New Delhi, OUP, 2001.

S.C. Gangal and Anurag Gangal : *Contemporary Global Problems : A Gandhian Perspective*, Jammu, Vinod, 1995.

Taneja, Anup : *Gandhi, Women, and the National Movement*, 1920-47, New Delhi, Har-Anand Pub., 2005.

Valecha, Simmi : *Gandhi's Law of Conscience*, New Delhi, Rajat Pub., 2002.

Veerraju, Gummadi : *Gandhian Philosophy : Its Relevance Today*, New Delhi, Decent Books, 1999.

Verma, B.R. and S.R. Bakshi : *Gandhian Satyagraha and His Technique (1920-1928)*, New Delhi, Commonwealth, 2005.

Vettickal, Thomas : *Gandhian Sarvodaya : Realizing a Realistic Utopia*, New Delhi, Gyan Publishing House, 2002.

Weber, Thomas : *Gandhi, Gandhism and the Gandhians*, New Delhi, Roli Books, 2006.

Yadav, K.C. : *Gandhi : The Spirit of India*, Gurgaon, Hope India Publications, 2003.

INDEX

N

P

Q

R

S

T

U

V

W

◆◆◆